Bicycle
HOBO

BY ROBERT DOWNES

The Wandering

PRESS

Published by
The Wandering Press
Traverse City, Michigan

Library of Congress Control Number: Pending

ISBN 978-0-9821344-8-1

First edition published by The Wandering Press in 2018
Printed in the United States of America

Books by Robert Downes are available at a discount
when purchased in bulk for educational or fundraising use,
or by organizations.

www.robertdownes.com

For Russ Barron & Alice Hauser

Also by Robert Downes

Planet Backpacker
I Promised You Adventure
(formerly Travels With My Wife)
Biking Northern Michigan
Windigo Moon

"Before you embark on a journey of revenge, dig two graves."

-- Confucius

"Thou saw'st the locked lovers when leaping from their flaming ship; heart to heart they sank beneath the exulting wave; true to each other, when heaven seemed false to them."

- Herman Melville,
Moby-Dick or, The Whale

The Trip of a Lifetime
Chapter 1

Like usual, I was awake by 4:30 and spent a couple of hours staring at the wall of my tent, struggling to fall back to sleep. At dawn's first light I crawled out of my bag and pissed on the nearest tree, stretched, yawned, fired up my butane stove and made coffee. Even at this early hour a light breeze was filtering through the dawn, blowing south.

I peeled the wrapper on a granola bar and mused on the wind. South? Where would that take me? A tall grove of threadbare pines swayed in the breeze, whispering my direction.

I follow the wind. On a bicycle. When it blows east, it means I might be heading for Boston, Charleston or Jacksonville, depending on my latitude. When it blows north, I could be riding toward Missoula, Chicago or Maine, depending on the longitude. The next day it might be blowing west toward Des Moines, Seattle or Yuma. If I hit a coastline and run out of land, I flip a coin and head north or south.

I literally bend with the wind. Where I go and when I turn all depends on the wind. I'm counting on it to lead me to the man who killed my wife.

Why on a bicycle? A lot of people ask me that and I don't have a good answer. If pressed, I'd say I'm trying to outrun myself. My head is full of obsessive thoughts that I can't escape except by OD-ing on exercise. It was either that or turn to booze, which was not an option, considering the hunt I've taken on. Some people try to ditch their demons by taking pills or joining 12-step groups, but the only thing that works for me is pushing lots of weight around. That's just how things worked out.

I ride more than 700 miles a week, often through killing heat, fog, darkness, rain, snow, I don't care. It's liberating; no one tells me what to do, where to go or when to do it. So far, there are more than 56,000 miles under my wheels and millions of turns at the pedals. Grinding on is the drug that keeps me sane.

Sane? That's a relative term. Partially sane is more like it. A little bit crazy too.

People ask me where I'm from, and these days the answer is, everywhere.

Once, the wind blew southwest for eight days straight and I rode a zigzagging course all the way to Tucumcari, New Mexico, population 5,363, before it shifted around to the northwest for another long blow. Riding nearly 200 miles a day with a strong tailwind I made it to Anacortes, Washington, and a taste of the breeze coming off the Pacific. That pushed me back east, over the Northern Cascades and Sherman Pass, rolling down to the Columbia River.

But the wind doesn't usually blow much more than four or five days in any one direction. Lately, I've been traveling in circles around northern Wisconsin with the breeze shifting every other day at right angles.

Wisconsin can be tough. It's got a lot more hills than you might think, short, but steep. Apparently, the glaciers of the last Ice Age missed a big chunk of Wisconsin when they crushed the Upper Midwest under a mile of ice, because much of the state follows a sawtooth terrain of up-and-down hills.

Hills matter when you're pushing 80 pounds of bike and camping gear, and obviously that means I'm not riding a Harley. The steel horse I ride is a touring bicycle with a chrome-molybdenum frame, strapped with panniers which hang like saddlebags over my front and back wheels. Even when I shift into a granny gear it's a struggle hauling this load up hills and over mountain passes of, say, 8,000 feet or more.

Back when I still had some roots, my friends would kid me with that old saying, "Everything's Jake." We'd meet for coffee or at a bar and I'd ask how things were going and they'd reply, "Everything's Jake," like we were in an old gangster movie. It means everything's great, cool. It dates back to the Roaring Twenties when everything was hunky-dory, jim-dandy, boy howdy... I don't know how that saying got started. There must have been another Jake back then, a guy like me, trying to figure things out. Maybe he rode around on a bicycle too or maybe he was some kind of bootlegger, I don't know. It's the kind of thing you think about when you're riding the back roads for 11 hours a day until it's time to make camp.

I didn't mean to be gone for so long. I thought I'd ride around for a year or so and then call it quits. That stretched into two years, and now, who knows? I was seduced by the sound of bird calls outside my tent in the morning, the sun on my face all day and the world turning inside-out under my wheels. I got used to not punching a time clock. Time passed and I found that I no longer had a home to go back to. Maybe I'll find a new home someday, but for now I'll just keep in riding.

Two years, three months and five days ago, everything was Jake. My wife Jill and I were five days into our first bike tour, riding the Natchez Trace Parkway. It's a national park as well as a highway, running 444 miles from just south of Nashville to Natchez, Mississippi through the heart of the South. The Parkway is touted as a designated cycle route, with no trucks or commercial traffic allowed.

After nearly seven years of marriage Jill and I had lost some common ground and I was hoping that the bike trip would bring us back together again. I don't believe in the "seven year itch," but even the best of couples tend to grow apart over time. You develop separate interests and morph into someone new, possibly into someone your partner no longer cares to know. For Jill an adventure was sharing a second bottle of Chardonnay at her book club, for me it was a night on the rock-climbing wall at the Y. I didn't expect that we'd stay joined at the hip forever, but over the years we'd drifted in different directions until it seemed we were strangers meeting at the back door on our way to other things.

I remember the moment we first met. She was wearing a white tennis skirt over lean, muscular legs, well-tanned and nestled in light gray running shoes with green trim and pink anklet socks. The legs are what did it for me. I've always had a thing for strong women.

She came breezing through the door of a coffeehouse where I was waiting in line. I'd turned with my cappuccino and banged into her, splashing her new shoes. I yammered out a string of "sorries" and fell to the floor, damping at her shoes with a napkin while her girlfriends crowded in behind her, looking over her shoulder all wide-eyed and cooing. I looked up into her big, blue eyes, taking care not to gaze beneath her too-short skirt and that's when she said, "How's it going cowboy?" in a husky voice, with her breasts rising beneath her silky gray singlet. Her honey-brown hair was dampened with a sheen of perspiration crossing her brow and she smelled so good with her perfume mingling with the warmth of her body fresh from the tennis court, it was love at first whiff. I got her shoe size and phone number that day and a date to go rollerblading the day after that. Then, we were off to the races.

We had our days of wine and roses. Jill liked to dance, so did I. She liked mystery novels and old horror movies, me too. We both preferred fish to red meat and liked wine more than beer. She liked to go bowling, as did I, and our lovemaking was good, very good. A woman who's a good dancer tends to be good in bed, and Jill moved like she was auditioning for "Dancing With the Stars."

Jill stood about two inches taller than me, something I never did quite get over. I barely scrape five-foot-six - barely - and was called Shortcake in high school. I did what I could to build myself up through weight-training and running, but that only goes so far. Jill never seemed to give a rip about me being shorter than her, but it gnawed at me a bit. She always said I looked a bit like Leonardo DiCaprio; maybe that's what cinched it for her.

Life was good, but we had our struggles. We were both 23 when we met and in the thick of creating our future selves. Some claim that your 20s is the best decade of your life, but that's bullshit. After years of low-grade poverty in college, Jill and I spent most of our 20s in a struggle to establish our careers and buy a home, laying the groundwork for starting a family. That's what you do when you marry young. We were going to be a picture-perfect middle class family like what you might see in a television commercial, with everything bright and new.

We had a big church wedding. Jill was a Lutheran and had a lot of relatives and friends, me, not so much. My dad was livid with the liquor bill for nearly 300 guests and I thought that spending more than $2,000 on wedding photos was crazy, but Jill insisted and said we were getting off easy. Looking back, I think that big, bloated wedding was our first stumble.

As newlyweds we settled into a routine. Jill worked days and I worked nights, which kept things fresh for a few years, if a bit lonely.

But by our late 20s we were drifting apart with other interests. Jill was in the medical field and started hanging with an elite crowd, while I was a blue collar worker whose buddies still smoked cigarettes and liked to hunt and fish. Jill began taking weekend trips to Chicago with her girl-friends while I went fishing with the guys in Canada.

Jill had always been kind of preppy. She'd been a cheerleader in high school and on the student council, whereas I was more of a C student and a dead-ender. In retrospect, I think she would have been more com-fortable with a clean-cut guy with nice hair who opted for Polo shirts and chino pants, but that wasn't me. Jill was a real head-turner and it was well-dressed jocks who lit up her smile at parties or when she dragged me along to church. God knows what kind of flirting went on when she was at the tennis club or the golf course where those kind of guys hang out.

In short, we were a mismatched species. Jill was a zebra and I was a stork and after the initial glow of our marriage faded we didn't quite know what to think of each other. On some level she didn't approve of me, nor I of her, but for half the country, at least, marriage is a three-act play that you must endure until the final curtain.

By the time we hit 30, days of silence fell upon us in which we no longer knew what to say to one-another beyond small talk that went nowhere. Often, the two of us sat over dinner poring over Facebook or Instagram on our respective tablets, not speaking a word. Gradually, it seemed it no longer mattered that we had a stake in staying together. In the back of my mind I did the calculus of selling our home and going my own way, and I think Jill felt much the same. There wouldn't be a big scene if we split up, it would be more like resignation.

But that didn't mean I didn't love her. This bike tour was supposed to help bring us back together and give us a rebirth. We'd gotten the idea from the travel section in the Sunday paper: "Bikeways of America" was the story, with the promise of a glorious time on two wheels for those who took the dare. The Natchez Trace Parkway was one of a half-dozen suggested routes.

Jill lobbied for a week of golf at Hilton Head, followed by an escorted bike tour of the Outer Banks. I should have listened, but I pressed for the more demanding trip down South under the notion that it would be more of an adventure.

"If anyone can handle this it's you," I said at the time. "I know you'll be kicking my ass." Jill was super-fit; in addition to playing tennis twice a week she was militant about her pilates and spinning classes.

But she wasn't keen on my bike tour idea. "I'm going, but under pro-test," was the best she could say.

We'd never done any serious biking. We were weekend riders at best, so most of our preparation had been gleaned off the web, followed by a trip to the biggest bike store in our hometown of Ann Arbor, Michigan. There, we learned that "traveling on the cheap" astride a bicycle comes at a hefty price. There were panniers to buy - saddlebags, really - along with arcane bike tools, lights, reflective clothing and helmets.

Then there was the matter of acquiring our bikes. We were steered toward heavy-duty touring machines with wide tires, beefy spokes, disc brakes and low-rise brackets that would lower the center of gravity for our gear, helping to balance our bikes. By the time we left the store we were more than $6,000 lighter.

"Think of it as an investment," I said at the time. "If we like doing this we'll ride a bunch of routes, and if we don't, we'll sell this stuff online."

Jill had rolled her eyes, as if humoring an idiot. So true, in retrospect.

A few weeks later we headed south.

"Are we crazy, or what?" I said as we drove through Kentucky on the interstate. "This is going to be the trip of a lifetime."

Jill didn't look up from her *Womens Fitness*.

"Are you there sugar babe?" I tried again.

"Whatever." I could tell she was fuming. "But my trip of a lifetime would be Paris, or Africa."

"What are you mad about?"

"I'm not mad."

"Well it seems like you are."

"You're just inconsiderate, that's all."

"What?"

"Are you deaf? I asked you not to put your trash in my cup holder, and you couldn't resist, could you?"

Sure enough, I'd wadded up a candy bar wrapper and tossed it in the space between us. Jill had been holding her coffee cup for the last half hour to make a point. We were heading into the kind of argument over nothing that's the specialty of married couples.

I scooped out the offending wrapper. "Yeah, sorry about that. I don't remember you telling me."

"That's because you never listen, Jake. You just go along like it's your way or the highway. I mean, this trip, the bikes — do you ever consider what I'd like to do?"

"Oh come on, you know I don't play golf, and your idea would have cost us a fortune. Hilton Head? Come on."

That really set her off. "What? You think this is cheaper!? Blowing ten thousand dollars on all of this crazy stuff for something we'll probably never do again?"

"Seriously? It wasn't that much. It was like half that amount."

"That's still halfway to crazy."

"Jill, please just give it a try before you trash it. If we do the ride and you don't like it, we'll sell the bikes and all this gear and move on."

But I had to admit, Jill had a point, we'd dumped a lot of cash into this bike tour scheme of mine and it was true that I'd dragged her along, knowing her heart wasn't into it. I wanted to tell her that I was hoping that some kind of adventure would bring us back together again, but I couldn't say the words. That would be admitting that our marriage was heading for the morgue.

A frost settled in over the next couple of hours and neither of us spoke. But we got along well enough in the motel that night and the next day we arrived 17 miles south of Nashville at the northern terminus of the Parkway. We unloaded our bikes and gazed down the road, decked out in our never-worn cycle shorts and fluorescent jerseys, ready to conquer the South.

Strange to say, we had never tried riding with the panniers attached to our bikes. They were still wrapped up in plastic in the trunk of our car. I figured it would be a cinch to simply hang them from our bike brackets and get going. Wrong.

I spent half an hour making false starts, cursing and reading the instructions before I had Jill's panniers attached to the rear of her bike. We loaded them up with her clothes and camping gear and she gave it a go, gliding as graceful as a swan around the parking lot.

"How is it?" I called out.

"It's okay. Feels kind of like I'm riding a little motorcycle with the extra weight," she called back.

Then it was my turn. I had both front and rear panniers to carry our food. Plus, our tent strapped to the back of my bike. I hefted my bike and found that Jill was right, it did seem a bit like hoisting a motorcycle, though lighter, of course.

I threw my leg over the frame, tangled my foot in the rear pannier and fell face first on top of my bike, scraping my arm on the asphalt. The first of many such wounds, as it turned out.

"Jake! Are you alright?"

"Not really," I called back, lying amid the tangle of my bike and the gear that had fallen every which-way.

"What happened?"

"I think I hurt my pride." That, and I'd banged myself in the nuts. Brilliant. I lay still for a minute or so before scrambling free.

But ten minutes later I was bandaged and we were off, both of us glid-ing along slowly down the road. Like swans.

We had a lot of ground to cover. The Natchez Trace Parkway winds through Tennessee, Alabama and Mississippi along a historic trail that was once traveled by Indians, pioneers and "land pirates." These were cutthroats and robbers who waylaid travelers. Some of them may have killed explorer Meriwether Lewis in 1809 as he made his way along a lonely stretch of the route. While staying at an inn called Grinder's Stand, about 70 miles south of Nashville, the hero of the 1804 Corps of Discovery expedition across North America suffered multiple gunshot wounds and a severed throat. Some historians believe it was a suicide, but how do you cut your own throat?

Back in when Abraham Lincoln was a young man and before the inven-tion of steamboats, he and other men would pilot flatboats full of cargo down the Mississippi and then walk all the way home along a pathway paralleling the river. Over the years their footsteps dug a trench that wandered all the way from Natchez to Pittsburgh. They called it the Trace.

The magnolias were blooming all along the Parkway that spring, with thousands of flowers blossoming pink and white in the trees. It was pleasantly warm as we rode southwest with the afternoon rains amount-ing to little more than a misting. We awoke to fog each morning, shroud-ing the forest like a fairyland. That, and an orchestra of bird calls as the sun scissored through the morning haze. We coasted over rolling hills past cotton fields of rich black dirt. We took side trips through ghost towns where every store was black with rot, with trees growing through their caved-in roofs and then past tumbledown barns, pig pens, barking dogs and scrambling chickens.

To my surprise, Jill seemed to be loving the ride. Two days into the trip and she seemed like the 23-year-old I'd met in the coffee shop, smiling, laughing and blasting past me on her bike, thanks to all of those spinning classes she took back home. Can love resurface with the simple immer-sion of a few days of cycling in the heart of nature? It sure felt that way. I felt closer to Jill than I had in years and she gave it right back to me.

Bicycles have the right-of-way on the Natchez Trace Parkway and for the most part motorists gave us a wide berth, swinging into the opposite lane and waving as they drove past. For our part, we hugged the shoulder of the road, but even then riding could be scary. The speed limit on the Parkway is 50 mph, but for most drivers a speed limit tends to be a starting point, rather than a top end, so some of the traffic was whipping by at 60 miles per hour or more. And though there were no semi trucks on the road, there were plenty of motor homes of monstrous proportions and pick-ups pulling boats or campers. With no shoulder along the road, we rode the white line as best we could, cringing when drivers got too close.

"How do we know these guys aren't texting or looking at Facebook while they're driving?" Jill wondered at a roadside park. "I worry about that more than people driving drunk." She was rattled, and I couldn't blame her.

"That's why we're wearing fluorescent clothing, so they can see us a long way off," I replied.

But privately, my concerns were mounting. Just before we'd left home I'd googled safety concerns for the Parkway and had read some alarming comments from cyclists who'd been clipped by passing vehicles or run off the road. There had been fatalities, a cyclist had been killed by a young guy going 78 miles an hour while texting. The Parkway apparently served as a mini-freeway for many locals, particularly in Mississippi.

Cycling along with the traffic whooshing by, I thought about pulling the plug and detouring all the way east to the Atlantic coast like Jill wanted in the first place. But by then we were in too deep, we'd spent too much money getting here and I was stubborn. I had something to prove, like we were going to conquer this ride and pull ourselves back together. The traffic was growing more intense but the scenery was glorious and for the most part we were enjoying the ride.

I made Jill ride ahead of me, figuring that she'd be safer up front.

At 31, Jill was in the prime of her womanhood. Strong, sure of herself and vise-gripped to a huge network of friends and family. Earlier that spring, she'd been made manager of her physical therapy unit, a promotion that came with a hefty raise. Our trip was intended to celebrate her success, and though I didn't know it at the time, she was also pregnant. I suppose she was waiting to tell me at some perfect night on our ride when the stars brimmed beneath the southern moon. I guess I'll never know.

Late in the day a massive motor home had brushed past me close enough to tickle the tendrils of my eardrum with the suction of its wake. It must have been doing 70 mph.

"Jill! I yelled, my voice lost in a wind filled with diesel fumes. She was 50 yards ahead of me on a curve and something made her turn around just as the RV reached her. The driver wasn't giving an inch, even though there was no one in the oncoming lane. It was as if he was bearing down on her on purpose, intending to hit her.

Jill disappeared behind the bulk of the speeding RV and my heart fell like a plummeting elevator. I was sure she'd been hit.

Almost. The tail-end of the motor home whipped past with the roar of an air horn in its wake and I saw Jill, still upright but whipsawing on her bike in the dirt alongside the road, struggling not to fall.

"You idiot!" she yelled at the fleeting vehicle, raising her middle finger in its direction.

"Christ! Are you alright?" I called, shuddering to a stop. "I thought he hit you!"

"He almost did!" she spat. "I got off the road a half-second in time. Otherwise..." she made a slicing sign across her throat. Then she had begun shaking and her face grew wet with tears. I held her for a long time by the roadside, neither one of us wanting to ride on.

But we did, feeling deflated and tense with the sound of every oncoming vehicle. Only 11 feet wide, the narrow lane now seemed an impossibly slim ribbon twisting its way to our mortality. Suddenly, the whole trip seemed like a crazy idea. What was I thinking, dragging my wife out here on a narrow highway, vulnerable to every vehicle careening down the road? She could have died and it would have been all my fault for talking her into going.

An hour later we reached a campground. The whole place was packed full with only two sites left. The first available site was perfect with a picnic table and a grill beneath a spreading oak tree. But it was alongside an extended family of yahoos who'd draped a Confederate flag across the tail gate of a pickup truck plastered with far-right bumper stickers. They had the whole shtick: two pit bulls capering amid a tribe of anemic kids, an open cooler stuffed with beer cans and loud music belching crusty Southern rock from a boombox. We moved on.

There was only one site left at the end of the campground and it was next to the motor home that had almost killed us.

"Let's go, we're not staying here," I said.

"Where then? I've had it for today," Jill said. She was red with exasperation; I could see she was at the end of her rope.

Just then the screen door of the RV snapped open and a giant with a horsey face emerged holding a beer can. He was about 45 with dark hair and a sallow complexion, standing maybe six-foot-eight, more than a foot taller than me, but slightly hunched as he stood on his rig's tiny porch.

Beyond that, the first thing I noticed was his hair, which was so black it looked like it had been dyed with shoe polish. He had a little boy's haircut, a page-boy in the style of Prince Valiant. He wore a pale yellow polyester shirt of the sort worn by the managers of cheap restaurants over black shorts with knee-high socks terminating in black penny loafers. He reminded me of a famous white basketball player, I can't remember who. That, or some hick you'd see at a mall in some obscure town like Saginaw. A dork.

His head jerked up in surprise and his eyes widened at the sight of us standing there in our helmets and fluorescent singlets, as strange on our loaded bikes as space aliens in a Mississippi swamp. He cocked his head and considered us with the affect of a praying mantis.

"Well, fuck me, it's you two," he said.

Like any white, middle-class man, I've been trained my whole life to avoid conflict. Cowardice has been drilled into me by the cautionary babble of parents, teachers, social workers, TV, the church... Whatever warrior vestige I had chained up in my soul from ten generations back had been milked dry by a suburban upbringing, the weight of feminism and a liberal arts education. I hadn't been in a fight since I was 16 years old. But Jill didn't have that sort of problem.

"You!" she accused, her voice rising to a shout. "You almost killed us!"

Slowly, deliberately, the stranger spat a gob of tobacco saliva into his beer can.

"Didn't mean to," he shrugged. "I was fiddling with the radio. Didn't even see you."

"You didn't see us from mile away wearing this stuff?" Jill stormed, flicking the straps of her jersey. "What are you, blind?"

The stranger pursed his lips. "Oh, I guess I saw you well enough, now that I think about it."

"Well?"

"Well what?" He glared back.

"You could have killed me."

He shrugged again. "I hit the horn, you got out of the way. All's well that ends well."

Jill looked back at him, speechless. That's when I jumped in.

"So, you're saying you buzzed us on purpose," I said. "You could have hit her with one of your mirrors and if she'd lost her balance you would have hit her for sure."

Angry as I was, my voice sounded reedy, shrill, impotent.

He spat again into his beer can, and for a long moment the spittle of his tobacco juice lingered like syrup, unwilling to disengage from his lips. Finally, he set it down on the metal grate of the RV's steps and wiped his mouth with his bare arm. Then he raised both hands up and outward like a beseeching preacher.

"Look here, little missy," he said, ignoring me. "You bicycle people have no business being on this road. Have some sense. This is an old carriage way designed way back for horses and buggies."

"Well, you're not driving a buggy," Jill said.

We stood 40 feet apart, glaring at each-other, he on his tiny metal porch and we at our picnic table. Yet, slowly, the anger melted from our neighbor's face, replaced with a wry grin. His voice took on a mild tone, as if reasoning with a couple of children.

"A buggy? No, but after the buggies came the vehicles, Model T's, tractors and then Cadillacs and pickup trucks," he said. "Through the years the vehicles got bigger and faster, but the road stayed just the same. So, today this road is for drivers who pay taxes to pay for its upkeep, understand? It's not for you bikies weaving all over the place like you own the road."

He paused to wave at the white wall of rolling aluminum behind him. The motor home stretched more than 30 feet and seemed as big as a ranch house. "When you drive a rig like this, you hold your line and keep it there and to hell with anything that gets in your way," he said. "Deer, bicycles, whatever."

"So you'd run over some kid on a tricycle?" Jill said, her voice wound to its highest pitch of sarcasm.

"I will if I have to," he shrugged. "It could be either him or me plowing into some oncoming truck. My point is, you keep the roads clear for those who belong. Those who don't belong take their chances."

Jill began muttering under her breath and I could tell she was winding up for a big "fuck you."

Things were escalating and I didn't know what to do. A stillness settled between us, an expectancy. Then, just as Jill was on the brink of unloading again, the stranger morphed into Mr. Nice Guy.

"But, look, what am I thinking? Look, I'm truly sorry," he said, wheedling like the stereotype of an old Jewish shopkeeper in a movie. "I missed you, I took care to give you space, there was no harm done. Come on, let's be friends now."

"Friends, sure," Jill said under her breath, disgusted.

"Put up your tent and stop in for a lemonade," he waved, insistently. "I'm just a lonely bachelor out here with no one to talk to. You can tell me about your trip; tell me about bicycling. Maybe I'll learn something, I'd like that."

Jill just groaned, shaking her head.

By then the sun was creeping rose-red toward the horizon and I realized that we'd barely have time to put up our tent and have dinner before darkness fell. The next campground was another 12 miles down the road and we were both dead tired from biking 63 miles in the hot sun. We were stuck here camping next to this weirdo. That, or the rednecks down the way.

But before we could reply, the screen door slammed shut as the guy scuttled back inside, leaving his spit-can on the RV's top step.

We put up our dome tent and had a cold supper of sub sandwiches purchased in the last town. Sitting at the picnic table as the sun faded away, our conversation fell to a whisper.

"So what do you think of all this?" I asked her.

"What do you mean?"

"I mean the bike touring thing. Are you still having fun?"

Jill gave me a wary look, her face half hidden in shadow.

"Sure, it's been a good time, better than I expected. But that was scary today," she said. "That guy's a creep."

I nodded. "Yeah."

"What an ignoramus."

"Yeah, big time."

"I thought you were going to punch him. You looked really mad."

"Did I?"

"Yup, pretty mad," she said, sipping at her tea.

"You looked like you were getting ready to scratch his eyes out," I said back.

"Next time, I'm going to let him have it."

"There isn't going to be a next time."

Ten minutes later the door of the RV snapped open and the stranger's voice called out: "Hey guys, I've got some lemonade for thirsty cyclists over here! Come on over."

Jill looked at me, no way. "No thanks," I called over.

"Come on, please? I want to make it up to you, show you my place."

He was standing there in the half darkness, looking like a hulking ghost in his white t-shirt.

"No thanks," I called out again.

"Come on, seriously. The ice is melting on these drinks, they'll go to waste. I want to make it up to you, just for a minute."

I groaned, got up from the table and walked over to where he hovered above me in the shadow of his RV.

"Hey, thanks for the offer, but we're both really tired and it's been a long day," I said.

"Come on, just for a second. Check out my place."

I hesitated. Just for a second? A bell rang deep in my mind with that old saying, keep your friends close and your enemies closer. It wouldn't hurt to see what this goofball was up to. It would be a bit of reconnaissance in the unlikely event that we bumped into him again.

"Just for a second," I said, mounting the metal steps.

"I'm Peter," he said, offering a moist hand. It was long, slender, and his fingers went on forever, like those of a basketball player.

"Jake," I nodded.

Peter's lair was uncomfortably warm and dimly lit. That, and the rank, sweet-sour smell of rotting garbage filled the air like the atmosphere surrounding a landfill. A tiny sink and kitchen counter was crammed full with beer cans and dirty dishes, some so crusted they looked like they'd been lying there unwashed for weeks. A waste basket dripping with brown stains overflowed with garbage attended by a smattering of flies. Crumpled bags and wrappers from fast food restaurants littered the floor. Jammed in between the trash can and a cabinet were a couple of pizza boxes, rank with the residue of moldering cheese and dried sauce. On the floor under the kitchen counter a half-eaten hamburger nestled with an almost-empty bottle of gin. Cheetos lurked until the sill of the counter, some mashed into the carpet, which was black with grease. I glimpsed a chicken bone floating amid unidentifiable crumbs.

For a moment, I thought I was going to retch.

It wasn't just the filth, my host also had piles of junk stacked up everywhere. There were stacks of yellowed newspapers and piles of magazines going back to the days of *Look* and *Life*. In one corner, a cascade of old crockery and china gave the appearance of a shrine; all that was missing were candles and statues of Virgin Mary. The place seemed the lair of a hoarder.

Further in, the stink settled into a musk like that of rotting cat food but otherwise, it was classic motorhome with vinyl swivel chairs cocked toward a tiny flat-screen TV and a plaid couch festered with rips and cigarette burn holes. A skein of cracks in the window above the kitchen sink was patched with masking tape gone black with mold at the edges. The bedroom door was shut at the far end of the rig, a blessing, no doubt.

Nestled atop a small table in front of the couch were three glasses of lemonade on ice, along with a pitcher of the same. Unlike everything about the place, the glasses and pitcher looked clean, but I could only imagine what sort of greasy rag had been used to polish them.

"Have a seat," Peter waved. "Your lady friend not coming?"

I shook my head. "No."

"She your wife?"

"Yeah."

"How long?"

"Seven years."

"Seven years, well, well, think of that, mmm, mmm. Hey, call her over. We could play some cards," Peter said, fidgeting. He seemed nervous, ill at ease, as antsy as a guy who needs to use to use a toilet in a hurry. At the time I took it to mean he was embarrassed by his behavior, or perhaps by his dump of a place.

"She's wiped out, probably asleep by now," I said.

"Well then."

"Yeah."

Peter reached down alongside his chair and drew forth a bottle of gin. "You want a little flavor with that?" he nodded toward my glass.

"No thanks."

"A little gin's good on a hot summer night."

"I just had a beer and mixing drinks gives me a headache, but thanks anyway."

"Suit yourself." He proceeded to fill his glass to the rim. "This is my own special recipe, two parts lemonade and one part gin, though sometimes my hand slips a bit when I'm pouring the gin, if you know what I mean."

"I do."

I looked around the RV's tiny living room. Other than the filth it was ordinary to a banal degree. There was a single photo of a duck on the wall, a 16" by 20" in a cheap, black frame, like something you'd find in a clearance rack at a dollar store. Otherwise, there were no family photos or mementoes of any kind. The place felt claustrophobic from all of the junk piled up in stacks.

"So, you're on your own?" I asked.

"Sure am, mister. Just me. I'm a lost highway kind of guy."

"Like in the Hank Williams song."

"You know it? Good man."

Peter took a long swallow on his lemonade, gulping it down noisily, followed by a belch and a starry gaze. He gazed into his glass and his eyes glistened. His chin was wet from where he'd slopped his drink.

I took a sip and studied the duck picture. You truly are an odd duck, Peter, I thought.

"Nope, all alone," he said abruptly. "I'm an IT guy, specializing in human resources. I travel around the country fixing software glitches. Been on the road for years."

I waited for Peter to ask me what I did for a living, but he didn't seem to be interested.

"Do you like to travel, Jake?" he went on.

"Sure."

"I mean, on a bicycle? That's a rough way to go."

"I like it fine, so far."

"Travel can be dangerous, don't you think?"

I shrugged. "I wouldn't know."

"These people you meet in campgrounds; you never know what they'll pull."

I thought of the rednecks a few campsites down the way. They looked like trouble.

"I suppose," I said.

"You haven't been around much, I take it?"

"About as much as anyone, I guess. Been to Cancun."

Peter nodded and gazed into his glass as if searching for something hidden in its depths. "Well I've been on the road since I was a boy in one way or another," he said at last.

Peter said he was born in Plano, Texas but had been raised in army bases around the world, never staying longer than a year or two. He'd majored in computer technology at A&M and after college he'd worked in information tech jobs at various hospitals and businesses. But eventually he'd gotten the travel bug and had set himself up as a wandering consultant.

Peter droned on and on in a low, sonorous voice. He'd been to Europe; loved Prague, hated Paris. He had once owned a 500-gallon aquarium, but all his fish died so he got rid of it. Hated cats, but loved smooth jazz and didn't care who knew it. He babbled on in a stream-of-consciousness way in a low, mellifluous voice, staring straight ahead at the wall as if I wasn't there. While in college he had flown radio-controlled model airplanes and was thinking about getting a drone. He still held a torch for The Beatles, but didn't much care for the Stones. He had managed a fast food restaurant once, hated it. He had never been to Canada and wouldn't dream of going to Mexico. His aunt was an heiress who owned a shopping mall, but he'd never seen a cent of her money. He didn't like staying in motels; that's why he drove a motor home. It was a sing-song monologue of the mundane, weaving along like a child's prattle. He seemed to have no filter, saying anything that popped into his head. He never asked a single question about me or Jill.

He wandered on like Mr. Magoo, the bumbling, mumbling, slit-eyed old man from a cartoon that was popular in the '60s, his monologue winding in an errant stream, here, there and everywhere for twenty minutes or more. I began to feel sleepy; it had been a long day in the saddle and his ceaseless drone began pulling my eyelids shut. Peter's stream of minutiae was strangely hypnotic.

Then I thought of Jill waiting for me and that gave me a jolt. She'd be worried. I pinched myself awake and squirmed in my seat, stifling a yawn.

Abruptly he said, "What's the matter? Don't you like your drink?"

I took a sip. "Good stuff."

"It's from a mix, not the best, but there's plenty more where that came from if you're thirsty."

I nodded. "Thanks."

"So drink up," he insisted. "You got to be thirsty from riding all day."

I took another sip and made a point of looking at my watch. "Got to get going."

He settled back in his chair and gave me an appraising look. "Hold on a minute, friend. I think I've got you figured out. I'm a polymath, you know."

"What?" For a moment I thought he said "psychopath."

"A polymath. To quote the dictionary, 'a person of wide-ranging knowledge or learning.'"

"Oh, right. Like Leonardo da Vinci." I suppressed a snigger.

"Well, not quite like him," Peter blustered. "More like Benjamin Franklin, I suppose. I speak six languages and have advanced degrees in chemistry and physics. I compose actuarial tables in my head when

I can't sleep."

"Really?"

"Oh, yes," he said, knitting his eyebrows. "I like to invent things. I like to invent scenarios."

"Ah, mais oui, c'est une bonne idee. Vous êtes très modeste," I said, offering a bit of my high school French.

"What? That's Portuguese, isn't it?" he replied. "I don't speak that one. What did you say?"

"I guess my pronunciation must be off. My mom is from Hungary and I was trying out a little Magyar on you."

"Magyar, you say? That's a language?"

I nodded solemnly. "Magyar, it's as Hungarian as goulash."

"Mmm, you don't say." He nodded solemnly.

It was bullshit, but I wanted to see how far Polymath Peter, the master of six languages, would bend on the goofy scale. It was clear that he was more of a loon than a genius, but I figured he'd be out of my life in a matter of minutes and it wasn't worth calling him out.

Instead, I said, "You were talking about scenarios."

"Yes, scenarios, little games that I play. They're my inventions. I'm kind of a mystery man, you know. I'd tell you why, but..."

He let the end of his sentence hang there with a goofy, expectant grin on his horsey face.

I played along. "Yeah? But what?"

"But if I told you, then I wouldn't be a mystery, would I?" Peter said triumphantly, slapping his hand on my knee like we were old buddies. He let it settle there.

"Wow, that's a zinger," I said drily, shifting my knee away.

"No charge," he said, "And, hey, you don't have to move away. We're just talking here, right?"

I had nothing to say to that. The gloom in Peter's RV had deepened with the dwindling sun, and with it came my sense of unease. He was a big guy, sitting there in the half dark, and at times he growled to himself, reminding me of a bear.

"I mean, men talk, right?" he went on. "We share things. Women think we don't, but we do."

"Sure, guy talk."

"Sometimes strangers share their deepest secrets because they know they'll be moving on," Peter mused. "Like with hitch-hikers or with someone you meet at a bar during a conference. You share a secret and move on."

"I guess so."

"Do you know, I once had a conversation with a guy for five minutes straight while we were both standing at a urinal?" Peter's eyes were wide as he made his confession.

"Hmm."

"Nice guy, in pharmaceutical sales from some town in Iowa. We just stood there talking for the longest time in the hotel john, holding onto our dicks, if you can believe that."

I could believe it. I made motions to leave. Peter had been a harmless bore up to now, but he was creeping me out and the conversation was heading somewhere I didn't care to go. My eyes swept over the sad photo of the duck on his wall, the mark of a lonely man. Without thinking, I asked the wrong question, aiming to change the subject.

"So, no family? You ever been married?" I regretted the words even as they left my lips.

The boozy smile on Peter's face shrank like dishwater going down a drain.

"What are you getting at?" he said.

"Just making conversation. No worries."

"No worries? What are you, some kind of hipster?"

"It's just a saying."

He glared at me, the rage we'd seen earlier in the day spreading across his face.

"You think I'm gay, don't you?"

"No," I said evenly. "I don't care what you do. I mean, it's none of my business."

"Well I'm not. I was raised Latter Day Saints."

"Mormon."

"You bet your ass I am," he said with a drunken snarl. "They don't like gay people in the LDS. Those guys in that play, 'The Book of Mormon'? I haven't seen it, but I bet they're all queer."

I saved my breath on pointing out that the Broadway hit was about a conflicted gay missionary. My head was starting to throb and Peter's weird scene was getting stranger by the minute.

He went quiet as a child and his face resumed its inward-looking expression, as if he was remembering some personal tragedy. "Gay people, give me a break," he mumbled. "You know what, my friend? I'm going to tell you a little secret."

"Yeah?" I recoiled. Peter was drunk and slurring his words. He leaned in close and I pulled back in response. I could smell his breath, heavy with gin and tobacco.

"I'm bisexual," he said in a breathy whisper, as if divulging some huge, dark secret.

I almost laughed, he seemed so melodramatic. "That right?"

"Yeah, that's right. But that doesn't mean I've got homosexual tendencies, does it? The church frowns on that."

I shrugged. My sister is a lesbian and the issues of sexual identity had been settled in our family years ago. I could give a rip what Peter did with his genitals. "Whatever turns your crank, I don't care."

Peter gave a crooked grin and slapped my knee again, an iron grip closing on my leg. "Turns your crank? That's a good one! I like you, Jake, and I'll tell you this: I like girls well enough, but if you can't get your hands on one sometimes it's good to have a little fun the other way around. Do you know what I mean?"

I wrenched free and stood up, stifling a curse.

He ignored it. "What? You're leaving?" his eyebrows arched in disbelief. "Hold on chief. You haven't finished your lemonade."

It was true, I'd only taken a few sips because of the beer I'd finished early on. Drinking anything else would mean having to crawl out of our tent in the middle of the night to trudge over to the restroom far across the campground.

Suddenly, I was dead tired, with a wave of fatigue washing over me. I'd been in Peter's rolling garbage dump for almost an hour and Jill would be worried.

"I'm going," I said, anxious to leave, "getting pretty tired."

"Well, if you gotta' go, I guess you gotta' go." His tone was moping, almost miserable.

"Yeah, thanks for the drink."

"Well hold on a minute, okay? I've got to pipe m' lizard."

"What?"

"The bathroom..." he waved.

He wove to his feet, stumbled sideways and headed down the hall to the RV's bathroom, banging into a small desk at the far end of what passed for the living room.

There was a laptop on the desk and it jittered to life out of sleep mode. Pictures of small faces flashed into view along with images of unspeakable things. No way... My eyes widened in disbelief and I quickly looked away.

I scrambled toward the door.

"Hey!"

Peter never made it to the bathroom. He weaved back around with the front of his pants soaked from where he'd pissed himself. He looked down at his laptop and snapped it shut.

"Y-you weren't meant to shee that," he said, slurring his words. "Tha's researsch I'm doin'. It's re... researsch fer... fer a med'cal journal." He hiccoughed, took a step forward and stumbled sideways into the wall.

"I didn't see anything," I lied.

"You sure about tha'?" he said, his eyes searching mine, "'cause I could get into a lot of trouble if someone gets the wrong idea."

"I don't give a shit what you do," I said, disgusted.

He came floating across the room, his eyes locked on mine.

"It's research, that's all," he said, clicking out of his stupor, as if he'd slapped himself. "I'm doing research for some guys I know; guys who want to stop this terrible plague. It's an affliction, you know?"

"Sure, whatever." But I was dialing 911 in my thoughts, rehearsing what I'd tell the cops.

Peter followed me out the door, looming over my shoulder. His face bobbed milky white in the vapor lamps of the campsite and the image of a vampire flashed through my thoughts. I felt myself shrinking before him. He was more than a foot taller than me and seemed even more so in the darkness.

"You rat me out and it means hard-time prison, all because you stuck your nose in where it don't belong," he said in a hissing whisper.

"I don't know what you're talking about," I said, hurrying. "I'm gone in the morning, you're gone too, right? Now get out of my face."

I pushed into the darkness toward our tent, my heart pounding hard in alarm.

He followed close behind.

"Hey, don't walk away from me, boy! We're friends now, right? If you let me, I'll show you..." He was begging now, assuming the wheedling voice we'd heard earlier, his face looming over my shoulder. A caressing hand ran down my spine.

It was too much. With a choking feeling rising at the back of my throat I turned and shoved him hard with both hands. He tripped and tumbled over backwards, hitting the ground.

"Cunt!" he called after me.

I stumbled over to our camp in the dark of the new moon and rummaged in the front bag of my bike for the pepper spray. It was something I carried in the unlikely event that we encountered a bear.

"What was that all about?" Jill asked as I crawled into our tent. "How did it go?" She'd been up reading by a pocket lantern.

"A little disagreement, that's all." I was too rattled to tell Jill what I'd seen on the stranger's laptop and there was no point getting her stirred up.

It took me a long time to calm down. I was still shaking from giving Peter a shove. Was that a fight? Had I overstepped? I wondered if we should abandon our tent and go sleep behind a tree, way off somewhere; for all I knew the guy had a gun. He seemed dangerously unhinged. But there were mosquitoes out that night and I had the bear spray within easy reach. Let that idiot try something, I thought, just let him.

How long I lay awake, I don't know, I was ripped with adrenaline. Then, somewhere in my dreams, maybe 4:00 a.m. or so, I heard the low, throaty rumble of a heavy engine. My head was pounding with a killer headache but I clawed my way up to wakefulness. A false dawn lit up the wall of our tent, growing brighter as the engine revved. The ground began to shake as our tent exploded with the light bouncing up and down. At the last second I realized it was the backup lights of an RV, thundering over rough terrain, coming on fast toward our tent.

"Jake?" Jill rustled in her sleeping bag beside me as the light rose in her face like the rising sun. It was the last thing she ever said to me.

Dead or alive
Chapter 2

"By the gods you shall digest the venom of your spleen, though it do split you."

— William Shakespeare, *Julius Caesar*

Jill was dead.

The double tires at the rear of Peter's RV had rolled over her abdomen, crushing her liver, ribs and lungs under two tons of pressure.

The rednecks we'd passed by in the campground were the first to respond, slashing away the fabric of our mangled tent and doing everything they could to save Jill as she bled out. The guy who had the rebel flag draped over the tailgate of his truck? He held Jill in his arms, whispering kind words into her ear as she died.

I died that day too, not physically, but inside. Jill's body had taken the brunt of the RV as it rolled over the two of us. It got me too, but the ramp of her body had taken most of the weight of the RV's rear axle. I guess you could say that Jill died saving me.

I woke up in the hospital eight days later, swimming up through the milky fog of an induced coma to a world that was utterly changed forever. Even in my daze, I knew Jill was dead before the doctor told me. The faces of the ICU nurses were too kind, their voices soft with compassion. There was no brusque joking around like usual with nurses. Deep down in my coma I had heard them whispering of Jill's death, heard every word. I don't remember what the doctor said, only that his face was a mask of sorrow. I couldn't make out his words but I saw his lips moving and understood him well enough.

Jill was gone.

Most, I suppose, would lie numb in shock and denial, unable to speak or move, paralyzed under the weight of such a blow, but I screamed, twisted and squirmed, kicking at the bed with confirmation of the horror

I'd been dreading. My limbs shook uncontrollably; I don't know what I said, it was all just gibberish and sobs. A squad of nurses rushed in on a Code Crazy call and strapped me down, to be sedated and then pumped with psychoactive drugs, the kind that light up your eyes with a silver-mercury sheen of lobotomized torment.

I'd ripped my stitches in my writhing; they told me later that bed was soaked with blood before they got me back under. They also said I'd had an emergency splenectomy, meaning they'd removed my spleen. That, a bruised kidney and four ribs had been broken, requiring a chest tube.

Turns out you don't need your spleen to live, although it's helpful enough. It's an organ lying below your lungs nestled against your liver on the left side of your body that filters red blood cells. Mine had ruptured under the weight of the RV's tires, and apparently, a ruptured spleen can kill you pretty fast unless it's removed. Right then I wished that it had. I didn't deserve to live.

I had a long red scar where they'd taken it out.

But years ago, spleen also defined a condition of melancholy or anger, as in to vent one's spleen. It's an archaic term, like something you'd read in Poe or Shakespeare. Like the organ itself, the emotional state of spleen is heartless, implacable and cruel. Soon enough, that would be me.

The next day, I swam up through druggy currents to find Dr. Werner silhouetted in the doorway. I didn't catch his first name, but he said he was a cardiologist.

"How are you feeling this morning?" he asked.

"Not so good."

"How do you mean?"

"I mean mentally and physically."

Dr. Werner was wearing a long white lab coat with a badge over the pocket where physicians used to keep their cigarettes back in the day. He gazed at my chart, fastened to a clipboard, but I didn't get the impression he was actually reading it. He looked a lot like a balding Rex Morgan, M.D., from the comic strip. What was left of his hair was black, brilliantined, and swept back beneath a face that wore a golf course tan.

Dr. Werner leaned up against the wall and crossed his arms. "You lost a lot of blood in the accident," he said, looking up. "Do you recall anything?"

"Yeah, I recall that it wasn't an accident," I said bitterly.

He nodded. "I understand. I mean, do you recall feeling anything?"

"Like what?"

"Like what happened after you were run over."

"Seriously?"

He nodded. "For the record."

"All I remember was waking up to the sound of nurses and a heart monitor," I said. "Colored lights, beeping, that sort of thing."

"That's it? Nothing else? I mean from the night this happened."

"I remember seeing the lights coming toward us in our tent." I shuddered, feeling a ripple of pain in my surgical wound.

Dr. Werner studied me, blank-faced, tapping a pen on my chart. "Well, you're a lucky man Jake, because you had an episode that few people live through."

"Lucky man, give me a break."

But it was true.

"You literally died out there," Dr. Werner said. "We believe you suffered from hypovolemic shock."

"Meaning?"

"Meaning you shouldn't be alive. Hypovolemic shock occurs when there's been too much blood loss for the heart to continue functioning, and you were lying in a pool of it an inch deep when EMS got there."

I let this settle in. It was hard to imagine, even with the thought of that big RV rolling over me in the night.

"You had an unusual response at the site of the event," he went on. "You stood up and walked. That's one for the medical journals in the condition you were in."

"I... I don't remember that," I said. "How do you know?" Suddenly, the room seemed to be spinning, awash in confusion.

"We've got you on a digital recording, Jake. You did something no man in your condition could possibly do. We've had a team of heart specialists in from Tulane to examine you. They'll have some questions when you're feeling up to it."

"Because I got up and walked?"

"Yes, while you were clinically dead."

Dr. Werner stared at me and I stared back, unable to speak. He had an expressionless face, robotic.

"Are you supposed to be telling me this?" I said at last.

He shrugged. "You deserve to know."

I faded out for a moment and when I came back, Dr. Werner was speaking again.

"...some of us believe that you also suffered from stress-cardiomyopathy," he went on.

"No idea," I said, running my fingers through my hair.

"It's called broken heart syndrome. Have you heard of it?"

I shook my head, no, feeling queasy.

"It happens when a massive release of adrenaline overwhelms the heart, shutting it down."

"I thought you said it was that other thing, hypo..."

"Yes, there's that," he interrupted, "but we believe that the shock of your wife's death resulted in cardiomyopathy as well. Most likely it was that rush of adrenaline that made it possible for you to reach for her."

"I can't remember." But I remembered being wound up after giving the stranger a shove and not being able to sleep. Maybe that had been the start of it.

"We don't expect you to remember much, if anything. But the specialists want to see you and run some tests. You're a medical marvel in these parts. We don't often use that word, but its seems you're something of a miracle."

"A med...?" I was spinning, losing it. I felt like crap, my stomach churned and a dark shadow crossed my eyes. "How 'bout that."

"Yes Jake. We believe you were dead for almost ten minutes before EMS brought you back. You're lucky there was a trauma center nearby because you were just a sliver inside the golden hour. The other good news is that your brain function seems to be fine. At least we think so. As soon as we complete some tests, we'll..."

"Okay," I gasped, "okay..." Dr. Werner's face began to melt, the lights of the room dimmed, and I sank back into darkness.

A day later, I was lucid enough to talk when the Mississippi State Police came calling.

"Jake? I'm the detective assigned to your case. Smith Freeman."

Smith Freeman had sleepy eyes and a polished complexion the shade of burnt cocoa. He had the same dimensions as a football, half again as round as he was tall, but looked to be all muscle, filling the frame of the door as if it wasn't big enough to contain him. He wore a crisp blue suit garnished with a cornflower-blue tie and a button-down shirt with pink pin stripes.

I got the impression he had all the time in the world.

"You look more like a naval officer than a cop from Jackson, Mississippi," I croaked, still groggy from the sedatives and psychotropic cocktail they'd given me.

He laughed. "No, I was straight Army. Just a grunt in the Gulf War. The first one."

"I hope you didn't dress up just for me."

"Course I did. You're the man of the hour."

That didn't feel good. "You got a first name?"

"It's Smith," he said, "just Smith. Detective Smith Freeman." The rumble in his voice seemed to fit his bulk. It was deep and slow with a burr of Southern honey.

"Sorry. My head's swimming laps. They've got me on some drugs."

"I heard you needed some. You okay to talk?" He sat down.

"Whatever."

"I'm sorry for your loss," he began.

"Yeah, me too."

"You don't mind if I record this, do you?" He set his phone on the tray table alongside a serving dish of green jello and marshmallows.

"I don't mind."

He hit the record button on his phone.

"You know, you're a celebrity here in the hospital," he said.

"That's what I heard."

"A dead man come back to life."

"Mmm-hmm." I nodded.

"What do you think about that?"

I shrugged. "It's what I do."

"Have they shown you the tape yet?"

I shook my head. "I've been kind of out of it."

"You ready for this?"

"Sure." But I wasn't.

Freeman fiddled with his phone. "This is from the body-cam taken by the first officer on the scene."

He hit a button and held the phone up to my face. A black and white video jittered into view showing me on a wheeled stretcher, bathed in the brilliant white light of the cop car's high beams. In the background there was a lot of yelling and two medics ran past me, like ghosts in the backdrop of the night. Another EMS guy was working on me, calling for compression; my chest and abdomen were bathed in black and I realized it was my own blood. It looked like I was dead, my face was white as a zombie in the glare of the headlights. Then in the video, I turned and looked off camera and my eyes widened. "Jill!" I cried, lurching off the stretcher. I stood up and stumbled forward. "Jill!" The video began lurching sideways back and forth as two medics grabbed me from behind and threw me down.

"Pretty dramatic stuff, don't you think?" Freeman said.

I swallowed hard and nodded. "I don't remember any of that."

Freeman snicked off his phone and tucked it away.

"You don't remember because there's no way any man could have got up from that stretcher with all the blood you lost," he said. "You were working on pure electricity or cussedness, something like that. You must have been pumping the same amount of adrenaline you'd expect from a horse."

I nodded. "I guess so."

"You're a lucky man."

"That's what they keep telling me, but it doesn't feel like it."

"How did it feel?"

"What?"

"Being dead," he said. "Did you see the long white tunnel? Did you walk it?"

"Give me a break."

"So, what do you remember?"

"I remember things going black and hearing voices... the nurses, I guess. I remember things before it happened."

"Tell me everything down to the small stuff. You up for it? Can you remember?"

"I remember everything," I said, staring at the ceiling. - My face was still streaked pale red with a delta of tears.

"Let's hear it."

So I did. The near miss on the parkway, the encounter in the campground, Peter's description and his story about working as an IT guy, the lemonade, his bisexuality and anger. The saltwater aquarium, the fast food gig, Prague and smooth jazz. His bullshit claim to be a polymath and my impromptu language test, which he failed miserably.

I told him about the things I'd seen on Peter's computer, two rows of six photos, three on top and three on the bottom, with a third row of photos cut off at the bottom of the screen.

"Tell me about that," Freeman said.

"It was kids, sick things being done to kids."

"What kind of things?"

I told him. It made me sick repeating what I'd seen.

Freeman grimaced and put his hand to his chin. "That's cold. You sure about that?"

I nodded. "It wasn't anything I wanted to see, believe me."

"So how long did you look at this stuff?"

I thought about it. "No more than two seconds, maybe three."

"That's not very long."

"No, but it was long enough for my mind to take a snapshot, you know? Like the saying goes, there are some things you can't unsee."

Freeman nodded. "I get you. So then what?"

"I got out of there and he followed me out the door in the dark. He said he was doing research and that if I turned him in he'd go to prison. Hard-time prison, that's what he said."

"He's right there," Freeman said. "Possession of child porn can get you fifteen to thirty years in Mississippi. It sounds like this cat's got his tail in the gravy."

"Yeah, well he got pretty freaked out when he saw that his laptop screen had opened."

"And what did you say?"

"I told him I hadn't seen anything. I just wanted to get away. I was dead tired, but I planned to call the cops in the morning and he must have known it. I told him I didn't give a shit what he did."

"So you came across as being hostile."

"Yeah. I couldn't help it after what I'd seen."

"Then what?"

"He grabbed my shoulder and I knocked him on his ass. Maybe that's why he ran over us."

"What do you mean, you knocked him on his ass?"

"I gave him a shove and he fell over backwards. End of story. But that wasn't the end of it. I could hear him howling in his motorhome. He sounded like a dog or something. He went on for more than half an hour and I had some bear spray handy in case he came charging over. We never thought... I never thought... I mean, who...?"

"Go on."

"Who would do such a thing? Jill was half asleep when I crawled into our tent. I stayed up for awhile, listening to him ranting across the way. The next thing I remember was hearing a roaring sound. I woke up in time to see his tail lights coming right at us. After that, nothing."

Through it all Freeman looked at me as intently as a dog waiting on a table scrap, his eyes never wavered. Now and then he looked down with a grunt to write something in a notebook, but he was a close listener, and I got the sense he'd be listening to his recording later on too.

"You should have moved," he said at last.

That stung. "I know that now."

"So, how do you know it was him?"

"Who else could it be? He was parked at the next campsite, maybe fifty feet away."

"Could it have been an accident? Like perhaps he was drunk and put his vehicle in reverse instead of drive?"

I thought of Jill, crushed beneath the RV that had come on like a hunting animal.

"No. It was no accident. He meant to kill us."

"How do you know?"

I struggled for words. "It's all of the above, you know? Buzzing us out on the highway and then all of his lies and the big charade of playing host. The guy was hostile as a hornet's nest. I could feel it the whole time we were talking. Then when he knew what I'd seen on his computer, that must have signed our death warrant."

Freeman nodded. "Tell me about the rig. What did it look like?"

"It was like an old cracker box or a big carton of cigarettes, all white, but old and streaked with rust and dirt, like something from the '70s, maybe."

"Did it have any distinguishing features?"

"Just dirt," I shrugged. "It had some brown rust streaks running down from the windows and some rust on the fenders. The kitchen window was cracked three ways. It was patched up with masking tape on the inside."

"Sounds like a hillbilly hooch,"

"Yeah, but he wasn't a redneck. He was a bullshitter, but he seemed smart enough."

Freeman nodded. "The motor home. How long would you say it was?"

"Thirty feet? Forty? It was the same as all of those big motor homes you see going down the highway."

"Did you get a photo of it? License plate?"

"I should have, but no."

"Why not?"

"I thought of it, but by then it was too dark to see and I was dead tired. I had a headache and figured I'd get it in the morning."

"Mmm."

I gave a feeble wave, my ribs still on fire with a cutting pain. "You think I'm an idiot, don't you?"

Freeman's face stayed as cool as stone. "Why do you say that?"

"For getting into this situation, for getting Jill killed. We should have moved on as soon as I figured the guy was psycho."

"You didn't know."

"You said yourself that I should have moved."

"Yeah, well, I wasn't choosing my words all that well. I'm sorry, Jake."

"I could have moved our picnic table, at least. I could have blocked his path."

"Look man, no one thinks they're going to get run over at a campsite. Don't go laying that on yourself."

"Yeah, I get that," I said, but I didn't.

"Come on, let's keep at it," Freeman said. "Did you catch what state his rig was from? Do you remember the color of the license plate? Anything like that could help."

"No, like I said, it was way past dark by the time I got the idea this guy was crazy. But I remember he had a couple of bumper stickers. Wall Drug was one of them, with white letters on a green background. There was another sticker with a star on it."

"What kind of star? Jewish?"

"No, it was just a five-pointed star, white on a black background."

Freeman tugged at the cuffs of his shirt and gave a little snort. "I don't know about the star, but half the motor homes in America have a Wall Drug sticker," he said of the tourist trap in South Dakota, "but it might help."

"Do you think you'll catch him?"

"Yeah, I do, assuming what he said about himself was true. He took off with his camp tag, but he wasn't able to get into the metal pipe where he placed his registration slip. He's from Shreveport; we've already contacted law enforcement there. It's a big town but it shouldn't be hard to track down an IT guy with a motor home. They're working on it."

The memory of Jill's death was still too raw for me to care about catching the stranger. What would I do without Jill? Where was she now? Her body, her soul? The nurse said her parents were waiting just outside the door to see me after Detective Freeman. They'd flown down a week ago and were there when I'd gone psychotic. I never even saw them. There would be a funeral; they'd take Jill home, but to where and to what? Old folks have funeral plans, plots, ideas on cremation, but we were young. Jill is only 31. Then, as would happen many times in the days ahead, I reminded myself that she *was* 31. Was.

Jill's parents came in after Freeman left. They were both in their 70s, gone deep gray, and they moved in the slow, stilted way of the elderly, unsure of their joints. Jill's dad, Bart, had been a firefighter and now he was stiff from a life of hard wear. He came in holding a small blue gift box with my mother-in-law, Mary, hovering over his shoulder.

"How are you son?" he began.

I gave him a gobsmacked look and opened my hands. "Sorry in every way. I'm so sorry, I..."

Mary drifted to my side, taking my hand. "We're sorry, too, Jake," she said, looking down on me. "We can only hope she's in a better place now. Someday we'll find her there, waiting for us with the Lord in heaven."

We talked. They said Jill's death wasn't my fault. I heard them, but they might as well have been speaking through a wall of glass for all I took in. All I could think was that it had been my fault for bringing Jill along. The whole world knew it was true.

Bart had placed the box on the bedside table and now he handed it to me.

"We didn't know how long you were going to be in a coma, Jake, or even if you were ever coming back to us, so..."

"You had the funeral."

Bart nodded. "Yes, Jake, and Jill has been cremated. We brought her remains here for you to, well, to say goodbye."

I opened the lid and there was a pewter urn containing all that was left of Jill, a strong, vital woman, dwindled down to a handful of ashes. Horror swept through me along with a black chill as it settled in that Jill wasn't with the Lord in some imaginary heaven; she was just in this urn.

The rest of that day and the next was a somber time as I reflected on Jill and explored the sensations of my damaged body. There was a certain raw thrill of pain whenever I twisted my scarred abdomen and my still-tender ribs. But my nurse said I'd be out of the hospital within three days.

Detective Freeman showed up again on the afternoon before my release with a forensic psychologist from the Mississippi State Police. Dr. Manning was a plump African-American woman with blue-black hair and a business-like manner, dressed in a baggy blue dress and wearing chunky black glasses. "Call me Vicki," she said.

"I got some news for you," Freeman began, handing me a clipboard. "We got the toxicity report back and it shows you had traces of GHB in your blood. It's a date-rape drug that made a lot of news back in the

'90s. Use enough of it and it will put you in a coma."

"Wow, let me guess," I said.

"Yeah, wow. So you've got to level with me here, are you a user?"

I answered with a grim laugh. "I'm riding a bike 400 miles through the South with my wife and you think I'd be messing around with some kind of animal tranquilizer?"

"Just had to ask," Freeman said. "We think this stuff was in the lemonade Peter gave you. You say you didn't drink much of it?"

"Just a few sips."

"Well, lord knows what would have happened if you'd drank the whole glass or even half of it. He turned and nodded. "Dr. Manning here would like to hear your story. She may have some ideas to share."

I went through the encounter with Peter again and Dr. Manning listened as intently as a child hearing a bedtime story.

"Detective Freeman says you saw some photos. What did you see?" she asked.

Reluctantly, I described them.

"That's some bad stuff, alright," she said. "So he figured he had to eliminate you or go to prison."

"He could have just thrown his laptop in the river," I pointed out. "He didn't have to run over us."

"Maybe he didn't want to lose it," she said quietly. "He may have had contacts and other information on his computer that he needed to keep. That, and the likelihood of prison pushed him into a corner."

Dr. Manning brushed off Peter's sexual kinks with a single comment: "Sounds like this guy could be a jailbird," she said to Freeman. "You might want to run through your list of ex-cons."

"Already on it," he answered.

She was more interested in Peter's rambling monologue about his past and his interests.

"How long would you say he went on?" she asked.

"It seemed like a long time, at least twenty minutes."

"And he never asked you any questions? Nothing about you or your wife?"

"Not a word. Toward the end he asked me a few things."

"And how would you characterize his voice? I mean the way he spoke to you."

"Kind of quiet, monotonous, sort of like a stream-of-consciousness thing, just sort of flowing on."

Dr. Manning looked up from her notes and nodded. "I think he was trying to hypnotize you," she said.

"Just by talking?"

She nodded. "Along with the help of the GHB. He was lulling you to sleep."

"It wasn't like he was looking in my eyes."

"That's an old myth. Most likely he was using what we call covert hypnosis or conversational hypnosis to make you relax. It's a way of connecting to the unconscious mind, lulling you into a deep trance."

"Seriously?"

"Yes. Let me explain it another way. Have you ever done any yoga?"

"A little."

"Are you familiar with the practice of yoga nidra?"

I shrugged. "I just tagged along to a few of Jill's classes. I don't know what they called it."

"Yoga nidra is a form of meditation where the instructor tells a long story in a low, soothing voice. It induces a deep state of meditation that puts you way under, far deeper than sleep. It's kind of like being in a trance where you're totally relaxed and out of it. I think your assailant was trying to do the same thing."

"So he was the cobra and I was the rabbit."

"That's right. Once you were unconscious with even a little bit of that G, he could have had you trussed up like a Christmas goose."

I didn't know what to say. The image of me tied up and unconscious while that psychopath went after Jill was too much.

"I'll tell you another thing," Dr. Manning said after a moment. "I think that everything this guy told you was a lie."

"All of it?"

"That's right. I believe he was just playing you the whole time. He even pretended he didn't know you were speaking French. He was making it all up as he went along, trying to put you under."

"Why do you think that?" Freeman asked.

"Because his goal was to leave a trail of bread crumbs that would take us nowhere," Dr. Manning said.

It made sense. Back in Peter's RV I had imagined that he didn't know I was speaking French when he claimed to know six languages, but he must have known; he was just playing the fool with me.

"There's one thing I don't think he was lying about," I said.

Dr. Manning's tattooed eyebrows arched up. "What's that?"

"He said he was into constructing scenarios. It seemed important to him, he emphasized it."

"What kind of scenarios?"

"I don't know, like games, I think. Like a spider weaving a web. He creates a scenario that ends up trapping his victims."

"If that's true, then maybe he kills for the fun of it," Freeman said. "Like some kind of thrill-killer."

"That's right," I said. "It's all just a game for him."

Dr. Manning studied me for several moments. "That's good, Jake. That's real good," she said. "But where do you see this scenario going?"

"I think he meant it as a game of hide and seek up to the point when he decided to run us over."

"So what would the game be now?"

Detective Freeman answered for me. "It's search and destroy," he said.

I didn't know what to think after they'd gone. Frankly, I didn't want to think about anything, not even Jill. The fact that we hadn't been getting along over the past year or so made her death seem even worse. There had been no closure or chance to tally up our marriage and say goodbye and good luck. I sat and stared out the window for the rest of the afternoon, watching the birds.

My brother John drove down from Michigan the next day to pick me up. When we got home, there was a memorial service for Jill with all of her friends and family gathered in a park outside of town. Her ashes were sprinkled in the Huron River.

I called detective Freeman a few days later; nothing had turned up yet, but he tossed me a crumb. Peter had written his name with a blunt pencil stub on the campsite registration, and though it was almost illegible, they'd figured out that his last name was Becker.

"We're confident we'll have this guy soon, very soon," Freeman said.

"Thanks for keeping me in the loop," I said.

I set the phone down with an involuntary laugh, more like a chuckle, I guess. Keeping me in the loop: what a funny thing to say about catching the guy who killed your wife. That's just how it felt, like I was caught in a loop going nowhere, impotent, powerless to do anything, just looping. Funny, that one.

But the days turned into weeks with me calling and no news coming back. I called the liaison officer in Shreveport. They had investigated every angle, checking every motor park, RV dealer and mechanic in town, but there was nothing yet. Possibly, the RV was parked down a two-track out in the woods or along some swampy river. They had eyes up and were working with the drug-snooping plane that combed the area in search of pot growers. They promised to keep me posted.

I got back to my job. The bosses had let me slide with a bereavement leave of absence, but if I missed any more days they'd have to let me go. Bills were piling up and Jill and I had a nut-buster of a mortgage. There were also expenses related to her funeral and my hospital stay. I needed money, I needed to get back to work.

After my fourth call to Freeman, something struck me. Peter, or whoever he was, claimed to be from Shreveport, Louisiana, but he didn't have a southern accent. There was some kind of shading to his voice, but I couldn't place it.

INCIDENT_____

THE PACKAGE HIT THE WATER beneath a low bridge in Louisiana and lingered on the surface for thirty seconds before sinking into the river. The sluggish waters were dyed a muddy brown from the tannic roots of a cypress forest upstream. The water flowed on, dark, concealing.

The driver watched it sink with satisfaction. He'd had his naughty fun with the prey chained up in his bedroom over the past three days, but had grown tired of changing the young man's diaper. He'd wrapped the heavily drugged man in a long sheet of polyethylene housewrap and half a roll of duct tape. There had been a mewling from the package as he dragged him down the steps of his RV, but the dude didn't have anything to complain about. He hadn't been kept in a fetid basement closet like his parents had kept him.

He felt nothing for him at all, only that given the circumstances, his prize had to go.

He'd been hoping for a dancer or a well-seasoned prostie when he staked out the back door of a strip club in Louisville at 3 a.m. Instead, this guy had popped out with a bag of trash, heading for the dumpster where he'd been waiting in the shadows.

He was angry with himself, not for the bartender with the thin mustache, but for what had happened at the campground. That had been stupid, he'd left traces of himself. He'd let his rage get the best of him. Again. People had seen him, and he wasn't the sort to go unnoticed. He'd driven the back roads of Mississippi and Louisiana for 12 straight hours at 35 mph, trusting that the police wouldn't be looking for a junker RV out in the sticks. They'd be watching the main roads.

Scenarios skittered through his brain like the footpads of a spider.

His rig was parked on the public access ramp, a muddy track leading down to the river, but there were no fishermen in sight and it was a golden Southern day. Around him magnolia trees blossomed in an eruption of pink and white and a wall of bougainvillea crept ruby red in the vines tangled over the old bridge. A live oak dripping with Spanish moss overshadowed the river, glorious in the sunlight. That tree had to be at least three hundred years old, he thought.

Casually, he strolled to his rig and fastened his seat belt. He pulled a ragged U.S. Atlas from behind his seat and paged through it to Louisiana, giving it a long look. None of the roads he was traveling on were on the map and he intended to keep it that way. He backed the RV onto the road and crept slowly across the crumbling bridge. The Texas border was only an hour away.

Going Postal
Chapter 3

"Can you remember who you were, before the world told you who you should be?"

- Charles Bukowski, *Post Office*

"Jake, I've got some news for you and it's not good." It was Freeman on the phone, six weeks after I'd made it home.

I sighed. "Give it to me."

"Sorry to say, we've searched every RV record in Louisiana, Mississippi and Arkansas, but there's no owner named Peter Becker," he said. "We've contacted motor services in Texas and we're going to search there too."

"But?"

"But now we think he was using an assumed name."

"Who's we?"

"We've got an interstate team working on this that includes the FBI," Freeman said. "We're trying, Jake, but we need to cast a wider net. You say this guy was some kind of gypsy fellow?"

"Yeah, he said he traveled the country as a consultant, fixing computer systems."

"Yeah, well if that's true, he may not even have a home base. I'm sorry, Jake, but it may take longer than we thought."

"So maybe Dr. Manning is right. Maybe everything he told me was a lie."

"Yeah, maybe. But we still have to follow up on those leads."

"One thing I wanted to tell you," I said. "It struck me that he didn't have a southern accent. I can't place it, but he didn't sound like he was from the South."

"Well, that's helpful," Freeman said.

"You think?"

"There aren't a lot of people who move to Shreveport unless they have to."

"Yeah, that's what I was thinking too."

"So, what did he sound like? You said he was raised in Texas."

I had a friend in college from Texas and he spoke with a bit of a drawl. There was nothing like that in Peter's voice, or whoever he was.

"He just sounded like a nerd," I said at last. "Like some nerd from the Midwest."

"Big area."

"Yeah."

We talked a bit more about how I was feeling and then about Freeman's own troubles. His 18-year-old nephew was supposed to be heading for his first semester at college but he'd gotten a DUI last week. Now, his entire family was tilted sideways with aggravation. Freeman felt bad about how my case was going; he'd expected it to be in the bag by now. But he let slip that he had a lot of other cases on his desk and mine was taking up a lot of time.

I knew what that meant.

"Let me know if there's anything I can do to help," I said.

"Will do, Jake. Got to let you go, there's another call coming in."

After hanging up, I thought of my file on Detective Freeman's desk, getting buried under all of the mayhem that went on each day in Jackson, Mississippi. My thoughts drifted on to Peter's accent and tried to place it. Like I said, I've got a good memory, but I'm no linguist. I can't tell an Australian from a Brit, and I've tried.

American accents are way easier. It's not hard to tell if someone is from New York, the South, Boston or out West, but the flat, featureless tones of the Midwest cover a lot of territory, ranging all the way from Connecticut to California. Peter Becker's non-accent took in most of the country.

I'd been numb at work even before Jill's murder, but now the joy of life crawled out of me, leaving only a shell behind to perform my monkey-see, monkey-do job at the post office. The old gang was happy to see me and threw a small, but somber, welcome back party. Then everyone drifted off to their work stations and things got back to normal.

But not for me.

I run a mail sorting machine at a postal distribution center outside Ann Arbor. Machine #6 is a clattering, jabbering, linear snake of a steel monster, about 80 feet long, which sorts up to 55,000 #10 envelopes per hour.

I didn't hate my job, but I didn't love it either. It was supposed to be a means to an end, but the end part hadn't come around yet.

When I graduated college with a B.A. in history, my goal was to head straight on to law school. But Jill and I got swept up in the peer pressure of most of our friends getting married in their 20s and we decided to take the plunge too. We had things all figured out; Jill had a good job as a physical therapist and she would support the both of us while I worked toward my law degree.

Then the Great Recession of 2008 hit and Jill's hours got cut. Suddenly the whole world was in flux, including my plans to go back to school. With millions of American laid off, it was a minor miracle that I was able to land a temporary seasonal job at the post office. Once I had my foot in the door, it stayed there.

My job is ministering to the machine. It's a dreary setting; the facility is painted in industrial shades of gray and urine yellow with a concrete floor throughout. It's a baleful place lit pale-green under sizzling fluorescent lights.

This, amid rows upon rows of linear machines. Scanners running optical character software read the addresses on the envelopes flying by, both printed and hand-written, and route the mail to their respective zip codes. Most of what we handle is third class junk mail, the life's blood of the U.S. Postal System; without it they'd be history in the age of email.

I say my machine clatters, but really, the sound it makes is more like a storm of whirring grasshoppers coming to devour the state of Kansas. Every few minutes it spits out an irregular envelope or jams up. It's my job to run back and forth, plucking bad mail from the stream to keep it flowing.

Like I said, it's monkey-see, monkey-do.

Legend has it that Buddha made peace with himself by sitting on the bank of a river and watching it flow on forever without a thought in his head. It's not like that at Postal Distribution Center #491. You spend hours watching the river of mail streaming by, but there's no meditative sense of bliss. Instead, the little snags in the current unleash a torrent of stress: a torn envelope, a bent corner, anything that jams up the machine.

The damaged and irregular mail that's kicked out of the machine has to be hand-sorted, like in the old days. I pull this duty a couple times a week and dread it. You spin in circles for hours like a chicken pecking corn, filing the shucked pieces of mail by zip codes in 28 baskets to destinations around the region. After awhile you start doing that chicken dance in your dreams.

But the pay's good for a college grad with a worthless lib arts degree in history. I hired in at $17.36 and after five years was making over $20 with extra pay for skipping breaks. Jill made a little more than me with her gig as a physical therapist. We did alright with our combined paychecks, even by Ann Arbor standards.

It's not easy getting in the post office. You have to take the postal exam, for starters. That means memorizing a slew of zip codes and addresses in rapid succession and repeating them under the gun of a time clock. Like I said, I've got a good memory, even for numbers, and hit the 90th percentile on the test, hiring in as temporary help at Christmas.

If you pass the postal exam you have a date with a drug testing facility to pee in a cup. You'd think that anyone applying to work at the post office for the princely sum of $17.36 per hour would give up smoking weed, meth or whatever for a month to pee a clear stream into a plastic cup. But out of 18 of us who passed the postal exam and made it through the hiring interview, only four of us passed the drug test.

After I passed the postal exam, the drug test and an interview, I was sworn in as a federal employee and pledged to uphold the Constitution against all enemies, foreign and domestic. Then I was in, a g-man with a job for life with Uncle Sam if I wanted it. Or at least until the level of automation and artificial intelligence caught up with the MS-21 machine and made my job as obsolete as those who sorted mail by hand in the last century.

After my first round on the midnight shift, I was exhausted beyond words, green in the gills and blue in the lips from standing for eight hours on a concrete floor in my steel-toe boots. When you work the graveyard shift from 10 p.m. to 6 a.m., your body starts screaming, "Go to sleep!" by about 2 o'clock in the morning. Then the light-sensing pineal gland at the center of your brain starts screaming, "Wake up!" at about 10 a.m. when you're back home and desperate to sleep. I took to wearing a ski cap to bed, covering my eyes in order to get some rest. It was a bummer working nights, but I kept going, saving what I could in the hope of attending law school someday.

My job training included lessons in foiling terrorists. In the weeks after 9/11, for instance, envelopes containing anthrax were mailed to two U.S. Senators and five media outlets. Twenty-two people were infected in the attack and five of them died.

Decontaminating the postal facility which processed the anthrax letters cost $130 million and took 26 months. Another postal facility in New Jersey was closed for four years and cost $65 million to clean up. It took almost $42 million to clean up the Senate offices in D.C. Overall, more than $1 billion was spent on the investigation and decontamination of a few letter sent through the U.S. mail.

Then there's the deadly poison, ricin, easily made from the pulp of the castor bean. In 2003 a letter packed with ricin was intercepted on its way to the White House. Another letter showed up at a postal facility in Greenville, South Carolina. The following year, an envelope containing ricin was sent to the Dirksen Senate Office Building in D.C. The sender, "Fallen Angel," claimed to be the owner of a trucking company who was angry enough to commit mass murder in response to changes in federal regulations for servicing trucks.

That's why today, the mail runs through an electronic sniffer called a Biohazard Detection System (BDS). It filters all incoming mail, collecting air samples from each envelope as it passes through, matching DNA samples with that of anthrax and the like. The machine's inventors relied on biological warfare research conducted by the military.

If a red stack light and a horn goes off on the BDS machine at any of the 321 postal distribution centers across the U.S., the whole place shuts down and we employees are supposed to march out of the building and wait for instructions. But by that time some us may be among the walking dead, since it takes about 90 minutes for the BDS to analyze the mail for toxins.

We're also trained to spot iffy mail, such as envelopes leaking white powder or oozing liquids. If we spot a package with smoke pouring out of the seams, that's a pretty good indication that it's time to run for cover.

Bombs are sent in the mail more often than you might think. The supreme madman of the mail was Unabomber Ted Kaczynksi, a former professor and anarchist who lived without electricity or running water in the woods near Lincoln, Montana. Kaczynksi sent letter bombs through the mail for 17 years from 1978 to 1995, killing three people and maiming 23 others in a crusade against technology. He was caught in 1995 after the most expensive manhunt in FBI history. His brother and his sister-in-law turned him in after recognizing his style and beliefs in the Unabomber Manifesto, which was published in the *New York Times* and *Washington Post*.

The Postal Service learned a lot from the Unabomber and his story was part of my training. We're taught to look for packages with no return address or phony addresses, along with packages that are obsessively wrapped in gobs of tape and plastered with stamps. Packages weighing more than 13 ounces are no longer accepted with stamps alone; they have to be checked in through a post office. If a package hasn't been inspected and tracked by a postal employee, it will likely be opened and examined.

Our facility covers a couple of acres under one roof, filled with mail sorting machinery and steel carts loaded with coming-and-going mail. Semi trucks would roll in after midnight with crews attacking endless bins of packages, all of which must be hand-sorted to dozens of communities. We'd tense as if awaiting a massacre and then start tossing priority parcels into ratty vinyl bags and bins for hours on end, bound for their respective zip codes.

It wasn't until I'd been on the job for a month or so that I commented on the row of dark windows that ran around the entire perimeter of our building about ten feet above the work area.

"That there is a walkway hidden behind dark glass," one of my co-workers said. "It's there so the managers can spy on us."

"Spy on us? Why would they do that? It's not like we've got time to slack off."

He laughed. "They're not worried about anyone loafing on the job. It's all about the money in the mail. Crooked postal employees have stolen millions of dollars in mail through the years."

"For real?"

"Seriously. Checks, Christmas gifts, birthday money and gift cards, all of that stuff is pretty easy to spot in the mail. If you're suspected of stealing, you get watched pretty closed, and if you're caught, you get fired on the spot."

I figured that the hidden walkway ran almost a quarter of a mile around the perimeter of the building, constructed at a huge expense. It seemed needless, but as it turned out, I was a replacement for a guy who'd been slipping envelopes into his coveralls when he thought no one was watching.

Given the time pressure of moving millions of pieces of mail every day, postal employees get anal to the nth degree over screw-ups. Dropping a package into a bag with the wrong zip code tends to earn you a caustic rebuke from a co-worker or management, igniting a sense of rage that seems beyond reason. There were times when I smoldered with anger for hours on end for being chided over a misplaced piece of junk mail.

Mostly, the job was stressful because there was never an end to it, no sense of completion. You'd tackle a mountain of junk mail flyers, newspapers, magazines and catalogs only to find that there was another mountain looming right behind it, in fact an entire mountain range of stuff that's mostly third-class crap bound for the addressee's trash can.

"Going postal" is what happens when an employee breaks under pressure. The phrase caught on in the '90s after a string of postal workers went berserk at a number of facilities. It started in Edmond, Oklahoma in 1986 when postman Patrick Sherrill killed 14 co-workers before shooting himself in the head. In the '90s, postal workers went on shooting rampages in Royal Oak and Dearborn, Michigan; Ridgewood, New Jersey; Dana and Goleta, California; and Baker City, Oregon. Dozens of people have been killed by employees going postal.

But the phrase adopted by the media is taboo at any postal facility.

"Don't ever use the term 'going postal' here, even if you're just kidding around," a manager warned us during our training. "It's tied to many painful experiences and can result in your termination."

Understood. But as I sat amid the whir of machine #6 that winter I slowly began going postal with thoughts of Jill and her death. Her killer was out there and I could nothing about it. I was just watching the river flow, possibly with a bit of Third Class junk mail addressed to Peter Becker streaming past. The stream of mail and the endless whir of the machine hypnotized me, stamping my brain with the indelible ink of revenge.

R.A.G.E.
Chapter 4

Dr. Johansson had a crown of frizzy dark hair piled up atop her head like an untrimmed bush from which small creatures might emerge at any moment. She was a big woman with green cat-eye glasses and a pillowy body canvased in a beige dress. She favored orange plastic clogs for shoes and had an aromatherapy diffuser that oozed essential oils in her office on the ground floor of a dilapidated mansion on Hill Street in Ann Arbor. She insisted that I call her Dr. Johansson, even though there was only an MSW degree displayed on the wall of her office. I called her on it once and she said she was "working on it."

Secretly, I called her Dr. Nerdingham.

"So, tell me about it," she said at our first visit.

"What?"

"It. Tell me about how you feel. How are things sorting out for you?" She leaned back in a black, high-backed office chair in front of a wall of books on therapy, social work, yoga, theosophy and pop psychology, most of which were paperbacks.

My brother, John, had guilt-tripped me into seeking therapy and I didn't want to be here. I smelled bullshit all over Dr. Johansson, but I marked that up to the bad attitude I had about therapy. It had failed Jill and me when we'd gone for marriage counseling, the end-game of mutually-assured destruction.

"I feel dead inside," I said.

"Explain."

"That sort of says it all, doesn't it? I'm stuck in neutral, not moving forward with my life. My wife died and it's my fault she's gone."

"Why is it your fault?"

I shifted in my chair and looked at the clock. "I talked her into going on a trip that led to her death."

Dr. Johansson leaned forward, arms on her desk, steepling her fingertips. "You talked her into this trip? Are you sure about that? Tell me about this trip; was it a guilt trip? A death trip? The trip of a lifetime?"

And so it went. Like with marriage counseling, I'd make a statement and Dr. Johansson would repeat it back to me as a question.

"We were having a hard time as a couple."

"You were having a hard time as a couple? Tell me about that."

"We were too young to get married."

"You were too young to get married? What do you mean by that?"

"It means what it means. Too young. We weren't right for each other."

"You weren't right for each other? How did that make you feel?"

That's the way things went every week all through the early fall. In between questioning, Dr. Johansson let on that she was $60,000 in debt for her MSW education at the University of Michigan. It occurred to me that she could have saved the whole bundle simply by learning that the gist of therapy seems to be repeating one's statements back as questions, ad infinitum.

Gradually, it dawned on me that Dr. Johansson was little more than a parrot, as disinterested in me as any weathered old bird, seeking only the cracker of the $80 per week that I paid for our visits. At times I caught her immersed in some other pursuit on her phone when she was supposed to be counseling me. But I had made a promise to John that I would get counseling and had signed on for Dr. Johansson's eight-week special for new clients, paid in advance.

All through September and October I came to Dr. Johansson's office once a week, playing Q&A with little result. Usually, I left her office feeling more unsettled than when I went in.

After one particularly exasperating session I blew up on her.

"How do you..." she began.

"Look, I'm looking for some direction here, not more questions," I said, cutting her off. "Do you think I like sitting her week after week answering my own questions? I'm looking for a way out of this..."

"This?" Her eyebrows went up.

"This pain, these feelings," I said in disgust.

Dr. Johansson settled back in her chair, drawing herself in like a cat. "Life is about answering our own questions," she said in a small voice.

"You think? That's the first solid advice you've given me."

"I'm trying to help you to help yourself."

"What? With these endless questions? Where will that lead us?"

She shrugged. "Search me. That's up to you."

"Well, I'm through," I said, getting up for the door.

"You are?"

"Yeah." I slammed the door behind me. There was a brewpub down the street and I downed three pints of bitter IPA, trying to stare a hole in the mirror beyond the bar. I stumbled home feeling lower than the street people begging in the cold on Liberty Street.

But the next day I sent flowers and an apology after a long night of beating myself up. Was I such a wuss that I couldn't deal with a few questions? I had talked on the phone with my brother John that night and he said to man-up, quit feeling sorry for myself. It only made me feel worse, bothering my brother, who had troubles of his own.

The next week I was back at our regular time. "Sorry about the hissy-fit," I mumbled.

"No pain, no gain, right?" Dr. Johansson said brightly. "We're making progress!"

By early November, Dr. Johansson began confessing her own troubles. She'd been a fat kid in elementary school and forced to wear coke-bottle glasses at an early age, which had ruined her sense of self worth. That, and her parents were rich, from an auto exec dynasty living in West Bloomfield. In this day and age they even had servants. "Black ones, can you imagine? From Haiti. I can't deal with that," she said.

"I'm living with the guilt of being born with a silver spoon in my mouth," she went on, clasping her head in her hands.

"So you were born rich?" I asked.

"Yes, and I hate it. But I love it too; flying first class, the nice car, the Blues Cruise in the Caribbean every year. It's nice, but at the same time it's loathsome."

"Poor little rich girl."

Dr. Johansson glowered at me.

"You don't know what it's like to be rich and not earn it," she said. "That's all I want, to earn my way, free of my parents. I want to do my own thing, make my mark on the world."

"You want to make your mark on the world?" Dr. Johansson didn't pick up on the fact that now, I was questioning her.

"Yes, I've got a plan."

"So you've got a plan?"

"Yes, I've got a plan."

"What is this plan?"

"It's a good plan."

"Tell me about it."

For once, Dr. Johansson looked timid and small. Her brown eyes peered tentatively at me over the frames of her glasses. "I'll think about it," she said.

A week later I made the long commute through traffic across town in the late-afternoon darkness and flopped down in the too-small chair across the carpet from her throne, intending to tell her once again that this was it. Therapy wasn't working for me; tormenting visions of Jill were still haunting my dreams and I couldn't stop replaying the scene from the campground in my head. I saw Becker spitting tobacco juice in his beer can, cajoling me into stopping by for a drink; I relived the scene outdoors by the light of his RV when I pushed him over backwards... it all replayed over and over again like a film on an endless loop.

"So how is it with you?" she asked, placing her hand on my knee and rubbing it back and forth.

"Real good," I lied.

"Coming along? Are you starting to find a little peace?"

"Not really."

"Really? How do you feel?"

"Like I felt when I walked in here a couple of months ago. Bad."

"You feel like shit?"

"Yeah, I feel like shit, and the questions aren't helping."

For a change, Dr. Johansson gazed at me and didn't respond with, "So my questions aren't helping you?"

"No."

"Hmm... Do you want drugs?"

"No."

She stuck a pencil in her mouth, eraser first, and chewed on it.

"Jake, I've been thinking."

I waited.

"We're like a couple on our third date," she said. "You know what that means."

"What?"

"That's when people usually get laid."

I shifted in my seat. "Thanks, but you've got this all wrong."

"Hold on Jake," she said, her eyes flaring into mine, as earnest as any lover. "I meant that metaphorically, like it's time to make a commitment to one-another. It's time to cross the Rubicon, know what I mean?"

"Not really." An uneasy feeling crept over me.

"I mean I want to share something with you, but it's kind of personal."

"Yeah?"

"Yeah. Truth or dare, Jake."

We sat there for 30 seconds with neither of us saying anything; just me looking down at the carpet and she looking at me.

"I don't want to have sex with you," I said at last.

"Oh, God *no!*" she said. "Jake, that was just an intro into a conversation I'd like to have with you. I mean, wrong foot, dig? Let's start over."

"Yeah, sure."

"I've got this thing I've been working on," she said slowly. "Actually, it's the thesis for my Ph.D."

"Hmm."

"It's called rage therapy. R.A.G.E. That stands for Revenge Alternative

Gaming Emersion."

"Rage."

"Yes, I've tried it on myself, Jake, but I need others to confirm its efficacy. Do you know what I mean?"

I nodded. "You know that immersion is spelled with an 'i' don't you?"

Dr. Johansson gave me a dumbstruck look. "No, it's the other kind of emersion," she sputtered. "I looked it up in the dictionary. It means to emerge from being submerged underwater, or when a celestial object emerges from an eclipse."

"I get it," I nodded.

"It's a nice metaphor, don't you think?" she went on, placing her hand on my knee. "But let me tell you about it."

For once, Dr. Johansson seemed totally present, as if the flywheel of her thoughts had finally engaged and was running full bore. The story of R.A.G.E. poured out of her in a rush.

It turned out she had a nephew, Ian, who was a whiz at creating apps and video games. "Ian's just a genie with technology," she said. "He builds castles in the clouds online, whole worlds. He really is a marvel in the strictest sense of the word."

I sipped at a mug of lemongrass tea and nodded.

Dr. Johansson said that under her professional guidance, Ian had devised a game specifically for persons who'd suffered at the hands of others, people seeking revenge.

"My ex-husband was a twisted bastard," she said. "He psychologically abused me and called me things I would never repeat."

She paused, and then, "Okay, I'll tell you. He called me a pig, and that hurt, you know? Then he cheated on me with my best friend who really was a pig. She was the maid of honor at our wedding and then she did this! It was a royal disaster."

"I'm sorry to hear it."

"Yeah, whatever," she waved it off, "but the upshot is, I developed this form of therapy to get over it, and it worked, Jake, it really worked!"

"Rage therapy." I was playing the therapist now, letting Dr. J unspool.

"Yes, R.A.G.E. therapy. I designed it for women who'd been cheated on by their husbands or boyfriends. It provides them with, oh, how

should I say it? A way to get even."

"It sounds very hands-on."

"You could say that." she nodded.

"But not quite."

"No, you're not literally beating someone on the head with an axe, if that's what you mean."

Dr. Johansson pulled a pack of cigarettes from her desk drawer and lit one. "Want one? You don't mind, do you? They're organic." She picked up a remote and sped up the fan on the office air purifier. "This is our little secret, okay? The smoking, I mean."

"Okay."

"Do you have any questions?" she asked, expelling a blue plume toward the ceiling.

"Well the obvious one is how does it work?"

"Easy. R.A.G.E. allows you to work out your revenge fantasies by killing whoever did you wrong through an online gaming modality."

"You mean a video game?"

"Precisely. No one actually dies, of course. It's all just make-believe, but for many of my clients it's quite healing and we believe it has a great deal of potential. Ian and I have even created a brochure; we call it a revolutionary blend of gaming and psychotherapy. He wanted to call it gametech therapy, but I came up with R.A.G.E. We're in phase two of testing it so far."

"So why me if this is meant for angry women?"

"I'd rather not say."

"You think my situation is similar to a jilted wife?"

"I'd rather not say." She took another drag, leaned back and exhaled toward the ceiling again.

"Well, I guess I'd rather not be involved then."

Dr. Johansson snorted, coughed. "Checkmate, I knew you'd say that. I've got your number."

"So tell me then."

"Okay," she sighed. "It's because women are unreliable and the results are inconclusive, in my study at least. Some are happy to kill their husbands over and over again forever. They can't get enough of it. But others break down and start crying after a few sessions, like they're reliving a bad car wreck. It's highly situational, depending on the woman and how angry she is, how emotional, or how much guilt she's taken on."

"So why me?"

"Because you're the bridge to wider implications, Jake. I believe that this could be helpful to crime victims such as yourself. Imagine if you're a victim of rape, domestic violence or an abused childhood..."

"Or your wife was murdered."

She nodded, gazing at me sideway and stubbing out her cigarette. "Precisely," she said. "I've been looking for someone like you to help me in a case study. You're perfect for this, Jake, and I'm sure it can help you. Truly, it can help both of us."

I don't know what made me say yes; maybe it was because I was powerless against the night visions, or because I felt like Dr. Johansson needed me at a time when I needed to reach out to someone. But I told her I'd give it a try in the hope of driving the demons from my head.

The next day I met with her nephew, Ian, who helped me create an avatar for Peter Becker. He had a palette of facial characteristics that we fiddled with for more than an hour, producing a face similar to the one

I'd created with the police artist in Jackson. Ian worked his coding magic and then there was Becker, leering at me from the screen of his laptop.

"So what do we do now?" I asked.

"You're going to kill this guy, over and over again," Ian said.

And that was the point of R.A.G.E. therapy. Dr. Johansson prescribed killing Becker's avatar in a dozen different ways for at least 60 minutes each night ("but no more than two hours") to work through my grief. There were a number of scripted scenarios; I could strangle Becker with my bare hands, blow him to bits with a machine gun, incinerate him with a flame thrower, toss him from a bridge, bomb him, cut his head off with an axe, and so on. Phase three, Ian told me, would allow me to construct my own scenarios, like if I wanted to drop Becker from an airplane into a volcano.

I got sucked in. For the first time in months the absurdity of it gave me a sincere laugh. The game, if you want to call it that, called for me to chase Becker's avatar down a dark alley in an urban environment through empty warehouses, storefronts, a Chinese restaurant and even a police station, eventually giving him his fatal comeuppance. Becker's avatar never stood a chance in any of the encounters; he always got caught and killed and I got points for each score.

I killed Becker 156 times in the first two days and more than 1,000 times before the week was out, racking up 126,000 points by the end of December.

"What are the points for?" I asked Dr. Johansson.

She shrugged. "It's just a gaming thing Ian came up with. It helps build self-esteem and pride in what you're doing."

Dr. Johansson followed my progress, asking me how many times I'd played R.A.G.E. during the week and for how long. How did I prefer to kill the antagonist? Strangling. How would I improve the game?

Concurrently, I pursued an online search for Becker, combing the Internet in the hope of tracking him down. I'd get home from work, settle in with a beer and plunge into R.A.G.E. for two hours, followed by a hasty dinner wolfed down and then several hours online, tracking down leads until 1 a.m. or so. That went on for three months or so.

Gradually, it began driving me nuts. Gradually? Make that quickly. I began to wonder how the women had fared in Dr. Johansson's study.

"They got turned off after a month or so," she said primly. "After a woman has killed her husband a few times online most of them are ready to move on."

"So I guess it was a success then?"

"Yes, I think so, but I've only tried it on myself and two other women and the department head says that's not enough to qualify as a study. What does he know? But that's why your participation is so important."

"I've got to say, the edge is starting to wear off for me," I said.

"Oh? And why's that?"

"It's the same thing over and over again. Chasing him through the alley or the old warehouse; it's not the same as I recall. It's not satisfying."

"You met this guy in a campground while you were out bicycling, right?"

I nodded. "Yeah."

"So if we tweaked this thing to have you riding a bike after Becker down some endless highway, do you think that would make a difference?"

I shrugged. "Maybe."

INCIDENT_____

TWO THOUSAND, SEVEN HUNDRED AND FIFTY-SEVEN MILES AWAY, a lone cyclist inched his way up the mountain road above the waves of Bahia Concepcion in the 106-degree heat. The waves of heat radiating off the pavement made it seem 20 degrees hotter. His face was wrapped in white cotton beneath his helmet, giving him the appearance of a mummy behind his dark sunglasses.

Despite the heat, he wore long sleeves and pants to reflect the merciless sun and wind of the Baja desert. That's how the Mexicans dressed, they never exposed their skin like the clueless tourists. Below him the bay sparkled a brilliant topaz blue beneath the stark, treeless mountains. The mountains were ragged and tan, running like a row of sharpened teeth for as far as the eye could see. He glimpsed a beach a mile down the mountain slope, ringed with tents and RVs.

He'd been riding four days out of Ensenada, down the 1,000 miles of

Highway One through Baja California with the heat seeming to rise with every mile under his pedals. Before that it had been six weeks of hard riding from New York to the Mexican border on a diagonal route straight across the midsection of America. He had unpacked and assembled his bike at Kennedy Airport, aiming to ride across the U.S. and Mexico to meet his sweetheart, Celeste, in Costa Rica.

Yves DuBois had been on epic rides before. He'd cycled the Donau bike trail more than 500 kilometers down the Danube when he was only 12 and had since bike-toured the Sydney-Cairns route in Australia, the canal trails of Scandinavia and across Kazakhstan; what a trial with the wind that had been... He'd been struck twice by cars, robbed at gunpoint by gypsies, chased by a pack of drunken thugs in Byron Bay and had tumbled sideways off a mountain trail in Albania. At 27, his life had been one of adventure and scrapes which he'd survived with the relish of an extremely fit and bold young man. And now, he was immersed in one last big adventure before he married.

But Yves had never encountered the heat akin to that of the Baja peninsula, not even in Australia, where he'd been wise enough to ride in the Austral winter. He figured on another day of hard riding to the oasis town of Loreto where he'd rest up for a few days, sucking down margaritas and tacos *ajo camarones* before the last sprint to La Paz and the ferry to mainland Mexico.

Despite the heat, he was grateful for the tranquility of Highway One. Billions of saguaro cacti rising ten feet tall or more stood mute witness to his ride along the mostly empty highway, with the pitiless desert and the bleak mountains running in an endless wall to the west. It was a narrow road, but often it was ten minutes before any vehicle came along and the trucks and buses he encountered were respectful, giving him a wide berth. Highway One was a popular route for cyclists delving into Mexico and he'd come across at least a dozen other riders, many of them men and women biking together. Motorists knew to watch out for them, much as they watched for the many cows and goats which tended to wander into the roadway.

It had been good camping in the Baja. Every beach down the peninsula was crowded with motor homes, truck campers, vans and tents at sites that went for as little as 100 pesos per night, about five bucks, U.S. He'd spent the past three nights sharing beers and telling tales in his broken English around campfires on the beach. A couple of beautiful chicas had tempted him mightily, but he had remained true to Celeste.

The ride down the mountains past the bay was an exhilarating roller-coaster of hairpin curves, but once down from the heights he knew it would be a long, flat stretch straight to Loreto. He'd stocked up on three gallon jugs of water at the last tienda before a 50-mile stretch of desert. The water added 25 pounds to his already heavy touring bike and would be hot as bath water by the time he drank it, but it was better to be safe than sorry, as the Americans say. He strapped the jugs with bungee cords, two on the rear rack of his bike and one up front and grimaced at the awkwardness of the ride. It would have to do.

Yves was 35k shy of the military checkpoint north of Loreto on a long straightaway when he noticed the RV in his rear view mirror. The speed limit on Highway One is 80 kilometers per hour, or 50 mph, rarely enforced unless a motorist was unlucky enough to encounter the Policia Federal in a bad mood. But the RV was coming on fast; Yves estimated it was well beyond the speed limit, some crazy American, perhaps, who didn't know about the potholes and cattle. He watched it uncertainly in his mirror as it drew closer, its engine wound to a roaring pitch. It was a big, white, boxy vehicle with a set of bull bars on the front of the sort he'd seen many times in Australia, used to bash kangaroos off the road. Yves braced himself, keeping far to the right of the road; the RV would be past in a moment and then he'd be alone again with the cactus and the wind. His thoughts flashed on Celeste; she would be waiting for him on the beach in a town called Samara, just two days south of the Nicaraguan border. There, his relatives from Orleans would fly all the way across the sea from France to witness their wedding on the beach.

Behind him, Yves heard a sound like thunder.

Then came a tremendous roar and suddenly, Yves was wheeling high in the bright Mexican sun, spinning around and around in the air, his bike tumbling away below him. He caught a split second glimpse of jagged rocks coming up fast and a three-pronged cactus and then...

The Way
Chapter 5

By January I was deep into Facebook, Twitter, Linkdin and Instagram, casting nets each night in my search for Peter. I went through thousands of Peters, flashing on each face as it came up on the search function. All futile, since he probably used a picture of a monkey or a cartoon in his profile.

I went through every information tech guy I could find on Linkdin; there were thousands. Each night I spent hours at my laptop, patiently waiting for every photo to come up. Again, nothing.

I tried keywords: Prague, salt water aquarium, smooth jazz, RVs, drones and other things Peter said he liked. That was even more hopeless.

I combed through scores of dating sites for straight people, gays, bi-sexuals, farmers, Christians, satanists, Mormons, RV owners, bisexual Christian truckers, anything I could think of. I combed online want ads for bisexuals named Peter with ties to the RV life or Texas A&M. Again, nothing, and it was beyond exhausting, not to mention like wading up to your neck through a sewer.

Then I created an online alias, Joe Rogers, a freewheeling RV owner who was looking for romance without boundaries. I went fishing with Joe, dangling him as bait down any social media manhole I could find. I'm not proud of some of the posts I made in his name; mostly I lured in a bunch of deeply conflicted lonely hearts, but none who were a match for Becker.

This was in addition to getting an anonymous Dark Web browser through the Tor system and mucking around in the marketplace of illicit drugs, sex, weapons and criminal enterprises in the sea of trouble at the bottom of the Internet. I ignored the sites for stolen credit cards, counterfeit cash, fake passports and I.D.s. There were snuff porn videos down there, lurid things which I imagined might appeal to Becker, but I couldn't or wouldn't dare to look at them.

I did all that and hired a private investigator to boot who assured me that Becker would be caught within two weeks at a discount rate of $800 per day. It didn't happen.

Through all this I was hacking away at the D.A.R.E. game each night. Ian had tweaked the program so that I was now pursuing Becker's RV on a bike. I could make him crash in a fireball, drive off a cliff, get stuck on a railroad track or suffer four flat tires, whatever I could dream up. As Dr. Johansson had said, Ian was a virtuoso at making my revenge fantasies blossom.

But the long bouts of R.A.G.E. only made me feel worse. And between trolling the internet and playing the game I began to fill with anxiety and powerless feelings, growing sicker, pale and flabby.

One night I heard a bang at the back door, waking me from a deep sleep. "Jill! Jill? is that you?" I cried out, fighting with the tangled sheets to leap out of bed. I ran down the hall in a frenzy to where she'd be standing, but then with the moonlight flooding silver through the window, I realized it was only the wind, slamming at the screen door.

Then came the voices, sly ones that crept into my head in the space between sleep and wakefulness. Sometimes they'd shout, "Jake!" incredibly loud in my thoughts and sometimes they'd mutter accusations filled with guilt and shame, "What did you do, what did you do...?" They were terrifying, unpredictable, always ambushing me. Could schizophrenia be self-induced? My thoughts of Jill's death had been obsessive, inescapable; they were leading me beyond my control to a place filled with horror.

Freeman called during the first week in February. He sounded harried.

"Jake, we've given Texas and the whole South a good going-over but at this point, it's going to be dumb luck if we catch this guy, especially without a license or more of a description to go on."

"So what do you advise?" I asked, my hand trembling as it held the phone. "I need a lifeline, Smith, I'm about two steps beyond crazy right now between my job and trying to track this guy down online. It feels like I'm breaking down, I can't take it, you know? I've got bad dreams, I'm hearing voices, I've got all this pressure building in my head... it feels like my head is going to explode."

Freeman said nothing and there came a long pause. I could hear him breathing heavily over the phone.

"Have you thought of praying?" he said at last. "That's about the only thing I can think of right now. We'll keep trying at this end, I promise you that, but it's in God's hands now. You've got to pray."

"Say my prayers? I don't think that God is in the search and destroy business anymore."

"No, I mean for yourself, for your peace of mind. That might help get you through this thing."

I promised I would, indeed I had, but after hanging up it settled in that I was no better than a 12-stepper who'd hit bottom and was hoping for a hand-up from Jesus. I wanted more than that; there was a T-Rex inside me that needed something more than prayer. I needed something raw to sink my teeth into. That wasn't the kind of thing you could pray for.

I'd neglected my friends all through the winter, skipping all of the holiday parties in December and at New Years Eve. Jill and I had gone to those parties together and I couldn't bear the sad looks and whispers from our mutual friends, so I avoided them altogether.

But in late February, two of our old friends, Mike and Jessie Taylor, called and insisted that I meet them for dinner.

"I've got work to do," I told Mike, gazing into my laptop.

Jessie got on the phone. "Jake, you're coming out with us or we'll come over and break down your door," she said hotly. "Jill would have wanted you to get out and you know it!"

So, reluctantly, I agreed and we met at an Italian place out on Washtenaw Avenue. I nearly turned around and walked right back out, because there at the table with Mike and Jess was a woman that could only be a blind date.

Mike shot up from his chair and rushed me. "Relax," he murmured in my ear. "It's not what you think."

Introductions were made. Shirley Willis was a doctor of naturopathic medicine from Seattle who was visiting her mother in Ann Arbor. A brunette, she had wavy, shoulder-length hair and lively brown eyes. She stood about my height and I noticed she didn't have a wedding ring.

"Dr. Willis and I have known each other since the third grade," Jessie said.

"It's nice to meet you," she said, rising from her chair. "Please, call me Shirley."

"Just so this isn't a blind date," I said bluntly, casting an angry look at Mike and Jessie.

"Oh, dear!" Dr. Willis gave a merry laugh. "From what Mike and Jessie tell me you're nowhere near ready to date anyone, Jake, least of all me. You're still grieving, you need time to heal."

I blushed, feeling like an idiot. "Sorry, it's just that..."

"I completely understand," she said. "I just happened to be in town and couldn't resist joining you all."

We shared a bottle of wine and then another and I began to loosen up. Shirley shared some stories of whale-spotting in Puget Sound and the work she'd done as a college intern with orca pods in the San Padre islands.

"It sounds like a good time," I said.

"Yes, you really must get out there sometime," she replied. "Vancouver Island, especially. It has its own alps and rain forests and there's a wilderness park called Strathcona. It's a very healing place."

She toyed at her gluten-free pasta. "But tell me a bit about yourself, Jake," she went on. "Jessie tells me you're in therapy."

"Yes, I guess it's no secret," I said. I had told Mike about my sessions with Dr. Johansson back in December, begging off from his annual Christmas party. "I'm working on something called rage therapy."

"Oh?"

Shirley Willis was all ears. I told her about Dr. Johansson and her mad scientist nephew Ian and the theory behind Revenge Alternative Gaming Emersion, along with the progress I'd made.

"Progress?"

"I'm up to more than four million points," I said.

She snorted. "And this rage therapy is making you feel better? Better than when you started?"

"No," I said slowly. "Actually, I think it's making me feel worse. I'm starting to feel disconnected, like I'm coming down with some kind of sickness from spending too much time online."

"What kind of sickness?"

"I guess I'd call it electronic sickness."

"Electronic sickness, that's a good way of putting it," she mused. "It's what kids are getting from spending too much time on their devices, their tablets and phones. I'm seeing lots of kids suffering from severe anxiety and alienation. Goddess knows where the world is heading with this digital fixation."

"Yes, goddess knows."

"Now you're making fun of me," she bristled.

"Sorry, couldn't help it, but you're right. I'm thinking of calling it quits."

"That would be wise," she said over the rim of her wine glass. "Rage therapy sounds kind of evil, if you ask me."

"That's your professional opinion? You don't hear doctors dropping the word evil very often."

"I'm convinced that evil exists and I know it when I see it," she said. "This guy who killed your wife, don't you think he's evil?"

"Sure."

"But?"

"You're a naturopath," I reminded her. "There's no evil in nature, there's just predator and prey. When a coyote eats a squirrel alive, it's not because he's evil. That's just nature in action."

"True, evil is something only humans are capable of," she replied. "Evil is a construct of free will, something that's only possible through consciousness. Something only we possess."

"You don't need to convince me," I cut her off. "I know this man is evil, about as evil as it gets."

"Yes, but don't you see? This rage therapy crap is sucking you into his world. Seriously, you need to back away from this stuff. What you're dwelling on is only making you feel worse. It's consuming you, eating you alive. It's time to kill your computer."

"Shirley practices eco-therapy," Jessie butted in. "It's healing through nature."

"Isn't that what naturopathy is all about?" I asked.

"It's a sub-set of that," Shirley said. "Eco-therapy involves getting outside and healing yourself through physical experiences like climbing mountains or taking hikes. Instead of riding a bike in a video game, you should be outside riding a real bike. You should be out skiing every day or hiking the Inca Trail."

"So you think I should do the opposite of what my therapist is telling me."

"Exactly. Imagine if Michael Jackson or Kurt Cobain had fled their demons to go rafting for a few months down the Yukon River without their handlers and their drugs; they might still be alive today."

"They probably would have been eaten by a bear."

"Maybe, but more likely they would have been reborn, free of what tormented them."

Shirley had a big Outward Bound-style practice in Seattle where she was healing scores of patients with eco-therapy, or so she said. She spoke of yurts and sweat lodges, fording icy rivers and climbing trees. She had a program called Five Peaks to Climb for people suffering from depression.

"I had a couple of patients who made their own bows and arrows with the idea of hunting their own food out in the wild," she said. "One of them nearly starved, but I gave him credit for trying."

"What about the other guy?"

"He disappeared," she waved. "Probably went off to work in the oil fields up north or something. I couldn't reach him."

Or maybe he was dead with his bones lying somewhere out in the woods, I thought. It all sounded kind of loosey-goosey, but also a more likely way forward than R.A.G.E.

I got together with Shirley the next day and we went for a long hike down the river, tramping on snowshoes through the new-fallen snow. She was cute in a wholesome way and I guess you could say it sort of was a blind date, although we just talked about her ideas on therapy. We hugged at the end of the day and I promised to look her up if I ever got to Seattle.

The next week, I got to Dr. Johansson's office 15 minutes early, arriving while she was in the bathroom. Her laptop was open in sleep mode and on an impulse, I gave the touch pad a jiggle. The R.A.G.E. program lit up the screen, but instead of the image of a cheating husband or an abused spouse, an avatar that looked just like me melted onto the screen with an axe sticking out of its head. Was it really me? The face looked a bit rounder than mine, but maybe that's how Dr. Johansson and Ian saw me. I double-clicked on the avatar and my name came up.

What could I do but smile? For whatever twisted reason it was clear that Dr. Johansson had begun raging against me, and with more than 60,000 points on the digital counter it was clear that her game had been going on for quite some time. Somehow, it all seemed to fit with her crazy scheme. I heard the toilet flush next door and crept backwards out of her office, quietly closing the door behind me.

So I gave up R.A.G.E. along with answering my phone on the dozens of times that Dr. J called, but my electronic sickness lingered on. I started taking long hikes around town at Shirley's suggestion, but got the feeling that if eco-therapy was going to work for me, I'd need massive doses of it, like something on par with skiing to the North Pole or climbing K-2. Then, in mid-March just as I had reached a place beyond despair with my online search, Jesus came through for me.

Ann Arbor is a hot town for cyclists. God knows why because the city that hosts the University of Michigan is hopelessly congested with traffic. Hulking SUVs jostle with schools of Prius drivers and the occasional Volt or Tesla along streets that are virtual canyons of parked cars on either side. Nonetheless, it's a town that seems to turn up on the Top Ten lists of various bicycling magazines on a perennial basis, probably because there are legions of well-off yuppies in A2 who prefer cycling to golf.

Late one afternoon, I was piloting my mountain bike around the icy puddles along State Street through town when a white RV swept past me in the other direction with a hulking, dark-haired shadow at the wheel. In profile, he looked exactly like Peter Becker. The beast lumbered slowly down the street, barely squeezing past the cars on either side of the narrow way.

It was him, I knew it was, and some chemical cocktail of endorphins and elation flooded my brain like the ecstasy of an onrushing LSD trip. I whirled around and gave chase, taking to the sidewalk and standing on my pedals in a furious dash down the blocks to where the RV was stalled at the long light near the stadium. College kids scattered in my path, their curses and cautions trailing in my wake. Reaching the light, I jumped the curb, landing with a splash in a pond of brown slush, fishtailing around the side of the rig. I narrowly missed a head-on collision with oncoming traffic as I rounded the RV.

Triumph shot through me like an electrical current. I had him! I hammered at the side of the RV, pulling even with the driver's side window. Standing on my pedals and breathing hard, I looked right at him.

But it wasn't Becker, not even close. The driver was just some big guy in his 20s with dark hair wearing a pair of nerd glasses. Sitting in the passenger seat was another young guy whose head was swathed in dirty blond dreads.

"Help you, man?" The tone of the dreadlocks dude was mild, unhurried.

"No... I thought you..." I stuttered, my bike began weaving as blood hammered into my head in a near faint. I put a leg down, steadied myself. The light was still red.

"We're playing tonight at Mr. Flood's," the guy said, handing me a card. "Five dollar cover, but this will get you in free. We've got CDs."

I looked at the card. It said Careless Whisker, Ska Specialists, a traveling band based in Tucson, Arizona. They were playing at a popular bar in town.

I put my hand to my forehead and waved half-hearted with the other as the light went green and the RV pulled ahead. On a whim, I looked up to see if there was a Wall Drug sticker on the rig's tail. There were a couple of stickers on the back of the RV, one being a D.A.R.E. bumper sticker, the acronym for Drug Abuse Resistance Education that teenage stoners plaster on their cars, hoping to throw off the cops.

The other was a picture of Jesus in his modern, surfer-dude incarnation stuck over the exhaust pipe and smiling self-confidently with a message promising salvation: "I Am the Way."

That night as I lay on the couch skipping the social media search for the first time in three months, those words came back to me along with Freeman's advice to pray for answers. I drifted off to the realm of visions, halfway between sleep and wakefulness, still thinking, I am the way... That's what I was looking for, a way. But what way?

Jill had kept an old family Bible on a desk we shared. I forced myself awake and stumbled in a half-sleep to where it lay, stabbing a finger at the onionskin pages within its cover. It landed on Matthew 7.7-8:

"Ask, and it shall be given you; seek, and ye shall find; knock, and it shall be opened unto you: For every one that asketh receiveth; and he that seeketh findeth..."

I looked up and saw my bicycle helmet and riding gloves resting on the bookshelf where I'd placed them months before. An icy current ran through me; I'd found the way and it had nothing to do with prayer or going to church. Maybe I'd never find Peter Becker, but perhaps I could find my way back to sanity.

I put our house on the market the next day and gave my two week's notice at work.

After the crash of 2008, Jill and I had scooped up a foreclosed home that the owners had trashed in a fit of rage when their skyrocketing mortgage put them underwater. They'd busted some windows, punched holes in the dry wall, and had torn the garage door off its track, among other things. The living room carpeting had to be torn out because it reeked of dog shit and cat piss. Such scenes were the backstory of America in the late '00s.

We got the house for a fraction of its worth and I'd spent a year fixing it up in my spare time. Now it was worth a small fortune, by our lights, anyway. Our house sold in two days for $749,499 in the rebounding real estate market. Less the seven percent sales commission netted me a little over $453,000 after the mortgage was settled.

Jill and I had been quite a team, real estate-wise. We'd made double payments on a 15-year mortgage, planning to pay off the place by our mid-30s. It was a four bedroom, three-bath ranch on a half-acre near the river just outside of town, a very desirable neighborhood. But I didn't want to live there anymore. I'd found my way forward.

The payout on our house would keep me on the road for the rest of my life if I traveled as a bicycle hobo. I divvied it up $53,000 of my stash into three bank accounts with debit cards linked to each one. I threw the rest of it - $400,000 - into an equity fund tied to the Standard & Poors Index. Then I forgot about it.

I trucked most of my possessions to Goodwill and sold anything of value on Craigslist. Some things were too dear to part with: family heirlooms, photos of Jill, some of her jewelry and personal items. I boxed it up and left it at my brother's place, keeping a photo of Jill for my wallet. I peeled off my steel-toe boots from the post office and set them atop the last box of my possessions; they were the last remnants of my old life.

Jill came to me at night in those final days at home, not as a ghost, but in my memories. I'd lay on the couch thinking of her and how she deserved better than me, regretting the times I'd been unkind or said something stupid. Sometimes I'd wake up laughing in recollection of some trip we'd taken or some joke we had shared. On those times I'd think she was right there beside me, snuggling on the couch, and it would take me by surprise when I came around to realize that she was gone. That went on for a long time.

Jill never spoke to me like Hamlet's father, crying for revenge, but that was a promise I made anyway; not revenge, but retribution, justice. During the process of going postal I had made a holy vow that Peter Becker, or whoever he was, would pay for Jill's life with his own. No torture or drawn-out beating with a pipe, just a quick death, like the Bible suggests: just an eye for an eye, a tooth for a tooth, no more, no less.

With the last days of March came splinters of sunshine through the bare trees after the long Michigan winter. It was still cold enough to wear ski gloves and there were still mounds of blackened, honeycombed snow piled up in the parking lots around town; but the wind was at my back, blowing out of the north. I got on my bike and headed toward Indiana.

The Land of Nod
Chapter 6

"As for me, I am tormented with an everlasting itch for things remote. I love to sail forbidden seas, and land on barbarous coasts."

- Herman Melville
Moby-Dick; or The Whale

Thus, I became a citizen of the Land of Nod, which means "Nowhere in Particular" in the Bible. Just another guy on a bike floating around the highways of America.

That first week was hell. It rained for three days straight and the roads out of Ann Arbor were narrow and filled with traffic. I was terrified, thinking I was going to die at any minute as an endless stream of cars whipped by at high speed in the gray curtain of the rain. Sometimes they seemed to be only inches away and a passing truck threatened to suck me into its slipstream. Could the drivers even see me, pedaling as if my life depended on it on the white line at the edge of the road? Soaking wet and shivering with hundreds of cars streaming by, I nearly called it quits on the second day. But then I came across a highway that had a four-foot wide shoulder marked by a white line, offering a measure of safety. From then on I resolved to ride only on roads that had a shoulder at least two feet wide, the blue highways of America.

I came to a crossroads in South Bend, Indiana. Which way to go? The wind was blowing south and the town itself suggested a direction. South, to Kentucky, Tennessee, Alabama and beyond.

Bicycling saved my life that spring. The endless miles under my wheels and the effort it took to produce them built a wall against the blackness that threatened to engulf me. Valentine's Day had stabbed at my heart with a thousand knives; it was our anniversary. How stupid was that, getting married on Valentine's Day? It was the sort of thing couples do to tempt fate.

But a few weeks of 11-hour days on the road began making me right

again as the endorphins generated by pedaling all day began streaming through my body. On my tenth day out, I found myself smiling at sunset, something I hadn't done for a long time.

Months went by and I found myself smiling more often. I had found a new way to live out on the highways, and if there seemed to be no end in sight, I no longer cared.

But from the very first day I learned that biking around the country is a raw way to go. At times there are powerful winds in your face which slow you to a crawl. You endure killing heat that bakes your brain and drains your body of fluids. Cold, damp weather pries at your knees and whispers of hypothermia. You're always out in the weather and even protective clothing doesn't always help. Rain gear tends to be useless because of the infiltrating dampness and sweat; often I wound up soaking wet inside my rain jacket. As for dealing with hot weather, when you strip down to some biking shorts and a singlet you're prey to the sun and the wind.

You just have to get used to living outdoors like an animal.

Many times, every cell in my body ached for the sight of the onion stalk of a water tower rising above the trees of some distant town as I rolled on, desperate for relief from the ever-churning pedals; yet so often finding only farms, disappointment and more hills. It was brutal, but I loved it.

For a change I was in real physical pain instead of what was going on inside my head. It was the pain of my calves, swelling like gourds without enough water to nurture the multiplying strands of muscle. It was the pain in my neck as I craned forward over the handlebars, the awkward position settling like a vise grip tightening down on my shoulders and clavicle. It was my ass worn raw on the seat that never seemed to have enough padding.

But most of all it was my arms, stretching out, bracing me up, shifting to different positions on the handlebars, but radiating with an intense pain up to the hinge of my shoulders, which seemed incapable of relief. Slowly, my arms toughened up, growing as rock-hard as my legs.

It took two months of riding before I managed to jigger my bike and the miscellaneous parts of my body into a smooth-flowing machine.

I read somewhere that you grow younger with extreme levels of exercise and it seemed true. Your body generates the precursors of human growth hormone, which are the chemistry of youth. Each day when I awoke after my muscles had mended in the night, I felt myself edging a little closer toward my youth. I was in my 30s, but it felt like I was riding back into my 20s.

I fell into a routine. I'd get up, make breakfast and hang my tent and sleeping bag from a post to dry out the dew while I drank my coffee. Then I'd pack my gear, placing each item in its place in my panniers. Then ride 30 miles, rest a spell, ride 30 more, and repeat. Along about 5 o'clock I'd start looking for a campsite and something to scrounge for dinner. I'd set up my tent, inflate my sleeping pad, eat dinner and try to read for an hour before my eyelids slammed shut like garage doors. I was usually asleep by 8:30 and wide awake by 4 a.m., waiting for the first rays of the sun to knock the chill from the morning mist. Each day brought something new, but the routine was always the same.

I had a lot of long days and some which were painfully short.

Like yesterday, I biked 139 miles over a roller coaster of long prairie hills, not bad considering I'm pushing more than 80 pounds of bike and gear.

But I had my face chewed off the day before that, pushing for 50 miles at five miles per hour against a raw, hot side-wind with temperatures in the 90s. I've run marathons faster than I could ride into that furnace. The wind finally turned late in the day and I made it 103 miles to a park in a small town by 10:30 at night, riding under lights. I set up camp in the dark and took a bird bath with what I had left in my water bottle. It wasn't much.

It wasn't long before I drifted into a fantasy that I was a knight on two wheels, although more on the Don Quixote side of things. Like Sir Gawain in search of the Holy Grail or a Crusader on the long march to Jerusalem, I didn't mind suffering. That was part of the gig. A lot of those old knights relished mortification, wearing hair shirts under their armor to make themselves itch and bleed as penance for their sins. And what were the tin-men of chivalry but angry lost souls like me?

I did a lot of reading while biking around. In fact, I was a used book store's best friend, browsing the shelves in every town I passed through and reading one or two books every week. There wasn't much else to do after I'd made camp for the day. I even got around to memorizing some stuff, like bits of Yeats, Homer, Rumi... nothing fancy, just bits here and there.

One of the books I read was *Le Morte d'Arthur*, written by Sir Thomas Malory in the 1400s. It got me going on the knight fantasy. Malory wrote that the furthest extreme for a knight was that of going "wood," as happened to Lancelot. Crazy in love with a married woman, Sir Lancelot went so far off his nut over Guinevere that he took to the forest, "as wild wood as ever was man," living naked and speechless like an animal for years until one of his knight friends came along and slapped some sense back into him. I didn't think that would happen to me. There was no way my friends back home could possibly find me.

I never ate well, instead I scavenged whatever the road had to offer. Mostly I ate gas station pizza, sub sandwiches and sad, wilted salads from fast food restaurants. Sometimes I'd make dinner with my butane stove, wolfing down canned ravioli or stew, canned chicken with instant rice, beans peppered with chunks of beef jerky. Food was never a priority.

Nor were my lodgings. Often I slept in town parks, pitching my tent behind a restroom or utility building for privacy or sleeping in a picnic pavilion if it was dark enough for no one to notice I was there. No one seemed to care out west where a bicyclist passing through is a daily occurrence. It was trickier camping in towns east of the Mississippi where the rules were doubled down. That, and the town parks of the east tended to be haunted with the indigent homeless suffering from mental problems or addictions, their presence making it difficult to sleep easy.

But once a week or so there was no alternative but to camp out rough beside some river, alongside a cornfield or down a two-track in the spooky mountains. Cyclists call it "stealth camping." I'd do my best to conceal my tent from the headlights of passing cars at these bandit sites, huddling in the silence of dusk, quiet as an Indian raider. Then, deep in the evening, I'd hear wild animals and birds fighting, hissing and screaming in the night as they preyed upon one-another only a stone's throw from my tent. Nature, red in tooth and claw, would remind me as to why I was out here.

One night, while riding through western Montana, I took shelter in the forest on a lonely mountaintop with a heavy rain and darkness coming on. All night I lay terrified in my billowing tent as the rain pounded down for hours and lightning rippled through the trees. The tent wracked and flapped in the wind like an angry seagull caught in a leg trap. That morning I rose at 5 a.m. and rode 30-some miles to the town of Dixon, eager for coffee and breakfast. But there was no restaurant in town and the sole grocery store had gone out of business.

"Grocery store coming soon," read a sign posted on the side of an abandoned building. It seemed overly optimistic because Dixon looked like a ghost town in which its 216 residents had not yet found the gumption to leave.

Scattered across the Great Plains and the Deep South were dead and dying towns bereft of every store except for a bunker-like bar and a post office. Often as not, the outskirts of town would offer pyramids of junk cars, trucks and farm machinery rusting in the sun, with rotting, aban-

doned grain silos hulking like tombstones warning passersby to keep on going. Even so, I'd see gaunt, impoverished women in their 20s trucking around with four or five anemic kids while their men were off some-where, beating at the earth with their machines. Why did they bear so many children in such bleak places? It wasn't for me to say.

Whenever possible I camped in state parks, circling through the camp-sites and looking over every RV. There were also numerous motor home campgrounds where the riff-raff of bicycle tourers weren't allowed to stay over. I'd offer a courteous salute to the front office and roll through anyway, making my inspection before riding onward.

Nothing.

A couple of times each month, rain or snow would make camping un-bearable, driving me indoors. I'd look for dive motels, to the type with big neon MOTEL signs from the '60s or '70s, never paying more than $50 for the likes of the Star Light, Sea Shell Inn or Galaxy. The disinfectant would hit you like a brick to the head when you walked through the door on these places, but it was always good to catch a shower and enjoy the novelty of a TV set. My motel visits reminded me that I was human.

Sometimes I lodged with other cyclists through a network of home stays known as Warm Showers. The hosts tended to be veteran bicycle tourers who opened their homes to other cyclists. The lodgings of the Warm Showers network included everything from bunkhouse barns to frilly guest rooms. I made a point to stay at a few of them each month in the vain hope that someone might have mentioned a run-in with Becker's RV. Nothing ever turned up.

Staying clean wasn't as tough as you might think. I wore quick-dry synthetic underwear that could be washed in any shower or sink along with my cycle clothes. Most mornings, I climbed into a clean set of duds.

Through all this I pedaled on, making 90-120 miles per day, depending on the wind and the vertical climb. In the Rockies there were days when I was lucky to make 65. But I figured if I could average at least 90 miles a day, I'd rack up more than 32,000 miles in a year. That would mean replacing my tires a few times each year, and maybe even my bike if it wore out before I did.

Above all I kept searching for that long white RV, stopping every time I saw one coming in the distance to give it a good look, or squinting whenever one passed me to see if it had a Wall Drug bumper sticker on the lower right corner. That, and for the inscrutable black & white sticker that I hadn't quite made out.

It turns out there are thousands of white RVs coasting the highways of America in dozens of variations of size and shape. A remarkable number of them bear Wall Drug bumper stickers along with shout-outs for Mammoth Cave, Pigeon Forge, Graceland and Branson, Missouri, the kind of places that motorhomes gathered like hippos around a waterhole.

Winters were brutal on my bike, even in the Deep South, where cold rains and heavy winds washed over me for days. On the endless staked plains of West Texas I shivered in the path of squarreling winds that scoured my face raw. The desert states of Arizona and New Mexico were little better; the days could be pleasant enough, but as soon as the sun went down the temperatures would drop into the 20s. From November to April I opted for criss-crossing the southern states from the Atlantic to the Pacific. That, and riding circles around Florida, where I figured Becker might show up during the winter.

One day I was riding a country road along the border of Texas and Arkansas amid a skittering of snow. It was cold that day and a chill crept through my ski gloves and wind gear, but traffic was light and there was nothing else to do but grind along toward the limitless western horizon. From time to time, drivers would flash their lights at me, slowing and casting strange looks my way. I looked myself over, there was nothing different about my appearance than usual. I was just a guy out riding on a winter day.

Late in the morning an ancient Ford 150 pickup truck pulled up alongside me and an old guy in a red plaid jacket gazed at me as we crept along. He leaned over and cranked the window down.

"How's it going there, friend?" the driver said. To my surprise, I realized it was a burly woman at the wheel. She looked to be in her sixties with close-cropped hair the color of old iron. She had a gruff voice and cool, appraising eyes.

"Doing good. How are you?" I called back.

"Kind of cold out here isn't it?" she said. "You got a home? Somewhere to be?"

"This is my home right here on this bike," I said. We were still rolling along slow, fingers of snow reaching forth across the road.

"Not today it isn't. Pull over."

She pulled up in front of me and came to a stop, stepping out of her truck, which idled on with a chugging cough.

"I'm Delores," she said, extending a hand in a buckskin work glove.

"Jake."

"You interested in dinner?"

"Dinner?"

"Yeah, we've got a little dinner planned for guys like you," she said. "I'm heading there now; it's the next town up over that hill. You can help out if you like."

"Guys like me?" I gave a little chuckle. "What, like guys out riding bikes?"

Delores gave me the kind of compassionate look reserved for simpletons. "You don't know, do you?"

By now it felt like we were playing some kind of game, but before I could say something smart, she said, "It's Christmas."

Delores helped lift my bike into the back of her truck and I eased into the warmth of her cab. Suddenly, memories of Christmas in Ann Arbor flooded back, with me lying warm in bed with Jill as dawn filtered through the window. We got to Delores's church with a lump in my throat. Inside was a long line of old folks and families of the working poor, Latinos, Indians and guys who looked like they slept out in picnic shelters all winter. Delores gave me a cotton apron and a big spoon.

"You're going to help out with the mashed potatoes," she said, directing me to a huge steel pot behind the counter where people were waiting. "I'll see that you get an extra helping of turkey when everyone's served."

The Animal Inside Me
Chapter 7

That was my first time eating at a church. Mostly, I dined at picnic tables at whatever park I happened to be passing by, or simply wolfed my food standing up outside of gas stations. I ate in bars a lot, dozens of them. After riding 90-120 miles in the extremes of heat, cold and wind, I was often ready for something besides canned ravioli. That, and I felt increasingly feral as the months rolled on; wrapping up the day in a bar gave me a chance to rub elbows with humankind and ease out of my own skin. When people asked, I let it be known that I was biking cross-country on a bet. That was sure to get them talking about themselves instead of me, which was just how I liked it.

The bars located in the back end of beyond tend to be squat, cinderblock buildings with a red neon BAR sign hanging in a small, dark window and a battered steel door for an entrance. Usually, they were the only places open in a small town anytime past 5:30. Sometimes they were the only business left in a dying town, period. Inside was always the same: darkness hiding the dirt, clusters of men in baseball caps and work clothes crouching over their beers in the amber twilight, and maybe a few diners, old folks or small families. Behind the bar were the same familiar characters that you find everywhere, glistening in a pool of light: Jack Daniels, Gordon's, Malibu, Captain Morgan...

I was always a bit on edge walking into a bar dressed in a skin-tight fluorescent jersey and cycle shorts. Mostly, the patrons were welcoming, especially on the major cycling routes, where guys passing through dressed like ballerinas are a common sight. I'd walk into a strange place with the air of someone who'd been there a thousand times, offer a rumbling, "How's it goin'?" to anyone who cared to look up from their beer, and make myself at home. Often, the patrons would tell me about other cyclists they'd seen passing through, and if someone was drunk enough I'd get a free beer.

But there are drunks and then there are drunks, and inevitably I met the wrong kind.

I'd been pushing into a heavy wind for three days, heading east across North Dakota. This was before I started following the wind around the country and it was my bad luck to be striving against it at 5 miles per hour. Conventional wisdom holds that the wind blows from the west to the east out on the Great Plains, but that's not true in the summertime when conflicting weather fronts have the wind swirling every whichway. The wind was literally a wall that I had pushed against for three long days.

So I was worn to the bone and in a bad mood when I finally rolled into a small town about 90 miles southeast of Bismarck. I didn't bother to check out the name of the place when I rolled past the town limits; all I wanted to see were the worlds, "BAR."

Like so many other dying towns, this place looked post-apocalyptic with "For Sale" signs on most of the businesses. The main street offered nothing but a succession of empty windows, all eerily black. There was a grocery store still holding its own, and far down the street were the lights of a gas station, but that was it except for the obligatory bar, Curly's. I leaned my bike up against the side of the building and pushed through the door into the darkness.

Inside were five scruffy guys in work clothes and baseball caps sitting around a high-top, hunched over a platter of chicken wings. I sized them up to be workers ending their day at the grain silo I'd passed on the way into town. Behind the bar was a big red-faced guy with sandy-blond hair and a walrus mustache. I took a seat at the bar and ordered a draft and the day's special, meatloaf.

I don't know if he was drunk or just a compulsive jerk, but one of the guys at the high top couldn't resist needling me.

"Well what do ya know? Looks like we got a visiting princess here," he said in a voice loud enough for me to hear. A couple of his buddies sniggered. One of them muttered, "Come on, shut up, man," but the guy kept gawking in my direction.

When I'm riding, I wear a bandanna around my neck to wipe my nose and serve as a mask against dust and bugs. Usually, I take it off before entering a business because it gives the impression of a gay caballero wearing a scarf. Suffice to say the drunk across the room honed in on that right away.

I glanced at the mirror above the bar and caught his reflection. He looked to be in his early 30s, rawboned, lean, and blackened by the sun with a shaved head beneath a ragged, red baseball cap. He had a stove-pipe beard that ended in a blunt cut four inches below his chin, which made him look like a cross between a biblical prophet and a violent jailbird. That, and dark eyes devoid of warmth, glaring over a wolfish smile of the sort worn by combative drunks. He looked like the kind of guy who liked to screw with people, a bully.

The drunk and his crew were temporarily diverted by a baseball game on one of the big screen TVs at the opposite end of the bar. But ten minutes later he was on me again, just as my dinner arrived from the back room.

"Hey Tinkerbell," he called out. "What'chu doin' in our town all dressed up like a little girl?" I heard snorting, giggles, and again, one of the guys telling him to be cool in a low voice.

I turned around slow in my seat and stared at him for 10 seconds without saying anything. "I'm trying to enjoy me dinner," I said at last. "Do you mind?" I hoped to sound menacing, but it came out with my usual luck sounding prissy, like Little Lord Fauntleroy.

The guy just stared back, chewing on a chicken bone with a look of dreamy insolence on his face, like he was contemplating how to mess with me even more.

I turned back to my meatloaf, lying half-eaten on my plate alongside a dam of mashed potatoes and gravy.

"Just trying to enjoy my dinner," I heard his mincing voice behind me as he shuffled over to the men's room.

"Ignore that guy," the bartender advised, wiping a glass with a damp rag. His face had gone a deeper shade of red, the sign of a bad case of high blood pressure. "He's the town asshole."

"Yeah, I figured."

A minute later, the guy was at my shoulder.

"Watcha' doin'? Same question as before. His breath stank of cigarettes, beer and gin.

I turned around and glared at him, saying nothing.

"I just thought a pretty boy like you might like to dance after dinner, know what I mean?" His voice had lowered to a husky growl.

A sick feeling settled in my stomach. I knew a roundhouse punch was called for, but I was exhausted from the day's ride. I felt suddenly weak, helpless.

The bartender wandered over from where he'd been rinsing glasses. "Dwayne, get back in your seat or get out," he barked.

Dwayne straightened up and backed off. "Just welcoming a stranger to our town," he said, drooping back to his seat.

I kept one eye on the mirror, considering my options. In the Jack Reacher novels, a bar fight against five bad guys is all quite simple. Reacher simply beats the shit out of all them in a well-choreographed sequence of elbow jabs and arm-busting in what used to be called fighting dirty. But in the novels, Reacher is 6'5" and has been beating people up since he was in kindergarten, whereas I'm 5'6" and haven't ever gotten around to beating anyone up lately, much less five rednecks in a bar fight.

But dinner was ruined and so was my mood. It had been black when I walked through the door, and now it was a few shades darker.

You've probably noticed by now that I tend to over-think things, even a bar fight. The only weapon at hand was the two beer bottles in front of me, one empty, one half full.

I'd read somewhere that Australia is the bar fight capital of the world, where there are hundreds of glassings each year involving drunken blokes who slash each other across the face with broken beer bottles. But beer bottles as a weapon have problems. If you bust one that's near empty, it tends to break off at the neck, leaving you with not much of a shard to get the job done. It's best to use a full or nearly full bottle, busting it over the other guy's head. I didn't have a nearly-full bottle of beer.

Then too, if you glass a guy across the face with a broken beer bottle, that's likely to result in a free ride to the state penitentiary for ten years or so. Or, the other guy could use it on you.

There was also the problem of this guy's four buddies who'd likely stomp the shit out of me even if I managed to overpower Dwayne. Massive head trauma was another thing I couldn't afford. I figured my best option would be to slink out of the bar without saying a word, get on my bike and hope that no one came after me.

But then I got to thinking, how could I bring myself to confront and possibly kill Peter Becker if I couldn't stand up to one loudmouth in a bar in North Dakota? What kind of man was I to think I could avenge Jill? A sadness settled over me as I stared at the leavings of my meatloaf and potatoes, now grown cold in a pool of grease in the yellow light of the bar. I was a pussy, Becker had said it himself, and now this drunken asshole Dwayne was proving it. Glumly, I motioned to the bartender for my bill, planning to slink out in defeat.

That's when the shit hit the fan.

It was a french fry. The drunk threw a congealed french fry at me, sopped with ketchup. It landed on my upper right arm, sticking to the clean jersey that I'd laundered just a day before. It lingered there for a second, and then peeled off, falling to the floor.

"Hey shithead," he called over, giggling.

I lost it, seeing red as the capillaries of my eyes flushed with blood.

Something awoke in me, its teeth bared and red with blood as a wave of mindless violence shivered through me, shaking me like I'd been electrocuted. I shot out of my seat and charged, hitting Dwayne with everything I had as he wobbled up from his high-top seat. His chair must have been three-and-a-half or four feet tall and I rocketed into him, hitting him full on with my shoulder. I'm short, but my legs have the power of a linebacker after biking 100 miles each day. The chair collapsed like a falling tower and he flew backwards, smashing into the barroom floor and banging his head against the jukebox, cracking its red glass.

But I wasn't finished. I came down hard on his knee with my right foot and he screamed as the kneecap cracked in two. He was lucky I was wearing running shoes instead of the metal cleats that most cyclists favor. I leaned over him and screamed into his face with a wild, inhuman cry of animal rage, *"Eeeeyaaaaaaaaagggghhhh!"* with my teeth bared like an animal. His arms came up, covering his head as I clawed for his throat, his eyes wide with terror. I whiplashed his head to the floor and turned to face his pals, who should have been piling on, beating the shit out of me. They were just sitting there, gaping stock still or staring into their beers. That's when I had an insight: they didn't like this guy any more than I did.

"Friggin' Wolverine, man," one of them mumbled. Another covered his eyes, laughing so hard into his beer that it spurted out of his nostrils. No one said a word.

I looked up at the bartender with my heart banging so hard it felt ready to tear through my chest. There was the matter of the bill. Forget it, he shrugged, motioning toward the door. "Get the hell out of here."

I ran out the door and took off down a side street, careening onto my bike. I heard the bar door bang open behind me and someone bellowing, but by then I was up around the corner and out of sight.

There was a two-track lane outside of town that headed off into a cornfield. I took it, bouncing along its knobby-back trace for a quarter mile until it opened onto untilled prairie. Then came another cornfield with the lane ending in some farmer's backyard. I blasted right through the farmyard to the road beyond with two dogs raging at my heels and my panniers flopping like wings. The wheels on my bike wobbled as I reached the road, whipping around toward the east.

I was frightened, not by the thought of anyone chasing me, but by what had happened back in town, specifically, the animal scream that had risen from my chest in the bar. Like the guy said, it was the werewolf scream of the X-man character, Wolverine. It was the howl of the horde of demons Jesus had exorcised from a possessed man into a herd of pigs. It wasn't me, I don't know who it was, but it made me wonder what I had become. For the first time in my life I was deeply frightened, of myself.

INCIDENT_____

THE INTRUDER had rented a car at Detroit Metro Airport after parking his rig at a truck stop on Middlebelt Road. It wouldn't do to pilot a motorhome around the suburbs of Ann Arbor; that would be too easy to recollect.

The rent-a-car girl at the airport counter had maintained a cheery front in the face of his sepulchral presence. Good girl. He'd stripped himself of his usual skin to present himself as he really was, yet she hadn't flinched. On another occasion, he would have enjoyed visiting her, but lucky for her, not today.

He made the 15-mile drive to Ann Arbor in a rented Charger, gunning it down I-94 for the thrill of driving fast for a change. Dinner was at a mid-level franchise on Washtenaw Avenue - chicken planks and fries with sweet and sour sauce - followed by several hours of nodding at the wheel and masturbating in the parking lot as the moon rose to the east. Then it was 2:39 in the morning and off to the races, following a set of GPS coordinates to the home on the Huron River.

He knew exactly where to go. He'd followed the online newspaper accounts of the campground killing with interest, and the husband's address and personal information was available for $4.99 on an internet directory.

He drove slowly, carefully, but not so slow as to arouse suspicion. There was no need to draw the attention of the local cops or whatever sort of neighborhood watch was on guard. Nothing, as it turned out. He rolled up on a sprawling ranch house glowing pale under the moonlight, killed the lights, and waited half an hour as the engine ticked.

Then he crept from the car, quiet as a cat.

There was a SOLD sign out front of the place, ushering a moment of disquiet, but he had to be sure. With his footsteps as soft as silk, he made his way to the back of the house where the river murmured amid the night wind. He could feel himself blending with the darkness; no one could see him, no one would know.

As he expected, there was a sliding door leading out onto a patio overlooking the river at the back of the house. He'd brought a long, slim blade to jimmy the flimsy lock, but he didn't need it. The door was unlatched. He reflected on how strange it was that so many people kept their doors unlocked at night, through which any monstrous incarnation of the human race might walk with ease.

The door slid open with a gravelly rasp. Inside was the kitchen, dimly lit by the green LED lights of the stove and a microwave. Now was the moment when a dog might appear, along with his cue to disappear back into the enfolding night. Again, nothing.

He crept into the room, holding the long knife before him like a wand or a torch. Beyond a long kitchen counter there was a living room to the right and a dark hallway to the left. Sitting there in the darkness no more than six feet before him was a dog after all, a cocker spaniel crouched at the entrance to the living room. It gave a low growl and fled in terror to a far corner, hiding beneath an end table.

He crept down the hallway past a bathroom, its pearl walls lit by the orange glow of a light switch. Beyond that was a bedroom, obviously the place where a child slept owing to the presence of a nightlight. The door was open and he peered in. There were two young girls sleeping in twin beds, their pillows strewn with curls.

He moved on to the master bedroom, dropping to the floor as he reached the doorway.

He loved this part, the crawling bit, going down on his hands and knees to snake his way into a bedroom at night with the sleeping innocents having no idea that he was just below their bed, like the monster they had feared as children.

He crawled toward the queen-sized bed and froze at the squeak of a floorboard, listening for any change in whoever was lying there. Nothing. He inched closer, near enough to grasp the bedding's comforter, and then rose up with the knife between his teeth, his eyes flaring to gather what little light remained in the darkness of the room. He suppressed a giggle, imagining how he'd look to anyone waking up at that moment. It had happened once before.

Two people were lying there, blissfully asleep, a balding man in his 40s and his plump wife snug up against him with her mouth open, breathing softly.

Disappointment seeped through him, but for a change, no sense of rage. It was just a scenario, that's all; his campground buddy had moved on. There would be another chance. It would keep things interesting. In a way he was happy, filled with the sweet torture of delayed gratification. It was something to savor.

Quietly, he made his way back down the hall, past the sleeping girls, the frightened dog, and out the sliding door. There was no time for tinkering. He had a long drive ahead of him, more than 1,500 miles to the southwest.

He heard the dog barking as he reached the door of his car.

The Long Rangers
Chapter 8

As the months rolled on, I got used to the animal inside me, knowing that I'd need that creature if and when I crossed Peter Becker's path.

But I also opened up a little space in my chest for human contact. Mostly the people I talked to were store clerks, bartenders and waitresses, people who'd comment on a stranger passing through on a bike.

Often, I encountered the gypsy tribe of cyclists crossing America, who tended to be a gabby bunch. They'd hail me from the other side of the road and we'd stop to trade stories on what was up ahead and what lay behind. I always asked if they'd had any near-death experiences with RVs. Most had a story to tell about being shaved within a whisker by a passing vehicle, getting cussed out, or having a bottle thrown at them.

One guy said that a year ago, he'd been fired upon by a redneck up in the hills of Idaho where a lot of white separatists lived. "It was just like in 'Easy Rider', man. This guy in the passenger seat leaned out at me with a pistol."

"What did you do?"

"What could I do?" he shrugged. "I called the police and they came up with nothing. But I tell you what, I hitchhiked out of there with my bike in the back of a pickup truck. I didn't want that guy coming around again."

We straddled our bikes on the side of the road outside Pueblo, Colorado. He told me his name was Dennis - "just like Dennis Hopper in 'Easy Rider'- and that he was riding the TransAmerica route from Oregon to Virginia. His ride around Idaho had been a warm-up for cycling across America.

The TransAmerica is a cross-country super highway for cyclists, attracting hundreds, maybe even thousands, of riders each year. The route was blazed in 1976 by the founders of the Adventure Cycling Association, an outfit based in Missoula, Montana. Back then, a ragtag group of cyclists had dreamed up a Bikecentennial ride across America to coincide with the country's 200th anniversary. That led to more than 2,000 cyclists riding all the way across the country that year. Many rode in large groups of college and church teams, some supported by sag wagons, and some going it all alone.

"It gave bike touring a huge boost," Dennis said. "My dad did the big ride back in '76 and I'm following in his tracks."

"He didn't want to ride along with you?"

"Well, he's 96 now, and it's 4,228 miles, so I'd have to pull him in a cart if we were doing it together. Even riding alone I figure it'll take me about two months."

"So you must be halfway there."

"Check that." Dennis said he'd ridden down the Pacific coast, then up over the Rockies, through Yellowstone and across the Great Plains. Ahead lay the Mississippi, the coal country of Kentucky and over the Appalachians to the Virginia coast.

Dennis filled me in on a number of other routes created by the ACA cartographers. The Northern and Southern Tier routes run from coast-to-coast over the top and bottom of America and in between are tendrils heading north and south: the Underground Railroad, Great Divide, Atlantic Coast and Great Rivers of the South routes, to name a few.

I rode most of them over the next year and a half. They were mostly on scenic, two-lane roads of the sort favored by RV drivers. I don't remember when I started riding with the wind. I guess it was when I ditched my last ACA map.

There were times that year when it felt like I was a character in Chaucer's *Canterbury Tales*, with little stories playing out on the road.

One day, I was cycling up near Crater Lake in Oregon when I came upon a row of white pavilion tents and a mob of 30 or so cyclists sitting down to a salmon dinner with asparagus and white wine at long folding tables. They had passed me earlier in the day, streaming by on their ultra-light bikes while I lugged my heavy gear up a long slope. A sag-wagon the size of a UPS truck followed close behind with all of their luggage and camping gear.

It had been a tough day with lots of hills and I decided to stop for a moment to say hello and compare notes. But just as I was climbing off my bike a guy hurried my way giving me a down-low wave with both hands. Like me, he was dressed in bike shorts and a jersey, but his were pristine fluorescent orange and black, whereas I was looking a bit rougher than usual that day.

"Sorry, sir, but this is a private event," he said.

"I just wanted to stop and say hello," I replied. "Fellow bikers, gentlemen of the road and all that."

"Well thanks, but we've got some company rules that I've got to abide by, and one of them is ensuring our clients' privacy."

I heard the clink of wine glasses and tableware. A few of the diners looked up and then quickly looked away. They were all wearing matching jerseys in orange and black. Suddenly, I realized that I looked like a bum by comparison. My own jersey had incurred an accident with a particularly gooey pizza a couple of days back and had been none too clean to begin with. My cycling shorts were in tatters as a result of taking a tumble on a bad stretch of asphalt a ways back. My hands were still black from changing a tire earlier in the day. Nor had I bothered with a haircut and a shave in several months. Not since I began riding, actually.

The guy's name was Bruce, team leader with a luxury cycle touring outfit called Elite Ramblers. By way of explanation, he handed me a brochure, the cover of which featured a picture of a well-off couple in their sunset years, toasting with wine glasses astride their bikes. For the price of a used Chevy, Elite Ramblers took its wealthy clientele on fully-supported bike tours, finishing the day with gourmet dinners, tents worthy of a Bedouin sheik, and comfortable cots topped with 1,500 thread-count sheets of Egyptian cotton. They had a staff of four, including a chef. It was the ultimate in bicycle glamping.

"Hey, bring that young feller over here," a stout, red-faced man in his cups bellowed from one of the tables. But he was shushed by some of his companions and I heard one of them mutter something about me being homeless. In any event, Bruce didn't extend an invitation, and after an awkward moment I rode on, making camp about 10 miles up the road.

The next day I rode into town and bought some new bike shorts. Then I hit the laundromat and washed all my clothes, shaving in the bathroom while they were in the dryer. I didn't care if the hoity-toity Elite Ramblers crowd accepted me, but it was embarrassing to think that I'd become such a slob. I vowed to clean up my act.

I got back on the road the next day, feeling a lot fresher and vowing not to let myself go in the future. By chance, I came upon Bruce and some of his riders at a picnic spot at mid-afternoon. It took Bruce a moment to recognize me in the wake of my makeover.

"What happened to your group?" I asked. There were less than half of them from the other day.

"We got ripped off," Bruce said dejectedly. "We figure some crew hit us the other night with bolt cutters. They got away with eighteen bikes."

I whistled. "Didn't you hear them? That would have made quite a racket."

"You'd think, but we were camping next to some railroad tracks only about fifty feet from our bikes. We had three trains pass by in the night and I figure that's when they hit us, like at three in the morning."

I had seen trains almost every day out west with many of them pulling hundreds of cars filled with coal or chemicals. Some were a mile long and could take 20 minutes or so to pass by, more than enough time for a well-oiled crew to steal a truckload of bikes.

Some of the riders had lost bikes worth five grand or more and now Elite Ramblers was in the doghouse, heading for small claims court at the least.

Of course, I was thinking, karma is a bitch, but I didn't say so. Instead I said, "I hope you have good insurance."

Bruce gave a nod, but he looked like a dog that had swallowed a toad. I wished him good luck and rode on.

Funny, but I never locked my bike in all of the time I was on the road. I just leaned it up against the side of a bar, a picnic table or restaurant, trusting that all of the gear I had strapped to the frame would dissuade anyone from trying to pedal off with it.

When you ride a bike 11 hours a day, you tend to see a lot of drivers texting at the wheel. Sometimes I'd see them blasting through red lights without a clue while chatting on the phone or whipsawing off the road in the middle of a text.

One afternoon, I made a stop at an ice cream stand and was licking at a cone when I saw a speeding pickup truck fishtail to a stop across the road. The guy was towing a huge fishing boat and hadn't noticed a gravel truck stopped at an intersection while making a left-hand turn. He must have been doing 60 miles per hour when he hit the brakes, with both his truck and his trailer careening wildly all over the road. It was a miracle his boat didn't flip over.

I shook my head. Idiot. The guy in the black pickup truck was either texting or fiddling with his radio because he'd come within a hair of killing himself.

An hour later I was huffing up a steep hill towards sundown, wondering where I was going to camp for the night. Up ahead I saw a wisp of smoke rising from down the hillside, and then tire tracks in the dirt alongside the road.

I stopped and peered over the bank. There, a hundred yards below, was the black pickup truck lying on its side and smoking. Its twisted trailer and shattered boat had been tossed upside down another hundred feet further on.

I threw down my bike and scrambled down the hill. The truck had tumbled over sideways and I had to climb up the bumper and stand on its frame to yank the door open. Inside, I could see the driver tangled up in the steering wheel, his head hanging at an ugly angle. I knew at a glance that he was dead.

He was a big-bellied guy with a black beard and skin as pale as milk. At the bottom of the cab I saw his baseball cap and his phone, still turned on and glowing. Maybe he'd been texting his wife, having an argument, or doing something that made him forget he was driving alongside a steep hill. That, or maybe he was in the habit of texting every time he drove. But not anymore.

I called 911 and waited by the road for nearly an hour before the lights of an EMS truck came speeding up from the valley. It wasn't easy getting the guy up the hill; six of us hoisted him on a stretcher, scrambling up through the brush and a scree of loose rock.

Then it was all quiet again, with the EMTs and the sheriff snaking off into the darkness, leaving me by the side of the road. I couldn't sleep, no way, I was too shook up. I got back on my bike and rode all night under the moonlight, thinking about the dead guy and the fragility of life. Better him though, than someone else.

Most of the long-rangers I met were men, but there were a fair number of women, too, some riding solo.

Like Lynda, fresh out of U-Cal Berkeley, who I met about a year into my search.

We met in a small town park in east Kansas. I'd just finished setting up my tent when she rolled in on a bike laden with front and back panniers, her face rosy with heat and sweat.

"Hey rider, want some company?" she called.

I took one look at her and decided that, yes, I very much wanted some company.

"Hell yes, I'd love some," I said. "Want some dinner?" I had a sub sandwich big enough for two, along with two tall cans of beer. It had been a hot day.

She hesitated, but not for long. "God, yes! I'm starving."

Lynda wolfed her food and her eyes glowed with a touch of gold when I pulled a chocolate bar from my front pack. "Thank you."

I helped set up her tent and then we went for a swim in the town pool. "God, it's so good to be clean!" she gushed as we lay on our towels, drying in the sun.

"What? You don't like being drenched in sweat all day?"

"Ha, ha," she said drily. "That's the one thing I don't like about bike touring. I need a shower every day or I go nuts."

I told her about my bird bath method, performed with a water bottle, to which she replied, "ugh."

"It beats rolling in the dirt like a warthog."

"Yeah? Well that's another thing I don't think I'll be trying."

I didn't have a swimsuit, so I hit the pool in my bike shorts, but Lynda had packed along a bikini, and it was only a matter of minutes before I had to roll onto my stomach and think about things like washing dishes and batting averages. When we talked, I was careful to meet her eyes.

It turned out that Lynda hadn't begun her ride alone.

"I started out riding with a guy I met in school," she said. "He said he was a big-time backpacker, but he hadn't done much cycling and had a tough time in the mountains. I think we spent half the day walking up some of those passes. He just couldn't handle it."

"I think you're bragging now," I said, though it was true that Lynda certainly had the legs for hill-climbing.

"Yeah, but if it's true, it's not bragging, right?" she said with a wicked smile. "Plus, it turned out he wasn't much of a camper either; he brought along way too much stuff and that was part of his problem."

"How do you mean?" I was still dwelling on Lynda's legs, which were sculpted pillars of hard muscle from her thighs to the base of her calves. I suspected that she'd kick my ass in the mountains, too.

"I mean he had too much stuff to truck up the Rockies and he didn't need half of it," she went on. "He packed along enough stuff to stock an REI store, stuff like a portable saw and a three-man tent."

"But he made it over the mountains," I pointed out.

"Yeah, but then there were the plains and the wind," she replied. "He was loaded down like a camel. I cut him loose a couple of days ago. He

caught a bus for home in Topeka."

"So why didn't you turn back too?" I asked, knowing the answer before I asked.

Lynda snorted. "You kidding? I came this far, I'm going all the way."

"It's hard to turn back when you've got a goal in mind."

"Impossible," she agreed.

"So how do you like Kansas?"

"It's like that movie, 'Groundhog Day', where the same thing happens every day. Flat, hot and windy."

"I've heard that from every other cyclist I've met out here," I said. "You've got to be a glutton for punishment to ride across it."

"A glutton? No, this is my trip of a lifetime," she replied. "I wouldn't miss Kansas for the world. I was hoping to see a tornado, or maybe Dorothy riding around on one, but not up close."

I grinned. "I've been looking for one too, at a distance. I saw one about a year ago in Alabama."

"Life can be a tornado, don't you think?"

"I guess so, if you're living on the edge, maybe."

Lynda seemed kind of young to be living a life similar to a tornado. " If you don't mind me asking, how old are you?" I asked.

"Twenty-three next month, August 15. I'm Leo the lioness," she said.

Indeed she was, petite and sleek, her body burnished gold with taut muscle. She had a tussle of sun-streaked curls that fell to her bronze shoulders, a blond Mexicana.

"Well, if you're only 23 then my guess is this is going to be the first of many trips of a lifetime, if your life doesn't turn into a tornado, that is."

"You think?" She nibbled at her chocolate, intent on making it last.

"Well, the biking part, anyway. It's addicting. Before you get done with this trip you'll be thinking about the next one."

"Yeah, maybe," she shrugged, licking a finger. "So tell me, how long have you been out riding?"

I tallied the months. "It's been a little over a year, fourteen months, just riding around here and there."

"Very impressive," she looked up, her eyes going wide. "So what are you, some kind of homeless person?"

That set me back a bit. Suddenly, I saw myself through Lynda's eyes: a 32-year-old man who lived in a tent, drifting around the country on a bicycle with no apparent destination in mind. A guy who showered with a water bottle.

"Truth or dare? Yeah, I guess I am homeless, for now, anyway," I said. "I don't know if I'll never stop riding. The earth is my home, this is my living room," I waved.

I meant it to be funny, but Lynda probably thought it was tragic.

"What kind of fuel makes a person do that?" she wondered.

"Fuel?"

"I mean, what's driving you?"

"Just gumption, I guess."

"Gumption?" Lynda made a face. "Lucky you. Just gumption, that's all?"

It was time to change the subject. "Yeah, that and sub sandwiches," I said awkwardly. "But enough about me, what about you?"

"Oh, I've got an internship lined up, doing some marketing with a boat company in San Diego that's likely to end with a job offer. I don't think I'll be doing much traveling for awhile."

"But someday."

"Someday, for sure," she said.

Lynda's last name was Martinez. She was a second-generation immigrant from a town called Mismaloya, just south of Puerto Vallarta. It was a sleepy little place where Richard Burton and Ava Gardner shot "The Night of the Iguana" back in the early '60s. Her parents still had a place there.

"Must be rough," I said.

"It's a nice switch from San Diego," she said lightly. "I go back every summer when San Diego gets the June Blues. You'd be surprised how cold and damp it gets there in June."

"I can hardly imagine," I said, thinking of winters in Ann Arbor.

The next day, we decided to ride together for a bit. For me it meant heading back the way I'd come, but that didn't matter much. It felt good to have some company for a change.

Like Dennis, Lynda was riding the TransAmerica route from Portland, Oregon to hook up with friends in D.C. We both agreed that biking across the country was a good way to go, a life of complete freedom.

She was rapturous, ticking off a checklist of reasons for riding.

"You get in great shape, meet cool people and have amazing adventures that cost next to nothing," she said as we rolled side-by-side over hills covered in corn. "It feels organic, like I'm part of what's happening instead of just someone passing by in a car."

"Connecting with the earth," I said, buoyed by her enthusiasm.

"Exactly. You're one with the earth and you can go where you want, when you want. What's not to like?"

"I can think of some things, like hills, heat, rain, flats, bugs and traffic," I said. "Also a sore butt and achy knees that you know are going to disintegrate sooner or later."

"Well, aren't you mister sunshine."

"Just keeping it real."

"Yeah, well there's all that too. But which way do you think the scales tip on balance?"

"You had it right the first time. The bad stuff just builds character."

I wanted to ask Lynda if she was ever afraid of riding alone. She was lithe, almost slight, and wouldn't stand a chance against the likes of the guys I'd run into at the bar. But she had a steely side, along with a 10-ounce can of pressurized grizzly bear spray capable of shooting up to 32 feet within easy reach in her front pack. I got the impression she wouldn't hesitate to use it. One blast of that stuff would have half a dozen thugs on the ground, vomiting their guts out.

We rode together for nearly a week, exiting Kansas and crossing Missouri. Lynda was good company and easy on the eyes. A time or two I found myself looking at her from behind and felt a twinge of guilt; she had a heart-shaped ass wrapped in skin-tight Lycra shorts - gorgeous - and it had been a long time since I'd been intimate with any woman other than Jill. I couldn't help getting a crush on Lynda, but I had made a vow to avenge Jill and I intended to keep it.

Still, we got along so well, it was tempting. We talked for hours in the late afternoons when we stopped to camp, and by the fourth evening we said an awkward good night to each other as we turned in for our respective tents. I thought of how good it would be to join her in her tent, if only to sleep snuggled up beside her. It was one of those moments where you both want to go for it, and we both knew it.

But it wasn't meant to be.

"You should ride on with me all the way to Virginia," Lynda said the next morning over coffee. "I'd really like some company; it's been tough riding all by myself."

"I'd like to, but there's something I have to take care of."

"Like what?" She asked, an innocent lilt to her voice.

I hadn't told anyone about my mad quest and I wasn't about to tell Lynda. I was afraid that she'd think that I was some kind of loon, a pitiful Don Quixote.

"It's personal," I said. "It's kind of hard to explain."

"What? Like a girlfriend or a wife?" There was a slice of frost to her voice and she stared into her coffee cup like it was the edge of a cliff.

"No, nothing like that. I had someone once, but not any more." I hesitated and then the words rose to my lips before I could stop them. "She died."

Her eyes rose with concern. "Oh, Jake, I'm so sorry."

"Yeah, it's sort of why I'm out here," I said. "I had a wife, Jill. She had a bad death about a year ago and it left me in a bad way. I'm still working things out."

"Do you want to talk about it?" She put her hand on mine and our eyes met.

I looked at her for a long moment and then back down at my coffee.

"It's like this," I said. "Has there ever been something you really had to do before you could get straight with yourself?"

Lynda nodded.

"Well, that's where I'm at now, and I can't talk about it yet, not just with you, but with anyone."

The words dropped out of my mouth and it felt as if they had fallen to the table, lame, incomplete, unsatisfying, but there it was.

"Okay, I guess," Lynda said with a taut smile and her eyes growing moist, but she didn't push. We held hands until it felt awkward, then got up to go. Lynda rode a quarter mile behind me for the whole day.

That afternoon we stopped in a small town for ice cream and there at the dairy dip we met two other cyclists heading east. Steve and Judy were platonic buddies who seemed to be mildly uncomfortable with one-another. They were thrilled to have Lynda join them, while I was sad to see her go. We spent the night with all of us camping together, and that meant the possibility of tumbling the night away with Lynda had flown.

"Well, it's been nice meeting you," she said the next day when it was time to say goodbye, her brown eyes gazing up at mine in a hopeful gaze. In that moment, her face was that of an angel, framed in cascades of sun-streaked hair.

"Yes," I said woodenly, my emotions whipping around like fighting cats. "I..., uh, you... You've meant a lot to me, more than you know."

"I hope things work out for you."

"They will. Good luck with your internship."

Our parting degenerated into small talk and promises to stay in touch on Facebook. I asked for one last picture, and she took one of me. Then we took a selfie and the sweet, delicious smell of her almost caved in my knees.

It was time for the goodbye hug. I took her in my arms and held her for a moment too long. She broke away, flushed and breathing hard. Then she was gone with the others and I watched them pedaling east until they were long out of sight. I cursed myself for the rest of the day for not kissing her, thinking of it over and over again.

But I was still on a mission and we'd come to the Mississippi.

I had a notion to check out the town of Carthage in Illinois where Joseph Smith, founder of the Mormons, had been hauled out of jail on July 27, 1844 by a mob with blackened faces. Smith got off a round from a pepperbox pistol a friend had given him, but was shot multiple times in return and ended up being a martyr for the church he founded. Becker had said that he was a Mormon, perhaps he'd traveled through.

I hit the local RV campsites, describing Becker to the proprietors. Nothing. Same deal in Nauvoo on the Mississippi where Smith is buried.

Heading west again I bumped into more cyclists, stopping to say hi to everyone I met.

Cross-country cyclists tend to fall into three groups: college kids who are geeked about their first big adventure; young guys in their 20s who have dedicated to lives of extreme-sports and adventure travel; and old folks spending their retirements biking around before bad joints and cancer catch up with them.

Then there were those cycling for causes, collecting pledges per mile to fight MS, breast cancer, child abuse and such. I came across old guys riding endlessly cross-country, still fighting Vietnam in their dreams with Missing In Action stickers on their bikes. There were young zealots proselytizing for Jesus and oddballs who seemed to be losing it in every sense of the word. Me, perhaps? I came across a guy with five-gallon pickle buckets strapped to his bike for panniers and a team of women riding recumbent bikes as low as race cars on the road. I met a woman who'd ridden around the world, and another who was soon to die from a hit-and-run.

On a long, uphill climb outside of Park Rapids, Washington, I met three dispirited Frenchmen from Nantes, a town at the mouth of the Loire River, who were cycling from New York to Vancouver. They barely knew any English and had endured their share of abuse from rednecks and motorhead drivers, not to mention the challenge of scaling the Rockies after 3,000 miles of riding cross-country.

"Voulez vous au vichyssoise?" I asked, struggling to recall my high school French.

All three gave me quizzical looks. "Thees thing, it is zee potato soup," one said.

"Oh, right, cancel that. Est tres bien, la voyage a la velocipede?" I tried again.

"Oh yes, I am thinking you mean to say the bicyclette, no?" said Phillip, who knew the most English among them. "Or perhaps the velo?"

"Oui, oui, le velo," I laughed. We exchanged a few more non sequiturs and passed by.

That's how it went time after time, with me making small talk with each passing rider hailed on the road and then asking if they'd had any trouble or near-misses with a white RV.

"I've had some close calls," said Dragon Chang, a college kid from Taiwan I met at a diner outside Spearfish, South Dakota. He was wolfing down two hotdogs and a pile of mac & cheese when I sidled up to his table. In between mouthfuls he said, "Sometimes I think they do it on purpose, passing as close as they can to scare you off the road."

I, of course, had thought about this many times, steaming with rage after every near-miss. A potentially fatal collision, with a driver passing inches away from me, happened every two weeks or so. It got me boiling mad, talking to myself and unable to sleep at night as I plotted various forms of revenge. The mildest I'd mete out would be piercing the driver's tire with my knife at a traffic stop, or whipping a rock through his windshield. If I was really pissed, I'd fantasize about sucker-punching the guy, and beyond that, hammering his head on the pavement, because with every near-miss I thought of the scenario that had led to Jill's death.

Why would anyone take a chance on killing a cyclist by clipping a rider with a mirror or front bumper? I thought a lot about that, too, and came to the conclusion that there's a murderous worm in the brain of some drivers, wriggling within the medulla of angry men, who shave cyclists to within an inch of their lives simply because they can, knowing that if they clip or kill a rider they can speed away with no one the wiser.

Chang's close encounter with death on the road had been more innocent. A less-than-nimble lumber truck had come swinging wide around a blind curve in Montana with no chance of veering out of his path. He'd ditched into a thicket of pine trees at the last second, falling off his bike and taking a wicked scrape down his right leg that was still angry and red with tattered scars. But he took his wounds with pride as a red badge of courage.

We rode together for a bit. He asked me where I was going as we pedaled along and I gave him my standard response. "Me? I'm just checking out different routes cross-country. Might write a guidebook."

"Have you ever written anything?" Chang asked politely.

"Just emails, but I know how to ride a bike. That's something. But enough about me, what about you?"

Chang told me he was riding cross-country on a spur-of-the-moment whim.

"All my friends are doing internships this summer. They think I'm crazy to miss out, but I decided to ride across America instead," he said. "Besides, I join my father's business in Taipei when I graduate. I don't need an internship."

"You'll get on-the-job training."

"Yeah. I bought a bike and took off from San Francisco a month ago. For me, it's the trip of a lifetime. When will I have a chance to ride across America again?"

"The trip of a lifetime. I've heard that before," I said, thinking of Lynda.

"Yeah, me too. Everyone says it."

It turned out that Dragon Chang had barely even ridden a bike before setting out on a journey of more than 4,000 miles to Bar Harbor, Maine.

"Most people I've met get some training miles under their belt before riding that far," I said as we rode along.

"Yes, but not me. I just toughened up as I rode along," Chang said. "At first I could do only 40 miles a day, but now, 75 or more."

Like with Lynda, we rode together for a few days and then parted. I wasn't on vacation and didn't want to be tied down with anyone. I turned down many invitations to ride along for the next 10,000 miles or so, including a couple from doe-eyed women who gave me a twinge or two. But I had determined to keep to my mission. My promise to avenge Jill crept over me like a ghost. At times I found myself muttering a mantra as I inched up one long hill after another. Stupid stuff, like:

> Jake and Jill went up the hill
> To fetch a pail of water,
> Jake fell down and broke his crown
> And Jill came tumbling after.

That, and there were songs that I couldn't get out of my head. That's a side-effect of being stressed for months on end: hypnotic songs rise in your thoughts and won't exit your brain. I won't name them because that will just start them up again. But they'd play on and on forever in my thoughts, some of them being songs that Jill and I had loved. They were "our" songs, but now they wouldn't go away, like a maddening swarm of flies that kept buzzing through my thoughts.

When things got rough, as they often did, I'd talk to Jill, who lived on in my thoughts. "This is another fine mess you got me into," I'd say, huddled with my bike on the side of a mountain with a bombardier rain soaking me bone-deep, cold as ice water.

"You asked for it, cowboy," she'd say. "Suck it up."

"Yeah, there's nothing like a good kick in the teeth."

"Mmm, out riding a bike in the great beyond, soaking up the rain. I hope I'm worth it."

"You are."

Then I'd imagine her standing there with me on the side of the mountain, the two of us pressed up under the half-shelter of an overhanging rock, slick as a black pearl with rain. Other times I'd summon her up when I failed to carry enough water with 30 miles of dry hills or desert plains yet to travel. Or when I was camped alone on a rainy night in grizzly country.

"What do you think of me now, Jill?" I'd say, staring hard into the drizzle by the glow of my headlight, hurriedly assembling my tent before it got soaked inside and out.

"I'd say you're something of a fool, Jake."

"Yes, but you married a fool, didn't you?"

"Go home Jake. Go home and lay in your bed and forget about me."

"Ain't gonna' happen."

"You don't want the bears to get you."

"By now I'm sure I'd taste like shit."

"But maybe bears like the taste of shit."

"Too funny, Jill, but I don't think so."

"Well don't say I didn't warn you."

My phantom lover Jill would tell me what an idiot I was and then I'd laugh and feel better.

"Yes, I am an idiot. Thank you for confirming that," I'd say, talking to the wind or the lonely night.

Jill came to me in dreams, too, talking about shopping for shoes or going out to dinner with friends, painting the bathroom or Thanksgiving with her parents. I'd wake up, busy making plans with her and there'd be a moment's confusion as I stared at the red membrane of my tent wall and wondered, what the hell? Then it would all come flooding back and I'd lay staring into the darkness for the rest of the night, once again reduced to a frightened rabbit in its burrow.

There were even times when I drifted into a reverie and found myself talking to her as I biked through the grasslands and endless prairies of the Great Plains. It was as if she was biking right alongside me. I'd ask, "So how's it going?" then look over and realize with a start that she wasn't there; it was just me and my shadow, the sun and the wind.

Jill's spirit came and went, but I kept on, rolling through Indian reservations, burned-over forests, arid prairie hills, drenching rainstorms, mossy Bigfoot haunts, grizzly territory and along sparkling rivers; up high mountain passes that plunged into screaming downhills. I met people at gas stations, diners and bars, chatting briefly before they slipped away as fast as they came around. I rolled past road-kill, kids on dirt bikes, deserted stores, forlorn-looking farms perched far across golden fields, combines trolling for grain at sunset, market towns bustling with life and ghost towns whispering their last breath. I saw a wolf loping across a field in southern Idaho and three elk does leaping across the road in front of my bike the day before that. I saw a stampeding herd of cattle and an antelope struggling to find a way beneath a fence. I rolled past dead rattlesnakes, hammered flat on the highway. I saw old men gathered at dawn in diners, pale skinny women who looked like frontier hookers, guys in cowboy hats, baseball caps and plastic hard hats. I saw Indians, Asians, Mormons and Mennonites. All this from the seat of a bicycle. Slowly, the roads of America filled my soul.

INCIDENT_____

FOUR CHILDREN HUDDLED IN THE DARKNESS OF THE RV, listening to the adults argue outside. Auntie Maria had told them to wait inside while the adults talked.

It had been an exhausting trip from the jungles of northern Guatemala, but not as bad as some. They had not ridden the infamous Death Train, like so many others fleeing Central America for El Norte. Instead, eight of them had been packed behind a false wall in a big truck hauling hundreds of bales of cotton. The hidden compartment had been only six by nine feet wide, but there had been a trap door in the floor that provided air and served as a toilet. They had been provided with a five-gallon jug of water and a supply of tortillas and bananas along with a flip phone to communicate with the driver. The cotton had been their protection while passing through the many checkpoints in Mexico where the internal immigration police scanned for illegals. No one had the time or patience to unload 2,000 bales of cotton from a rusted old truck to roust out a few wretched souls from Guatemala. Papa and Uncle Ciro had been skeptical of the plan, but had paid half their life savings on a bet that it would succeed. It had worked so far.

Somewhere far to the west of Ciudad Acuna they had dropped through the trap door in the darkness past midnight and waded across the Rio Grande to Texas. Josepha considered that it was a small river for such a legendary country; barely a creek with one deep spot in the middle where they had to lift their scant possessions over their heads. Papa and Uncle Ciro had carried the twins on their backs, ordering them to silence, but none could help laughing with joy when they reached the far side — America!

On the opposite bank, a man Papa called the coyote had introduced them to the tall white gringo, a giant who dwarfed even their parents. The children quaked under his gaze; they were diminutive and thin, of Mayan ancestry. Even Josepha, the tallest of them at 11, was less than four feet tall.

"These will do nicely," the big gringo had muttered, looking at the children. They were words that none of them understood, but Josepha felt with a shudder that he was staring at her the same way that Papa did when he was appraising goats at the livestock market in Paso Caballos.

Yet, despite their terror, the faces of the children betrayed no emotion, not even the six-year-olds, Lydia and Leon. They had learned the Mayan way of turning their faces to clay.

They were on the run because one of the rival gangs in their town had burned the small tienda owned by Papa and Uncle Ciro for refusing to pay up. It had been little more than a one-room shack, selling flour, tortillas, root vegetables and cheap soft drinks from Mexico, but the store had provided for their needs. Papa had protested that they were already paying another gang and couldn't live on anything less, but that had been met with a scornful laugh and a pistol in his face. That, and a promise that Josepha's brother, Santiago, would soon be joining them, though he was only nine years old.

Mama, Papa, Auntie and Uncle had packed a few things and crept out of town in the middle of the night with Josepha, Santiago and the twins, leaving their few possessions behind.

The coyote said the giant gringo with the long face was an angel they could trust with their lives. He ran a *subterraneo ferrocarril* for illegals fleeing the anarchy of El Salvadore, Guatemala, Nicaragua and Honduras. He said it was an Underground Railroad, just like the one Presidente Lincoln had built to free the negro slaves. He would take them deep into El Norte to a place called Oklahoma where they could ride the bus all the way to their relatives in Chicago.

The big man had a home on wheels like that of other gringos they had seen on the rare occasions that they had visited Flores near the ruins of Tikal. He sat them down in his small living room and gave them lemonade. It was a filthy place, but they had seen worse; perhaps this was how the gringos lived. Soon, they were all fast asleep.

The afternoon sun woke them, blasting through the thin windows like a hammer. The adults had crashing headaches and the men knew what that meant. Hurriedly, Mama and Auntie shook the children awoke, slapping them, dousing them with water. It took a long time to rouse the twins, whose eyes rolled in their heads, their tongues hanging out like cattle. They woke complaining that they had been beaten with hammers, though the men knew it was only the poison which the gringo had given them.

Gazing out the small windows of the RV they found a nightmare landscape unlike anything they'd ever experienced in the jungles of Guatemala. It was the great Chihuahuan Desert the coyote had spoken of, with nothing but sand and rocks stretching to distant sere mountains, buttes and mesas. The only vegetation was a dense thicket of thorny scrub that wandered up a side canyon. Otherwise, the desert was littered with cacti and a few ragged bushes, tearing in the wind.

The RV was parked in a dry riverbed in the shadow of a canyon. Somehow, the gringo had managed to cover the huge vehicle with camouflage netting, anchored with rocks. Uncle Ciro went for the door, only to find it padlocked from the inside. Behind them, they heard the gringo snoring in his room at the far end of the RV.

The adults talked among themselves while the children huddled in a corner. The coyote had told them they'd be traveling desert roads for at least two nights since the Border Patrol could search any vehicle within 100 miles of Mexico. But he had never said anything about being drugged.

"What can we do? We're stuck here." Mama had said. "The coyote said he was a good man, and he's our only way out."

"A good man doesn't poison his guests," Papa had replied. "He gave us something to put us out. There was something in the lemon drink, like what we use to tranquilize animals."

"But if he meant to kill us, he could have done so already," Auntie had said.

It was Uncle Ciro who came up with their plan. "We must be ready to flee if he tries anything, and to overwhelm him with our numbers, all of us, working together. Nor will we drink anything else that he gives us."

They filled their six plastic jugs with water and waited.

Near sundown, the gringo awoke and came out of his room, barely acknowledging them. Papa demanded to know what was going on, but the gringo waved him away. "Café," he muttered.

He poured some old coffee out of a pot and warmed it on the RV's small stove, groaning and stretching. Then he collapsed in a chair and stared out the window, sipping at his brew as the eight of them gathered in a small space by the door.

"Comida," Mama said at last, indicating that they needed food. The gringo stared at her as if she was an inanimate object, not a person at all. Then he gave a languid wave to a bag on the kitchen counter which held some cheap cookies, tortillas and a few bananas. Mama shared them out and they ate slowly, with dignity, though all of them were as famished as wolves.

"Senor," Papa began again, struggling with his English. "What is to do now?"

The big gringo knew only a few words in Spanish, and they knew next to nothing of English, but he waved irritably. "El camino es proximo," he pointed toward the front of the RV. "Muy proximo de aqui."

He indicated that the men should help him with the net that concealed the RV. It was growing dark and soon they would be traveling again to the road which he said was nearby.

The gringo unlocked the padlock with a ring of keys snapped to his belt. Papa and Uncle Ciro came to the door, eager to help. If the road was nearby, perhaps they would soon be shed of this diablo. Mama and Auntie demanded to go with them. At first the gringo had said no, but when they insisted, he shrugged and let them through the door. He motioned the children to stay put.

Outside the sun had disappeared far over the canyon wall and the RV was deep in shade. It would be a simple matter to toss the ropes holding the camouflage net back over the vehicle and be on their way.

"If there's trouble, take the water and run," Auntie whispered to Josepha as the adults passed through the door.

Josepha's father had stood in the doorway for a moment, looking back. "Tu eres el hombre ahora," he muttered. Josepha nodded to show that she understood.

The children gathered at the tiny window in the RV's living room, straining to look at the weights holding the net flying over the vehicle. Then it had been folded and stowed somewhere at the back of the vehicle. Then the adults had gathered at the front of the RV, led by the big gringo and they could see nothing. After a time, they heard voices raised and then shouting, and then a sound like corn popping and Auntie's voice shouting, "No!"

Then, Uncle Ciro had stumbled into view, clutching his belly and falling to the ground, his shirt a mush of blood.

Minutes went by with no sound but that of a woman groaning. Then there was a popping noise again and the sound of the gringo whooping. Then through the window they heard him grunting, cursing, with his voice slowly receding. The children were frozen in place, quivering like rabbits. But as the oldest, Josepha knew that she must do something, and fast. She crept to the door and pushed it open, gazing out above the aluminum baseboard. The gringo was dragging the body of Auntie Maria by her legs up to a place behind some rocks, perhaps 100 meters away.

Quickly, Josepha passed a jug of water to Santiago and each of the twins, picking up two herself. Papa and Uncle Ciro had given each child a knife when they had left home; they were little more than paring knives used to peel carrots or scale fish, but now they seemed precious. Santiago held his in his right hand, his jug of water in his left, and they crept out the door.

The gringo had gone out of sight beyond the rocks. "Ahora," Josepha whispered. "Andele!" The four of them crept down the black metal stairs of the RV and scurried back down the dusty two-track from which they had come. She felt a tug at her skirt and turned to find Santiago plunging his knife into the rear tire of the truck. The heavy rubber resisted at first, but Santiago put all of his weight on the hilt and it slid slowly in, like a blade into the back of an alligator. The tire gave a long, wheezing hiss, and then they ran back up the way from which the RV had come, scrambling as fast as their legs could run.

"Hey!"

Josepha turned to see the big gringo running fast behind them, his legs pounding at the dust. He seemed incredibly fast, gaining on them, and they could only run as fast as the twins.

"Drop your water and run!" she ordered. Leon and Lydia needed no encouragement. Their gallon jugs fell to the dust and they shot ahead. Behind her, Josepha could hear the big gringo's feet hammering closer; she could hear him wheezing, cursing. She knew he could only be a few feet away. She pushed the young ones ahead of her, expecting to feel his hands on her legs at any second.

With the instinct of rabbits the children fled into the scrub running up the canyon. For once in their lives their short stature was a benefit, for even Josepha made it under the shelter of the thorny branches by stooping only a little. The gringo would have to crawl on his hands and knees to reach them in the forest of thorns.

But her ankles were only an arm's length from the gringo devil's grasp. She was barely inside the safety of the brush when the gringo ran headlong into the branches in a last, desperate bid to seize her. He gave a horrible shriek and then screamed again as the branches of gray thorn, mesquite and ocotillo engulfed him in a trap of thousands of needle-sharp thorns an inch long or more. The children scrambled on, then, barely twenty feet away, they watched agog as the gringo twisted and cursed in the brush. They could see only his legs, but driblets of blood were falling like raindrops through the branches.

Josepha motioned for them to move out, scrabbling beneath the thicket further up the canyon. They stooped and crawled, tortured by the thorns which had fallen to the ground, yet fortunately few of them, since for the most part they were able to walk upright or slightly stooped beneath the rending branches. Behind them they heard the big gringo cursing and shouting, then the sound of shots fired blindly into the brush.

"Push on," Josepha ordered. Her brothers and sister needed no encouragement. They burrowed a quarter-mile through the brush, a fortress of thorns, then huddled together for warmth against the cold of the cruel desert. Somberly, Josepha reflected that the desert was much like the jungles of her homeland: everything here either bit, scratched or had a sting.

Then, several hours after midnight, yet well before dawn, the gringo moved on with his vehicle limping cockeyed in the moonlight. They heard the vehicle wheezing lopsided as it crawled deeper into the desert. After hearing the last whisper of its engine fading far off beneath the desert stars they had crept forth as timid as rabbits. By the light of the stars, they set off in search of their parents.

Big Star Casino
Chapter 9

Another year rolled by, the seasons changed, and I took to riding the South again in the winter, zig-zagging across Alabama, Louisiana, Texas... I had adventures, close calls. Sometimes I rode along narrow roads with barely any shoulder, my bike shuddering in the wake of a passing coal hauler or dump truck. I no longer cared. God would protect me, or not. As winter rolled into spring, I edged steadily north, still following the major bike routes.

One day through that second year on the road I headed down a bike trail in Wisconsin to skirt a line of hills. The dirt trail was heavily overgrown and as the miles passed on it dwindled to a dirt two-track with the fronds of small trees slapping me on either side. As the miles rolled on the trail grew rougher, intended mostly for snowmobiles.

I hoped to make camp in the town of Amery, but as darkness fell it was still miles ahead and nothing along the trail offered any hope of a camp-site. A cloud bank covered the sky, low and heavy as a sheet of iron, deepening the gloom.

Suddenly, a huge shape bounded out of a cornfield less than fifty feet ahead of me.

That looks like a bear, but it can't be a bear, I thought. It was too big. It looked as big as an elephant.

But it was a bear, looming as a black silhouette against the deepening gloom. I'd seen a number of bears by now in my travels up and down the country, but never this close, and never this big.

The bear looked at me and I looked at him, both of us in a state of won-der and puzzlement. He gave a loud *wooof!*, shook his head and shot down the trail ahead of me.

Who knew a bear could run that fast? I say run, but in fact he galloped, his massive front legs propelling him forward at what I took to be 20-25 miles per hour.

I fumbled in my front bag and gave chase, hoping to snap a photo with my phone, but it was hopeless; about a quarter-mile down the trail he crashed off to the right through the brush and into another cornfield.

It's one thing to chase a bear that's running away from you as fast as he can go and quite another to roll up on where he might be lurking. I fished around for my radio and cranked up the volume on a girly-pop station. Some honey-voiced crooner was singing something about his momma didn't like his girlfriend and now he didn't much like her either. I didn't know if the music would scare the bear off, but at least he'd know I was coming.

But by then I suppose he was long gone. A couple of miles up the trail I met a woman out walking and stopped to warn her. She was older and had the thin, hawklike features of someone who did a lot of hiking, a bird-watcher, perhaps.

"Did he look to be about 400 pounds?" she asked in a querulous voice, a bit cross and not the least bit alarmed.

"I'd say so, as big as my bike, at least."

"Yeah, well that's our boy. We've had reports about him from other

cyclists, only a lot further up the trail. He's a local legend."

"Does he have a name?"

She made a face and scoffed. "You kidding? He's a bear, for Christ's sake!"

"He told me his name was Brutus."

The mouth of her turtle face snapped open and shut. "Well, I suppose."

That wasn't my only encounter with the bear tribe. One night something big brushed the side of my tent while I was sleeping in the woods off the Blue Ridge Parkway in North Carolina. I shot straight up in my sleeping bag, straining to listen. There came a rustling by my bike, and then the sound of it tipping over. It occurred to me that my bear spray was in the front handlebar bag.

I switched on my head lamp and peeked out of my tent to find two red eyes burning in the darkness.

"Shit!" I scrambled deep into my sleeping bag, pulling it over my head like a cocoon. But the bear wasn't interested in me; he was too busy gobbling the contents of my food bag, which I'd forgotten to hang from a tree earlier that evening.

Soon after the bear ate my lunch in North Carolina I started riding northwest, climbing up and over the Smoky Mountains and on through Kentucky. The green hills of the bluegrass state gradually gave way to the cornfields of southern Indiana, upon which settled a sump of steaming heat and humidity.

It was a long day riding in what cycle racers call "black flag" conditions due to the threat of heatstroke. Checking my thermometer, I saw that it was 95 F., but it seemed much hotter due to the humidity rising from miles of cornfields and sorghum. I was in a hurry to hook up with some old friends in Illinois, so I pushed on, soaking wet from my own sweat.

I started shaking around the time my odometer hit the 123-mile mark and decided it was time to make camp, but for the last 10 miles there had been nothing but corn and sorghum on either side of the road, with the green fields stretching far out of sight over the hills. Darkness began to settle in; it was 9 o'clock at night, about the time the last rays of the sun dwindle away in the northern latitudes at high summer. Yet still there was no campsite nor even a river or a quiet woods where I could bed down. I began to wobble a bit and after another five miles or so decided that it was time to take anything I could find.

Then I spotted a faint trail marking a break in the corn. With no cars coming from either direction, I pushed my bike into the tall stalks to a clearing about a hundred yards in. Night had fallen by then and I could barely see, but that's the perfect situation when you're bandit camping because I figured that no one could see me either. I drained my last half bottle of water, too thirsty to waste any on a bird bath. For a change there weren't any mosquitoes and I was dead tired. Instead of setting up my tent, I just unrolled my sleeping bag and dropped off to sleep as soon as my head hit the bundle of clothes that served as my pillow. The stars swirled around the sky in my vision and I was out.

The sun was well up for a change when I awoke to the sound of something snuffling. Thoughts of the bear tearing into my panniers a couple nights back swept through me and I froze, not daring to look up. Slowly, I opened my eyes to find a mutt sniffing the ground close by my face.

"Hey dude." A slow, laconic voice called out over my shoulder.

Oh crap, busted. I pushed myself up on my elbows and turned around. There was a young guy standing there in the center of the clearing, which was nothing more than a circle of old, beaten-down corn stalks. He didn't look any older than 18, wearing denim overalls with no shirt and cheap high-top sneakers with no socks. A nest of curly dark hair spilled out of his straw hat to his shoulders and he gazed down on me, chewing on a sprig of grass. He looked exactly like I'd picture Huckleberry Finn, except that he had ear spacers big enough to accommodate my thumb. That, and a double-barreled shotgun hung easy in the crook of his arm.

"You know yer trespassin'?" he drawled.

"Yeah, sorry. I was riding through and couldn't find a campsite," I said, pointing to my bike, laden with gear. "It got too dark to ride and I was wiped out. I didn't know what to do."

"That so."

"Yeah, sorry."

"So you just happened to find this place, just like that."

"I did."

"Where you from?"

I told him.

"Where you goin'?"

I gave him my standard story about riding cross country on a bet.

"A bet? That sounds like bullshit."

"Yeah, but people believe it in bars. Mostly I'm riding around because I feel like it."

He gave a snort and his thumb caressed the barrel of his shotgun at the break where it accepts its shells. I wanted to crawl out of my sleeping bag, but the way things were going, it seemed best to just sit tight.

"So you never been here and don't know nothing about my place," he said at last.

"All I know is that I'm somewhere in Indiana, just riding through."

"A bicycle tourist."

"I suppose."

"In Indiana."

I nodded.

"Just you, all alone."

"What better company?" I shrugged.

"It takes all kinds."

"I guess."

Around us I could hear the corn growing, a gentle rustling sound. But all else was still, quiet as only the country can be.

"I seen some of you guys out riding before," he said. "A bunch of bike packers rode into Bloomington for the bike races last month. They had saddle bags, the whole bit, just like you."

"We're not all that hard to find these days," I replied.

He looked up suddenly and called out, "Jake, come here!"

"What?"

"Jake!"

His dog jumped up from where he'd been sniffing at my panniers and ran to his waiting hand. It was one of those indeterminate mutts, a brown mongrel mix of a half-dozen breeds with long, floppy ears and an eager nose.

I forced a little laugh. "Your dog is named Jake? That's my name too."

"That right?"

"Since the day I was born."

In the distance, the sound of a truck came humming down the road beyond the corn. We stopped to listen as it drew closer. It flashed by the narrow pathway through the cornfield and continued on down the road.

I started making some small talk about corn farming in Indiana, but the kid waved me off.

"I don't bother with all that," he said. "You smoke?"

"Smoke? Not since I was a kid. I got up to a pack a day and called it quits."

"Naw, I mean herb, weed."

It was an odd question and seemed even odder with me sitting up in my sleeping bag, under the kid's gun in a cornfield. "Well yeah, in college," I said, "but not anymore."

"Well you do now," he replied, tapping the barrel of his gun.

He circled over to my left and for the first time I noticed the back bench of a ruined car seat lying on the ground in the clearing, surrounded by a circle of beer cans. It looked like it had been picked at by animals, tattered and worn by the sun and the rain.

"Come on," he waved, "you're going to prove you're not a cop."

What the hell. I crawled out of my sleeping bag and joined him on the car seat with the sun creeping over the top of the corn stalks. The upholstery was still wet from passing rains. My host pulled a lighter and a spliff the size of a clothespin from the top pocket of his overalls, firing it up.

"I'm Charlie," he said in a strangled voice as he inhaled. "And this is some powerful righteous Indiana skunk, right here."

So we sat and smoked and Charlie told me he was seeking a degree in sustainable agriculture at Ball State University, paying his way through school as a grower with a loyal clientele both on and off campus in Muncie, Indiana.

We talked of many things, cats and kings, the fate of the earth, life on a bicycle and all of the usual stuff the comes up when you get high. Charlie told me that skunk was a crossbreed of cannabis sativa and cannabis indica.

"You learn something new every day," I said, marveling at this revelation.

"I never did think you were DEA," he said after a bit. "Besides, herb is practically legal now anyway."

"Smoking it, anyway," I said, feeling dreamier by the minute. Charlie wasn't kidding about the power of his product and it had been years since I'd indulged.

"So where do you grow?" I asked, imagining an indoor operation under lights, like the medical marijuana growers I knew back in Michigan.

"What do you mean?"

"I mean, do you have your stuff set up in a barn or something?"

Charlie took another toke and grimaced. "I'd tell ya, but then I'd have to kill ya," he said.

He gave me a dead serious look and then broke out laughing. "It's right over there," he waved.

I looked to where he was pointing, but saw only a wall of corn.

"Come on," he said. We pushed into the corn, its leaves tickling my arms and its tassels dancing overhead in a dazzle of gold. It was like we were on a magical expedition, though I knew it was only because I was as high as Jupiter. We only pushed in five rows or so, and there was Charlie's crop, towering as tall as the corn, a more emerald shade of green amid their stalks.

I fingered one of the narrow leaves and then on an impulse, plucked it and stuck it in my hair.

"That's a good look for you," Charlie said, "just don't tell anyone where you got that."

"How many plants you got out here?"

"Only about sixty. I ain't greedy; I'm just growing enough to make it through school without any debt. That, and I got payments on a truck."

We talked a bit more and then attacked my supply of fig bars, devouring them. Charlie wished me luck and pressed another joint on me for later. I offered to pay him five bucks for camping on his dad's farm and he just laughed. "Yer gonna need that money for the munchies."

I wobbled my bike back down the narrow path through the corn and headed west, my head humming with pleasant thoughts beneath cumulous clouds that streamed by like steamboats in the sky. After a bit, I found a roadside picnic stop and the shade of a vast oak tree. I tumbled off my bike and sat propped up against it for the next couple of hours, feeling powerless to move.

I shared the bear story with Freeman the next time we spoke on the phone, leaving out my subsequent adventure in the cornfields of Indiana. By now our calls were a mere formality, just checking in.

"So, I guess you're out riding for the long haul," he said.

"Yeah, just looking around," I said, suddenly abashed. I had never told Freeman about my bicycle odyssey in all the times we'd spoken on the phone over the past year and a half. I didn't want him to think I'd gone crazy.

"Seeing anything?"

"Just the world turning around, like always."

"Well, I wish there was something new, but things have gone kind of cold."

"They started cold and stayed cold," I said bitterly.

"Don't give up."

I vowed not to, but had to admit, it seemed hopeless. By then I'd begun riding whichever way the wind was blowing. It was a lot easier riding with the wind than beating against it on the ACA routes and I figured I was getting nowhere anyway, biking through the Land of Nod as it were. As it turned out, that led to my first lucky break.

Near a small town in central Illinois, a dusty beater van rolled up on me. At the wheel was a young guy with sparkling blue eyes and a headful of red-gold curls. Clustered behind him were four kids in their late teens and early 20s sucking on colas and cigarettes, giddy with the novelty of talking with a dude on a bicycle loaded with camping gear.

I could see that they meant no harm. Also, that they'd never seen a touring cyclist before. By now I was well off the route of America's bikeways, wandering with the wind.

Where you going? What you doing? He looked out his window, squinting in the sun. The kid had a lot of questions and they came in a rush.

"Whichever way the wind blows," I said.

"Really? You're riding across the country? You're doing it alone, just by yourself?"

"I've got nothing else to do," I shrugged. "You could do it yourself. Just get a bike and go wherever you want."

"And you just camp out? Where do you stay?"

"Wherever I end up that day. Mostly it's in campgrounds or in town parks, but sometimes it's under a bridge or a bush."

"Someplace where people can't see you."

"Yeah. That and someplace free always works for me."

Beyond his eyes, I could see the wheels of his imagination churning with the possibilities. I assured him that life as a wandering bicyclist was an unfettered blast of freedom and adventure, leaving out the parts about the wind, hills, heat, bugs, traffic, crappy food and days without a shower.

"Start out with a backpack and a short trip," I advised.

He nodded, a drowsy expression settling over his face. His passengers just sat there giggling, in no hurry to clear the side of the road.

"Yeeeah, I could do that," he said.

As an afterthought, I asked where he and his tattooed friends were off to.

"Oh, just going to our NA meeting," he said, his smile fading.

"What's NA?" I asked.

"Narcotics Anonymous."

There didn't seem to be much more to say after that. I wished him good luck and the kids sped off while I labored on into the town in search of a cup of coffee. I arrived around 6 p.m. to find downtown locked up tight with the main street as quiet as a mime's graveyard. Rolling through town I noted that there were no coffee houses, brew pubs or nightclubs, the kind of places where young people might find healthier outlets than doing drugs. There's nothing more forlorn than a town without a coffee house.

But just out of town was a park with campsites gathered around a lake. I pitched my tent, made some coffee and settled in for a feast of Ramen noodles when up drove the occupants of the neighboring tent. Out of an old, low-slung Plymouth sedan popped a couple of pit bulls and two heavily-tattooed young guys, as thin as razors, shirtless in skin tight jeans and cowboy boots. Accompanied by a plump young woman dressed in black, they looked like extras from *Breaking Bad.*

As I expected, later on there was a party with other young people showing up around their camp fire. Rumbling in around 8 p.m. was the van I'd encountered on the road a few hours earlier.

"Hey, biker dude! Do you socialize?" It was my buddy, the golden-haired driver. He made the universal sign for smoking weed, holding an imaginary joint to his lips.

I demurred. "No thanks, I'm pretty wiped out."

"From biking, right?"

"Yeah, but have a toke for me, okay?"

"No problem!"

He turned to go, then turned again. "I'm Luke, by the way."

"Jake." We shook hands.

As I drifted off to sleep I overheard Luke and his friends talking across the way about how they liked to get high before attending their court-ordered NA meetings. One of the bunch opined that he liked to smoke weed, while others vouched that they preferred to endure the meetings high on crystal meth. I gleaned that they were cooking methamphetamine in an abandoned barn out by the town dump.

No worries, owing to past encounters with the tweaker tribe, I knew that meth users tend to avoid calling attention to themselves and were unlikely to "meth" with me unless they got so stupid-stoned they didn't know what they were doing.

Sometime after midnight, I awoke to the metallic fumes of crystal meth being smoked just a hat-toss away, followed by hysterical giggling that went on for some time. As I drifted back to sleep it was almost as if I could hear that manic giggling in my dreams.

Whatever. I was up by six and had packed my gear, drank my coffee and hit the road south out of the park, well before the druggies arose.

My buddy Luke was sleeping upright at the wheel of his van, gently snoring with his mouth open. I had an impulse to say goodbye. It occurred to me that he had such sparkling eyes because he and his jolly companions had been as high as Cheech and Chong when I met them by the road yesterday. Just a carful of small town druggies out driving impaired on their way to a Narcotics Anonymous meeting that probably wasn't offering the kind of direction they needed.

Perhaps I could urge him to get addicted to something else, like bicycling, maybe. He could start out riding an old junker bike out west beyond the Mississippi to the West Coast and get a job in a coffee shop, away from this stultifying town and the dead-end life of drugs and the criminal justice system.

But Luke slept blissfully on as the sun rose in his face and I suspected he wouldn't listen anyway. Plus, there was no lack of drugs out west; he'd have to figure things out for himself. I pushed forward with my bike, got tripped up on a crumbling patch of driveway, and fell heavily into the gravel.

"Motherfucker!" I cursed, pulling my bike up and brushing myself off.

It was then I noticed that the back gate of Luke's van was slathered with dozens of bumper stickers like you sometimes see driven by folks who are all wound up about politics or the environment. There was a D.A.R.E. sticker, of course and a Grateful Deadhead skull along with the wise sayings of Indians and Noam Chomsky. Also a CO-EXIST sticker, some Save-the-Whales stuff and the like. But one leapt out at me, a bumper sticker that Luke must have chosen for its symbol: BIG STAR CASINO. It had a black background with white lettering and the star symbol was formed to look like something at the end of a branding iron. I recognized it at once; it was the same pattern as the sticker I'd seen on Becker's RV.

The Bicycle Bums
Chapter 10

"Well I guess we know he likes to gamble," Smith Freeman said over the phone when I called him. "Are you sure about that?"

"I'm sure," I said. "The second I saw it, it clicked. It's the same bumper sticker I saw on Becker's RV."

"Big Star Casino. Where's that at?"

"It's little place down in Oklahama with less than a hundred slots. They don't even have a web page. I found it on Facebook."

"Well, that'll help," Freeman said. "Could help a lot."

"Right, I mean, how many dorks are there out driving around with that combination of bumper stickers? Wall Drug and Big Star Casino?"

"That's rhetorical."

"What?"

"I mean, who knows? Could be a lot from what I've seen of the RV crowd. But it's a solid lead and I'll get it out there."

I rang off. The next day I bivouacked in Springfield and its public library, scouring the Internet for the casino and its connection to RVs. It turned out that the Big Star Casino had a small RV park and a steak restaurant, but the whole operation had gone out of business two years ago, about the same time as its last entry on Facebook. As for my hot tip to Freeman, I imagined it would end up on a sheet of paper in his file cabinet instead of an all-points bulletin to the sharp-eyed cops of America.

Still, my spirits had buoyed, and with the wind blowing southwest I took off on a wandering path towards Missouri.

The wind was loving the west that month, pushing me on and on. I hit St. Louis and rolled under the Arch. On a whim, I took the Katy Trail for more than 230 miles up the Missouri. It's a bike path paved with crushed limestone that runs beneath the same high bluffs overlooking the route Lewis and Clark took on their expedition across the country. There was little chance I'd spot RVs of any kind paralleling the trail, but I needed a break from dodging cars after enduring the traffic of St. Louis.

Riding west from St. Charles, I reminded myself that this was the route I should have chosen for my bike tour with Jill. There were no vehicles on the old rail-trail and it would have been completely safe. Jill would still be alive if I'd opted for a route that carried a little less "adventure." It took me back a few years to other trips we'd taken and all of the things we'd dreamed of.

Like most couples muddling through the 20s, Jill and I had had a few small adventures. During our first winter together we went to Panama Beach, neither of us mentioning what we'd done there in the arms of others while still in college.

We went Cancun the next year, then Disneyworld and Rocky Mountain National Park. But our biggest adventure had been climbing Mt. Adams in Washington State. We flew out to Portland for our fifth anniversary, planning to celebrate on a mountaintop.

It had been a two-day hike up the south face of the mountain, and at 12,276 feet it had been a bit tough on a couple of rookies from the flatlands of the Midwest. But Jill and I had taken a course that included a couple of guides and we set out weighed down under heavy packs, outfitted with helmets, crampons and ice picks.

We labored up the long slope, tramping through the snow in full sun and camped at a high meadow called the Lunch Counter with two other groups of hikers. Then we were up before dawn for the last, high stretch, reaching the summit in time to catch the sun lighting up the distant mountains as if they were flames rising from the earth.

We took selfies, hugged each other and gazed out on Mt. Hood, Mt. St. Helen and Mt Rainier. "This is living," Jill said, a red angel in her snowsuit.

"Yes it is."

"Those mountains are like all of the big things we're going to do with our life together," she said, waving her arm dramatically to sweep them all in.

"What?"

"I mean, they represent all the mountains that two people can climb together. Family, a home, careers..."

"Oh, we're going to climb more than that," I said, smiling.

"More than that? What is there?"

I shrugged. "New Zealand?"

Jill crept in close, nuzzling me. She looked up, gazing with her big blue eyes into mine. "We'll go to New Zealand? she said, "Promise?"

"Oh yeah, Alaska too."

"Africa?"

"We'll buy a boat and sail there."

"Can we take our kids?" she teased.

I gazed over her shoulder where Mt. Rainier rose up, as radiant as a diamond in the sun. "Well, I guess we'll have to make some first."

Ah, but that had been years ago now and the only hope Jill had of making it to New Zealand was if some particle of her ashes drifted down the long river to the sea and was swept to the other side of the earth.

I shook my head to clear my thoughts. Truthfully, by now my memories of Jill were starting to slip away, even though I held on as best I could. I felt guilt, even shock at times with the realization that I seemed to barely remember her. Maybe it's a natural reaction, the erosion of memory after the loss of a loved-one, but at times it was as if she never existed.

If the conscious mind is a ship floating on the sea of something dark and deep, then Jill had slipped overboard in the ocean of my memories. On many nights while lying in my tent I'd summon her back, reviewing our times together, sometimes laughing, sometimes staring transfixed

into the darkness, breathing shallow like a rabbit that knows it's been spotted. Then she'd come back to me, but in fragments, mere patches of our life together that had come unstitched in my memory.

Strangely, I had no problem remembering the horse-faced monster Peter Becker.

In a patch of woods outside the burg of Treloar, I stopped to help a cyclist fix a flat. He was sitting alongside the trail with his back propped up against a tree, trying to wrestle his tire off the rim with his bare hands.

"That isn't going to work," I said, rolling to a stop.

"Tell me about it." He threw the wheel down in disgust and looked at his hands, covered with grease. "This ain't no good."

"Where's your tire spoons?" I asked.

"Tire spoons?"

"Yeah, they're the levers you use to get a tire off the rim."

"I never changed a tire before."

I had to laugh. "Yeah, I can see that. Do you even have a pump?"

He shrugged. "Aw man, my pump fell off way back and I haven't gotten around to buying a new one."

I'd seen hundreds of cyclists making their way across the country over the past two years, but none like this one, a big guy in baggy shorts and high-top sneakers. His skin was a shade paler than chocolate milk, but most of it was covered with tattoos. A screaming eagle spanned his chest, while his back was mirrored with a thunderbird of some tribal origin. A devil peered out from the meat of his upper right arm, with an angel riding on his left. He had the sun and moon tattooed on either leg. All this I knew because he wasn't wearing a shirt; he was dressed only in basketball shorts and shoes.

He stood up and looked down on me, hands on his hips. He was maybe six-foot-four and heavily muscled with a ladder of sinew climbing his abdomen. His shoulders were massive, climbing to the trunk of a thick neck, around which he wore a gold chain with an NBA medallion. A mass of braids fell to his shoulders with strips of cloth tethering the ends, reminding me of a lion, or perhaps an African warrior who hunted lions. His features were vaguely Oriental, giving his face a rather delicate look, yet he wore a menacing expression, lips tight and eyes glaring. He looked like what the rappers call a thug.

That feeling dug a little deeper as he crept around behind me, peering over my shoulder as I levered his tire from its rim. I could hear him breathing softly as he watched me working. It occurred to me that we were miles out of town, hunkered down in a tunnel of trees and brush in the shadow of the bluffs. If he wanted to get the jump on me, this would be a good place to do it.

I glanced back, finding only curiosity in his face, like a kid gazing at a turtle. His face had gone soft; if he really was a thug, he was an amiable one.

"Pay attention," I said. "You've got to pry both spoons under the tire and then zip it off like this."

By now I was a master at changing high-pressure tires, which tend to grip their rims like they've been welded on. Within ten minutes, I had his tire patched and back on his bike. He didn't have a spare.

"Thanks man, I owe you," he murmured. He had a high, piping voice as soft as that of a woman, or maybe Michael Jackson.

"De nada."

"Huh?"

"Don't mention it."

We made some small talk with me trying to suss him out. At last I said, "How's it going for you riding around the country?"

"What do you mean?"

"Well, I mean, I haven't seen many African-Americans out bike touring. A few, but not many."

He gave me a shocked look.

"What makes you think I'm an African-American?" He seemed a bit indignant.

"Whoa!" I just..."

"I'm biracial," he said drily, "like Meghan Markle."

"Who?"

"The gal who married Prince Harry."

"Never heard of him," I said, thinking he was some rap artist.

"Well she's biracial like me. We're practically cousins."

"Or like Tiger Woods."

"Yeah, but don't push it."

"Or Barack Obama."

"Yeah, him too."

"Or The Rock."

"Enough."

"Sorry."

"I'm a little of this and a little of that," he said. "Part black and part Japanese or something Eurasian. And you? What are you?"

"Scotch-Irish and some other stuff, a mutt, I guess."

"Mmm." The stranger nodded his head, looking off into the distance and pursing his lips.

"The oppressor," he said after a bit.

I scoffed at this. "You mean the guy who changed your tire?"

"Yeah," he gave a crooked smile, "my hero for today. I owe you one."

It was time to change the subject. "So, how's your trip going?"

"It's going," he said, followed by a heavy sigh. "But sometimes it can be a bitch, know what I mean?"

"I guess so. Life's a bitch."

"And then you die," he said quietly.

"Yeah, sure. Which way you heading?" I asked, hoping it was in the other direction.

"Same way as you."

He stuck out a limp, clammy hand. "I'm Jimmy Christmas."

"Jake," I shook back.

So we rode on down the trail cluttered with the leaves of a passing storm, pedaling past Hermann, Rhineland, Portland and Mokane. It transpired that Jimmy had been having a rough time since leaving his home in Chicago. He'd endured heavy rains, unfriendly people spooked by his appearance and racist teens shouting from passing cars and trucks. Like Chang, the cyclist I'd met from Taiwan, he hadn't done much cycling outside of pedaling around on a one-speed BMX bike as a kid. His kit showed it too; his tent and sleeping bag were tied in an unbalanced pile on the back of his bike which tended to make him wobble as he rode along.

"I could use a friend, you know?" he said after laying out his litany of troubles.

"Sure sounds like it," I replied, knowing that Jimmy had picked the wrong guy for the position. He was likable enough, but I was headed off to God knows where and friends weren't in the picture.

We started out riding, but soon enough Jimmy begged to stop for a water break, a leg cramp, and then to rest his sore ass. I began to lose patience. It wasn't like I needed a tag-along. The afternoon progressed and Jimmy kept falling behind. I waited for him a time or two, once for a long time at a town called Tebbetts, and then pressed on. I didn't expect to see him again. Through all the months of riding my legs had grown incredibly strong, hammering like pistons, and there was no way to turn them off.

Toward dusk I made it to the turnoff for Jefferson City, the capital of Missouri, which sprawled across a high hill beyond the river about two miles off the trail. Even though the Katy Trail hosts thousands of touring cyclists each year, there aren't many campsites along its length. But I found a clearing in the brush about a hundred yards down the connecting trail into town and figured it would do for the night.

I pitched my tent, inflated my mattress and was spreading out my sleeping bag when I heard a hooting and rattling coming down the trail from the city.

It was a couple of bicycle bums on beater bikes, dragging their worldly possessions along on the kind of trailers designed for carting toddlers around town.

I'd run into them before in city parks and hobo jungles hidden away down railroad tracks outside a number of towns. Generally, they rode donated or stolen bikes with a bolus of sleeping bags, rank clothing and winter coats packed into cast-off bike trailers.

I call them bums, but the polite term is indigents, gentlemen who are down on their luck, mostly through a combination of alcohol and mental illness. Most were the beneficiaries of Good Samaritans who set them up with bikes and trailers in order to make their lives a little easier.

They were a different tribe than the homeless families who lived out of their cars or in shelters. Those folks of the working poor might be homeless for a few weeks or months until they got back on their feet. Often as not, they were the victims of medical disasters, a lost job or prescription drug abuse.

But the hard-core indigents often seemed to be in for the long haul. Some were harmless, the meek of the earth, but others were vultures who'd sell their grandmother for half a bottle of Mad Dog 20-20.

Such was the case with two who showed up at my bandit camp.

"Hey, fella', you want some comp'ny?" They stood in shadow against the last rays of the sun, as still as deer at the far side of the clearing. The one who called out was tall and rough as a cornstalk, crowned with matted, greasy hair in a disarray that ranged about his head like horns.

The other guy hung back a bit behind him. He was dark, stocky, and about my height with a bad case of the stares. He looked a bit like Boris Karloff in a bad mood. He was either humming or growling as he swayed from side to side, I couldn't make it out.

"No thanks," I said.

He ignored me and they drew closer, their gear bumping back and forth behind them.

"I'm Ferns, this is Bob," he said. "You got anything to eat?" He eyed my gear with his head poking up and down like an ostrich.

I gave him a flat, expressionless look and growled. "Are you kidding? I'm traveling around on a bicycle."

"That don't mean much. Bob and I meet lots of folks who like to share. We like to socialize, pass the bottle around when we got one. Know what I mean?" He winked, baring a broken fence of corn-yellow teeth.

"Yeah, well, sorry but I've got nothing for you." At best I had a little beef jerky and half a bagel from lunch. That, and after thousands of miles of hard riding, I had become someone who, as the saying goes, could not suffer a fool. Ferns struck me as a fool. I was tired, crabby, arrogant; I wanted these guys to get lost.

"Well, okay then. Mind if we camp here, Mr. high and mighty?" Ferns asked. To this, Bob scoffed and gave a husky laugh.

"I was looking for some time alone, but thanks for the offer."

"Huh?" His eyes bugged out in mock disbelief.

"I'm not looking for any company."

A hateful look crossed Ferns's face and he threw down his bike. It hit the ground with a bang, jerking his trailer sideways.

"Whoa, fella'! Why you want to be so mean? You got something agin' those who got nothin' while you's sittin' there like the king of England?"

I said nothing.

Ferns began to mutter and pace while Bob stared at me.

"This here's a free country and we camp where we want," Ferns went on, glaring at me. His sallow face was tight with rage. "I figure we'll set up right here, nice and tidy, and there ain't a thing you can do about it."

Again, Bob gave a huffing laugh. He was wrapped in a heavy down jacket over a sweater in the stifling heat. I figured it to be in the low 80s even with the sun going down.

"What's wrong with your buddy?" I asked, changing the subject. I was feeling antagonistic. "Does he talk?"

Bob came alive. "I talk plenty, you pussy-ass fucker!" he spat. He went off with a long stream of obscenities and insults, shouting and waving his arms, like the hostile crazy men you see haranguing people passing by on city streets. Abruptly, he stopped swearing and started growling instead, clenching his fists and grinding his teeth. He shuffled from side to side, his eyes roiling with hostility.

I sized him up as borderline psychotic and a combative drunk with Ferns being a simple product of child abuse and alcoholism. I'd read somewhere that in terms of animal behavior, it's best to be completely non-reactive when man or beast crosses a line. It befuddles them and has a calming effect, so I said nothing to Bob; didn't make a face, smile, frown, nothing. I turned to fiddle with my tent stakes, drawing one out. It was about 10 inches of hardened plastic with a tapered point at the end.

"Hey, watcha' doing with that?" Ferns was hovering over me.

I said nothing.

"You fixin' to stick that tent stake in my eye or somethin'?"

"No man," I said calmly, "why would I do that? I just want you two to buzz off."

The events of the day had warmed me to a slow burn. First there had been wondering how to ditch the tag-along Jimmy Christmas and now these guys. I'd ridden more than 70 miles of crushed limestone trail that day under an 85-degree sun and all I wanted was to be left alone.

"Ohhh..., big man!" Ferns cooed. "Like you think you can just blow us off? This is our place, bicycle man. You're in our living room now and we call the shots here. How do you like that? How do you like it? Huh? What do you think? You want us to go away? It ain't gonna happen you little bitch. You'd better think about giving us something to make amends, little man, or we'll rip you a new asshole. What do you think about that, huh? What do you..."

Ferns was sidewinding into my comfort zone while spooky Bob angled behind me. The sun had fallen below the horizon and we stood in a tableau now, frozen in the half-dark on the brink of the first move. My plastic tent stake suddenly seemed a ridiculous weapon and my antagonism turned traitor and fled. Normally, I'd consider myself up to the task of taking on these two slouches, but that's the sort of delusion you tell yourself when you've had a couple of beers and no one's barking in your face. The reality was I had attackers looming front and back, closing in on me in the darkness and my knees were starting to shake.

That's when Ferns pulled a knife. A broad grin creased his face as he held it up, waggling it back and forth like a sword. "Let's see where this goes, little man," he said.

I glanced over my shoulder to where Bob had blended with the night in his black winter coat. By the light of the moon I could see he was holding a bottle.

Just then I heard the crunch of tires on the gravel trail and a light bobbing along 100 yards away.

"Jake? Is that you?" It was Jimmy Christmas.

"Over here!" I yelled. "Over here!"

The grin faded on Ferns' face. "Got the cavalry, huh? Well let's just see if he's a pussy like you."

"Yeah, pussy like you," Bob echoed. He had crept in close and was practically breathing down my neck. He gave me a half-shove on my shoulder and I turned, pushing back with both hands. Bob stumbled back and laughed. He was drunk.

Christmas had an LED lamp mounted on his handlebars, throwing a blinding glare on the situation. He loomed large in the headlight and his dreads gave him the silhouetted appearance of a towering lion, deep in shadow. He leaned his bike up against a sapling and stepped out of the light. Ferns was still holding his knife, it was something he'd cribbed from a kitchen, a good ten inches long, designed to carve turkeys.

"Mmmm, you two get going," he said in his soft voice, quiet as a woman crooning a lullabye. "Get going right now, you got it?"

Ferns was incredulous. "You got a nigger riding with you?"

He didn't get a chance to emote any further because a long stream of liquid shot from Jimmy's hand followed by a prolonged scream from Ferns, who dropped his knife and clutched at his eyes.

"My eyes! My eyes!" He cried. "What the fuck, man! What the fuck!"

"You want some of this?" Jimmy spoke to Bob, who stood there gaping. The scent of insecticide choked the clearing. "You better get some water on your buddy, then get the fuck out of here before I give you a dose too."

But Bob didn't stick around to wash out Ferns' eyes. He spat some obscenities and lumbered his bike trailer back down the trail, waddling toward Jefferson City.

"I'll be happy to give you a dose!" Jimmy called after him. "Come back around anytime, I'll be waiting for you."

We couldn't leave Ferns like he was. He was gagging, crying. We washed out his eyes with what was left in our water bottles, cleaned him up and gave him some beef jerky.

"Thanks man," he blubbered once we had him straight. "I didn't mean anything by that nigger thing. I got friends, right here in town. Black dudes, we's friends."

"No harm done," Jimmy said in his quiet way.

"What is that stuff?" I asked.

"Wasp spray. My grandma used it when things got serious 'round the neighborhood. Shoots twenty feet of snake venom."

"Yeah, I see that," I said. "Thanks, I don't know what I would have done without you."

"Maybe you don't want to know," Jimmy said darkly. "So we're even on the tire now, right?"

"Damn straight."

"So, what do we do now?"

"We can't stay here. We'd be dead meat in our tents if Bob came back, and he might have friends. Plus, we got Ferns here. We've got to head on down the trail a ways."

"He ain't gonna' come back," Jimmy said.

"You want to be lying on the ground fast asleep if he does?"

Jimmy groaned. "So tired, man."

"Yeah, me too, but let's go."

Through all this, I'd been packing up my gear, jamming it helter-skelter into my panniers. Ferns had sprawled out on the ground, still stinking of wasp spray with a bad rash on his face, but snoring. His sour breath stank of booze. I stuffed a five dollar bill in his collar, called him a shithead, and we took off down the Katy Trail, heading west. I tossed Ferns's knife in a gully about a mile down the trail.

Five miles on, we found a clearing in the woods alongside the trail that wasn't much more than a cubbyhole in the brush. We pulled out our sleeping bags, hunched up against a tree and called it a night with a half moon arcing west over the Missouri.

Jimmy Christmas
Chapter 11

So I guess I had a friend, whether I wanted one or not. With a strong wind blowing west, we pushed past the trail's end in Clinton and headed for Kansas.

Kansas was much the same as ever with the same flat cornfields running from horizon to horizon, but we made over 120 miles a day with the wind at our back. We came to the same small town where I'd met Lynda more than a year before and I thought wistfully of her, wondering where she was now. I'd sent a friend request on Facebook, but she hadn't acknowledged it. Maybe she was trying to push me out of her thoughts, or just didn't think about me at all. I tried to give up thinking about her, but it wasn't easy. She probably thought I was some kind of weenie.

"So, what's with the name?" I asked Jimmy as we pedaled on.

"What name?"

"Your family name."

"Christmas? That's a big family name down South," Jimmy said. "After the emancipation, a lot of folks didn't want to keep their slave names, so they fixed on something else, like Washington."

"Or Freeman," I added, thinking of my detective pal.

"That's right. The story goes that my great-great grandfather wanted every day to be Christmas when he escaped bondage, so that's why I'm Jimmy Christmas today."

"Nice. Better than Halloween," I said.

Jimmy laughed. "Yeah. And you, what about you?"

"Just call me Jake."

"Jake. What? Like Madonna or Prince? Eminem, Bono, Fifty Cent? What's your last name?"

"Can't remember anymore," I said. "I just go by Jake for now. You can make up a name if you want."

"Well, okay, Jake Madonna, or whoever you are."

Jimmy's story unreeled as we pedaled side-by-side. He'd been raised by his grandmother, "just like Barack Obama," on a street on the south side of Chicago just a few doors down from where Muddy Waters once lived. He'd been sucked into a gang at the age of 13.

But I got the impression that Jimmy had been play-acting at being a gangster.

"I got some tats and got into a little trouble, but I kept up with my studies," he said. "I was a private school kid, thanks to Grandma."

Jimmy's gangland days had been crowded out by his skill at basketball. He'd earned a scholarship at Northwestern University in Chicago, playing right-forward. His dream was to play with the NBA, thus the pendant around his neck.

"And you know, you got to have tats these days to play in the leagues," he said, half serious. "I'm halfway there."

"So, what are you doing out here, riding around on a bike? Is that just a summer fun thing?"

Jimmy pursed his lips and whistled.

"No, boss. It's more like I'm on the run. I couldn't get away from my past, know what I'm sayin'? My old boys came around from the gang days and started putting pressure on me."

"What kind of pressure?"

"What did they want? They wanted me! They had this idea that a college boy might be valuable, like maybe I could throw some games or something they could bet on. They made me an offer I couldn't refuse."

He thought about it a bit, then laughed. "They wanted me to be their accountant because I was going to college! Can you imagine that? And I'm majoring in computer forensics. I don't know shit about accounting."

"So you took off."

"Yeah."

"On a bike?"

"Why not on a bike?" Jimmy said. "There was no place for me to go, no relatives down south or anything like that. Me and Grandma, our whole world was about five miles square; that's the way it is for people who live in the hood. If it wasn't for my studies and the bus trips I made with the team, I wouldn't know anything about the world beyond Chicago. I got the itch to get out and look around, know what I'm sayin'?"

"I do. But bike packing requires a particular set of skills," I said. "Even people who ride a lot don't have a clue about what it means to go bike camping around the country."

"Particular set of skills? Come on, I learned that pretty fast," Jimmy scoffed. "But this is how it happened. One day, I'm walking down the street to the store and here comes the guys, six, seven of them, coming straight at me.

"So we have this meeting, right there on the corner of Racine and 63rd Street and they're going hard at me to get back with them. I couldn't say yes, but I was afraid to say no. Maybe they was just bullshitting, but they made out like it was a one-way street with no other way. I told them I'd think about it and get back to them later that day. Jabazz, the guy in charge, handed me something like five hundred dollars and said it was a taste of the sugar to help make up my mind.

"Well, just then, who comes along but this guy on a bike, riding all around lost in the south side of Chicago," he went on. "It was some guy from Switzerland who had the idea he was going to see the most dangerous city on earth, like you might ride around to the same places in Europe with no worries. The guy barely spoke English, but somehow he'd figured out a way into town.

"Except this guy was plenty worried by the time my boys stopped him. He'd gone, as you might say, a whiter shade of pale. My boys started poking at him and saying shit, having a good time, and things weren't going his way, know what I'm sayin'? Like a dumbass, he had his wallet in his back pocket, and that went right away, along with his passport."

"So, what did you do?"

Jimmy gave a low laugh. "Aw, man, I don't know how right this was, but I made him an offer he couldn't refuse."

"You took his bike?"

"Yeah. I made up some bullshit about his passport being worth thou-sands of dollars on the black market and Jabazz and the boys swallowed it like fish bait. They took off down the street leaving me to get rid of the Swiss guy and fence his passport. I told them I'd handle it and they believed that too. They didn't know what to do with a guy from Switzer-land, so let the college boy figure it out, right?

"By this time the guy was all crying and shit; he just wanted to get out of there. Didn't even care about his bike! So I put him on a bus up to the Miracle Mile where his hostel was and told him good luck."

"Buena suerte."

"Yeah, buena suerte, amigo. And that's when I started riding, right then, right out of town in my basketball shorts."

"What about your grandma?"

"Oh, blessed soul, she's gone. I was living with my girlfriend by then. She's got all my stuff, waiting on me this fall."

"But how are you going to get back in town if these gangster dudes are waiting around for you?"

"That has a way of falling apart, know what I'm sayin'? Plus, I ain't going back to the old neighborhood, least not in this lifetime. Me and Sheila are moving up north to around Wrigley Field. We're going to be buppies, black, urban professionals."

"Sure, you can hang out with the Obamas."

"Probably. It could happen. He likes basketball."

"So this all turned out like a summer vacation for you."

"Yeah, summer vacation."

"But you robbed that Swiss guy."

"No! I only borrowed his stuff, man! I got plans to give it back. I even got his card with his email and all. It's just that he's going to have to fly back from Lausanne to get his stuff," he finished with a laugh.

"Well, I guess he was asking for it," I said.

"That's right, be careful you don't get what you ask for," Jimmy nodded.

"One good deed deserves another."

"No good deed goes unpunished."

"So true."

I didn't say anything for a long time, trying to parse out what Jimmy had told me. Why didn't he just point the Swiss guy in the other direction and tell him to ride on out of there? He'd robbed the guy, there was no other way around it. Jimmy's grandma might have placed him on the right path, but he was still capable of mugging a snowflake from Switzerland.

But, thug or not, I didn't think that Jimmy would try anything funny with me. Whether he was some kind of latent gangster or a college kid seeking a fresh direction, Jimmy needed me. He was a stranger in a strange land, and I was his way through it.

So on we rode.

On our second day together, Jimmy insisted we stop in town to buy a basketball.

"You've got to be kidding me."

"I don't kid about basketball," he said. "I got to keep in shape. Coach gave me the summer off to go biking; he said it would build up my legs. But I can't stop doing my drills, know what I mean?"

Good, I thought. I'd be able to shuck Jimmy while he did his basketball drills.

But that's not how it turned out. Instead, we stopped at every town on the way west and scrimmaged in the school basketball courts. Jimmy was a foot taller than me, so invariably he blocked every shot, but often as not, I ran circles around underneath him.

"You's like chasing a chicken," he grumbled after I made a break down-court and scored.

"Takes one to know one, I guess."

Despite myself, I began looking forward to basketball practice. It had been nearly three years since I'd done anything other than riding a bicycle. I quickly discovered a host of muscles that hadn't been used in years, feeling as sore as a chewed bone when I bedded down for the night.

The West has miles of hills that go on forever. We'd grind and grind under the heat of the flaming sun until we could bear it no longer, climbing off our bikes to push our gear up over the crest of a hill followed by miles of soaring downhill and the respite of flat terrain before starting another climb all over again.

For me, even worse than the high mountain passes were the screaming downhills, clutching my brakes with a death grip until it seemed they were burning as I plunged five, ten, even fifteen miles downhill. All this while riding a white line at the edge of the road at 35-40 mph with cars, trucks and motor homes whooshing by. At that speed on a loaded touring bike, a speed bump or a rock in the road could hit you like a land mine.

Through it all, Jimmy kept on my tail, resolute, never wavering. He was an athlete, after all, and the death-dealing plunges down from the mountain tops that scared the hell out of me were just a thrill to him.

INCIDENT_____

"IT'S THAT SAME CREEP FROM LAST YEAR."

"Yeah, I see him. The guy we called Frankenstein."

Smokey and Jagger were members of the Black Rock Rangers security team at the Burning Man festival that sprawled across the Nevada desert in early September.

It was a good gig and they were proud to be part of a radical way forward for the human race. The festival was all about freedom and self-expression with ten principles that emphasized sharing, responsibility and other high-flying ideals. But mostly, Burning Man was about getting loose and having a good time. What started as a small bonfire ritual on a beach in San Francisco in 1986 had morphed and migrated into a global event in the Black Rock Desert with 70,000 partyers from all over the world.

Dressed, pierced, tattooed and bejeweled like a lost tribe of gypsies and hippies, the Burning Man pilgrims swarmed 300,000 acres of alkaline desert to the north of Reno each year around Labor Day. At its peak, a colossal semblance of a male hominid went up in flames, no different than the wicker men of the ancient Celts, lighting up the desert sky for 30 miles or more.

Smokey and Jagger were an odd couple with more than 30 years' distance between them, but they had one thing in common. Smokey had served in the infantry in Vietnam, and Jagger had done the same in Iraq's Operation Enduring Freedom. For most of the festival-goers they were little more than polite nannies, reminding people to pick up their trash or helping those on bad trips to the medical tent. But both of them still worked out, and when they were crossed they didn't take shit from no one.

Still, they were happy to have each other for backup, because the guy known as Frankenstein was one ugly hulk, standing maybe six-foot-eight and despite his goofy grin, or perhaps because of it, he looked like bad news.

It wasn't easy to get tossed out of Burning Man, where no rules tended to be the rule. But any scene that tended toward public nudity and free-wheeling ravers dancing in dreamy cartwheels tended to draw the kind of pervy dudes that could make your skin crawl. Peeping Tom types, dirty old men who strolled around in their underwear or a gross thong and a bag on a sling. A lot of them liked to take photos, which tended to kill the vibe.

That's what Frankenstein was up to, the same as last year. He didn't make any attempt to blend in, dressed in plaid shorts, calf-high white socks and penny loafers. Instead of a shirt, he wore an old SLR with a telephoto lens around his neck. For the past two days he'd been creeping around taking photos of children, especially the hippie kids who ran around naked.

They caught up with him heading back to Camp Nomadia, one of several campgrounds that served more than 70,000 attendees.

"Hey," Smokey called out. "Hey you, we need to discuss something."

Just ahead, the big dude turned around with a nutty professor grin frozen to his face.

"I guess you know who we are," Smokey went on, speaking gruffly with his no-bullshit voice. "We've had complaints, same as last year."

"Complaints?" The big guy craned forward, sticking his neck out in confusion. It wasn't convincing.

"Yeah. About you taking pictures of the young girls. Kids. We can't have that here."

"But these are just art photos," the stranger protested. "I work for a gallery in New York. I have showings..."

"Yeah, cut the shit," Jagger broke in. "You've got ten minutes to get in your rig and hit the road or we call the real cops, the state police."

The stranger kept his grin, but a harsh gleam crept into his right eye. "Oh, please, we don't need to go to all that trouble. Look, it's hotter'n a bonfire in hell out here today. What say you stop by my place for a drink and we talk it over?"

"I don't drink," Jagger replied, "and neither does he."

"Well that suits me fine! I've got a fresh batch of ice cold lemonade in my fridge and plenty of ice and..."

"Just get the fuck out of here," Smokey said.

The stranger turned without another word with the grin still on his face and they marched him another 200 yards or so to his RV. They watched without a word as he tucked his steel porch into its nest under the vehicle before climbing in. Slowly, he pulled out and they could see through his smoked glass that he was no longer smiling. If anything, his face was contorted in a mask of rage.

The RV purred down the long line of motor homes, trailers and pop-up campers on either side of the playa until it was the size of a pea in the distance, shaded in a fog of alkaline dust.

The Great White Road Whale
Chapter 12

Two weeks passed as we made our way 600 miles across the Great Plains and up through the foothills of the Rockies. The Plains had spread out before us like a bowl of grass floating beneath a cumulus sea. Golden fields of wheat and barley stretched for miles over the horizon, caressed by combines as big as two-story houses. That gave way to sere, sandy prairies with only power lines for sentinels, snaking on and on over the highway heading west. Across these plains only three lifetimes ago, the Sioux, Cheyenne and Kiowa had migrated in dogged pursuit of the buffalo. You could no longer see those huddled tribes dragging their travois over the belly of the world if you were passing by in a car, but you could feel their ghosts if you were on a bike, gliding silently alongside them.

Our barroom encounters grew more interesting with Jimmy along. He was terrified of entering those bunker-like drinking halls out on the Plains, but I assured him he'd be safe with me; as safe as I'd be if he were squiring me around the black side of Chicago. To this he seemed uncertain, yet sure enough, we'd walk into some darkened pit with the sunlight at our backs and be treated like visiting princes by the farmers, ranchers and silo men of the Great Plains, who were astounded to find a black basketball player from Chicago in their midst. I knew that by dint of culture and isolation that these men were legacy racists by default, but given an unexpected confrontation with the Other, they were as gracious as Bedouin tribesmen greeting travelers through the desert. Seldom did we leave without someone buying us a round.

It helped that Jimmy always carried his basketball into the bars. He kept it criss-crossed to his back of his bike with bungee cords while we were riding, but carried it everywhere when we stopped.

By and by we reached the Continental Divide in western Colorado and stood on the backbone of the West. You could see for fifty miles from up there, and in the distance more mountains, buttes and towering cloud banks.

"The wind's angling northwest," I said. "I guess that means Montana."

Jimmy groaned. "Seriously? What's the plan? Where we goin'? What's with the wind?"

"It's where I'm going, amigo. You're the tag-along here, remember?"

"Yee-aah..., but why? What's with always riding with the wind?"

"It's just what I do."

That night, I had one beer too many and let Jimmy in on it. I told him the whole story; how I'd met Jill, our seven years together and the slow disintegration of our marriage. I told him about my big idea to do a bike tour to pull ourselves out of the doldrums of a marriage gone stale. I told him about the near-miss with the motor home, then my time with Becker. Then of the backup lights of the RV coming on fast and waking up from a coma eight days later with Jill dead. That, and the claim that I'd been dead myself for ten minutes or so.

I told him about Dr. Johansson and the R.A.G.E. experiment. I told him about going postal, the detectives and the Internet search that had gone nowhere. I even told him about bumper sticker Jesus and the batshit idea of biking around the country, following the wind in the hope of tracking down Jill's killer.

"So you're doing all this on a bicycle?"

I nodded.

"That's crazy."

"Well, yeah, I get that."

"You know, what you're doing is like searching through all the billions of stars in the Milky Way in an Apollo 10 rocket," he went on. "There are billions of places this guy could be lurking and you'd have to land within a hundred yards of him to even get a clue. For all you know, he's half a mile from us right now, sucking on a slurpy."

I nodded again. "You're right, it's a stupid idea, it's just..."

"So why the bicycle? Why not a car or something you could camp out of?" Jimmy interrupted. "You'd cover a lot more ground."

"I know, I know," I said wearily, "but all my life I've been given to obsessive thinking, you know? There are women I've obsessed about every day for five years. I've obsessed over minor slights, old scrapes from high school, disagreements at work. I'm messed up! I can't drive a car because I'd think too much just sitting on my ass driving around. It would drive me crazy. I need exercise, lots of exercise. Riding the bike keeps me sane, you know what I mean? I have to have faith that it will lead me somewhere, somehow."

Jimmy studied me in a dispassionate way, like I was a bug trapped under a glass. I could tell he thought I was pathetic; an old guy at the age of 34 with nothing on the horizon.

"You know, it could be a thousand years before you'd ever find this guy. It could be ten thousand years. You're going to be riding for the rest of your life. You know that, don't you?

"That's the plan. This all must seem pretty stupid to you, huh?"

"I don't think it's stupid," Jimmy. "It's crazy, but not stupid. Well, maybe kind of stupid... I liked that bit about you being a dead man."

"Yeah, I guess that's a bit different." I gave a weak smile.

"You're the Crow, come back from the dead."

"Yeah, the Crow," a freak from a graphic novel and a cult film.

"For revenge."

"Mmm-hmm."

"Have you ever considered that this might all be just a dream?"

"What do you mean?"

"I mean the whole walking dead man thing and you being in a coma. Have you ever considered that you might still be in that coma, lying in some medical facility, making all this stuff up in your head?"

"Did riding over the Rockies feel like a dream to you?" I shot back.

"Yeah, it kind of did."

"Well, here's to dreams coming true then," I said, raising my beer can to his.

By now the sun had gone down and we sat in the dark with the quiet burr of mosquitoes settling over the table at our campsite. I lit a candle and our faces glowed red and gold by its light.

"So, how's that wind thing going for you? Following the wind, I mean,"

Jimmy said at last.

"I guess I won't know until I know," I said. "It's like finding something that's lost; it's always in the last place you look."

"That's zen, man, pure zen, trusting in fate to guide you. Trusting in the wind."

"Something like that."

"That's bad, losing your wife like that."

"Yeah."

"So, what are you gonna' do?"

"What?"

"What are you gonna' do when you catch this guy?"

"I don't know. Get even, call the cops. Split his skull, maybe. I haven't really thought about it. I've spent all this time just trying to catch him."

"Well, you better figure that out sooner than later."

"Yeah, I'll think about it. Good idea."

Jimmy took a pull on his tall boy and cocked his head sideways and back.

"So really, I should call you Ishmael," he said. "Or Ahab."

"Mmm."

"Hunting the great white whale."

"Yeah."

"The great white *road* whale, right? That's what they call those RVs. Road whales."

"I've thought of it before," I said. "How could I not?" Peter's RV was Moby Dick, a behemoth slipping through a tangled sea of highways, and I had become a lone harpooner, searching millions of miles of roadways that might as well be all the oceans of the earth itself, trusting only that God and the wind would guide my path.

"You're chasing Moby Dick," Jimmy said.

"Whatever."

"But you ain't Ahab, you got two legs."

"I lost a lot more than a leg. I'd gladly give a leg to have Jill alive."

"Right, but that's what made that a dumb book," Jimmy said, his voice hurrying on. "This Captain Ahab loses his mind because some dumbass whale chewed his leg off and then he goes all around the seven seas, gimping on an ivory peg looking out for his revenge."

"His leg was made out of whale bone."

"Whatever."

"He lost a ship, too," I reminded.

"Yeah, but in the book he doesn't care about the ship and the men he lost. It's his leg, man, his leg! I mean, a leg is something, I wouldn't want to lose mine, but who could get that crazy about losing a leg?"

"People go off over different things."

"Yeah, but a leg? My uncle lost his leg in Vietnam and he got on with his life," Jimmy said, his voice rising. "I mean, thousands of soldiers lost their arms and legs in the Civil War 'round about Melville's time. They got shot in the leg or broke that thing and - boom! - it was sawed off, no anesthetic or nothing! Just straight whiskey, a bite-stick and a saw-bones with guys holding you down to make it happen!"

I was going to make the point that Herman Melville published Moby-Dick in 1851, ten years before the Civil War, but something told me Jimmy already knew that. Instead I asked, "How do you know about Moby Dick? I thought you were a thug."

Jimmy snorted and slapped my back sideways. "A thug? Come on, man, that don't mean I'm stupid! We had to read Moby-Dick in freshman lit."

"Really? Truly?" I scoffed. "No one makes it all the way through Moby-Dick."

"I did," he said, his voice going soft in the memory. "Most of the class just skipped around in it, they said the book was heavier than a boat full of blubber, but I had to prove something to myself and made it all the way through."

Then Jimmy gathered himself and bellowed, "'The ship! Great God! Where is the ship?' That's a line I remember. Best line in the book."

Jimmy savored the phrase and I could read his thoughts, imagining the stricken sailors in a rowboat who scanned the horizon in vain for the ship claimed by the great white whale.

"Where is the ship? He chuckled. "You know that part where Ahab finally catches up with the whale and its swimming around with a harpoon broke off in its back? At last, he's going to get his revenge! But you know, it's almost like Moby has been looking for him, instead of the other way around. It's the whale who wins in the end, not Ahab. Ahab ends up being fish food."

I couldn't resist reciting my own little bit:

"'For Moby Dick, the huge white sperm whale: who is old, hoary, monstrous, and swims alone; who is unspeakably terrible in his wrath, having so often been attacked; and snow-white.'"

"That's sweet," Jimmy said, nodding, "nice."

It was a line I had memorized from D.H. Lawrence's essay on the forgotten masterpiece. Lawrence's had rediscovered *Moby-Dick* in the 1910s, making it a bestseller years after Melville's death. Melville never knew that his epic work, which flopped at the book stores, would some-day be hailed as America's greatest novel. In that way, he was like Van Gogh, who sold only two paintings in his life; they'd been purchased as a joke.

I'd read Lawrences's essay while browsing *Moby-Dick* on my e-tablet, where America's greatest novel was now a free download. Like their authors, literary treasures fade to ghosts over time, worth nothing at all on in the age of Twitter and Pokemon.

"You're a spooky guy, Jimmy," I said. "Maybe you should forget bas-ketball and become an English lit professor."

Jimmy took another swig. "I read, I ain't dumb. You just think I'm dumb because I'm biracial. You want a piece of Huckleberry Finn, Homer? The Gettysburg Address? I got a thing for memorizing; been practicing since I was a kid. It's a rap thing, you listen for the rhythms and the rhymes. Listen, I'll say it back to you."

Then, composing himself and looking off into the distance, Jimmy repeated my own words back to me: "For Moby-Dick, the huge white sperm whale: who is old, whorey, monstrous, and swims alone; who is unspeakably terrible in his wrath, having been snow-white, like Jake.'"

He grinned, I gaped.

"Damn! You got that dead right until the last bit."

"Yeah, that was just to mess with you. I don't know why you're a whore, but that's you man," he said. "You're Moby-Dick, swimming alone, unspeakably terrible in your wrath."

"I thought I was Ahab."

"You're a little of both."

What Jimmy said rang true. At the age of 33 I had become "old, hoary, monstrous."

"Just don't be thinking of me as Queequeg," he said as an afterthought, "or asking me to join you in your tent."

"Yeah, I get that. Rest your mind." We both knew of Ishmael's unspoken love for a South Seas cannibal whose coffin-making skills saved him from a watery death.

But that night a heavy rain began falling and Jimmy was drenched under the sagging wreck of his tent which he'd stretched between his bike and the bench of a picnic table. Late in the evening I heard his bike fall over and a soft curse as his makeshift tent collapsed.

"Come on in out of the rain," I called, unzipping the fly of the mosquito net.

"You sure man?"

"Yeah, come on. Why suffer?

"Jimmy pushed his wet bag through the narrow opening and crawled in behind, shivering.

"Thanks."

"Don't mention it."

"You smell funky, man."

"Look who's talking."

"Don't you use deodorant?"

"Just when ladies are present. Are you a lady?"

"Do I look like a lady?" He kicked his way into his bag, making a pillow of his jacket as the overhead lamp rocked violent shadows against the tent walls. "This riding around is a bitch sometime, isn't it?"

"Yeah, totally."

"But it's a good bitch."

"Yeah, sometimes."

I'd been thinking about what I'd do to Becker if and when I caught up with him; like Jimmy said, I'd never given it much thought, yet lying in my tent, it was all I could think about. I weighed what Jill was worth to me now that she was nearly three years in her grave. What did I owe her? What price should I set on Becker?

Jimmy lay quiet for five or ten minutes, then just as I was trickling off to the land of dreams he began a soliloquy about his grandmother from Mississippi who'd come north when the Freedom Riders kicked up such a stir with the white people down South. She'd raised six kids, mostly all alone in the rough side of Chicago, including his Moms, who... I didn't hear the rest, instead, much later, I found myself in a black place deep beneath what could only be the sea with a vast white shadow of a thing ghosting in the darkness far away, so dim it could only be lit by starlight piercing the waves.

Jimmy started to bug me a bit after that. He kept calling me Ishmael, then Ahab, and then Moby-Dick. It was the kind of good-natured kidding that friends banter back and forth, but it had an edge to it and I could see that the college kid in Jimmy hadn't completely severed his gangster roots.

"You know, there's a singer named Moby," he said as we rode along. "He plays some kind of electronic shit."

"Yeah, yeah, I know."

"Maybe you could be Moby too. Moby Jake."

"Ha-ha. Maybe you could be a dick," I said. We came to a hill and I sprinted ahead, but Jimmy caught up easily. He'd gotten stronger in our days of pushing 90 miles or so and he was a basketball player, after all.

"Maybe I'll call you Jimmy Christmas Tree," I shot back.

"Heh, I'd like that. Jimmy Christmas Tree," he savored the notion. Then, "Moby Jake."

"Jimmy Dick."

"Ha-ha, white whale boy."

But Jimmy lost his fascination with moniker possibilities as we pushed up the Million Dollar Highway north of Silverton. It's a narrow ribbon of road that hugs the San Juan Mountains on one side of the highway, with steep cliffs and no guard rails on the other. We made our way through the Uncompahgre Gorge, hugging the wall of the mountains as best we could as gawking drivers and RVs rolled past, their thoughts aflame with the possibility of tumbling over the cliffs.

We pushed on to the mountain bike nirvana of Moab, Utah. In the days before Jill's death I would have been delirious to go scooting around the canyons and razorback trails of Moab, but now it was just another signpost with squadrons of mountain bikes flying by as we huffed on through town.

Still, it had been three days since we'd played basketball and Jimmy insisted we stop for a day to play some pickup games; he could be like a mule locked in his tracks when it came to his routine. Kind of like me. We made camp at the high school and rounded up some of the visiting cyclists, playing all-out for the rest of the day. At one point, Jimmy called out, "Moby Jake!" amid a knot of players while passing the ball to me. It pissed me off.

He caught my eye and knew he'd transgressed. "Sorry man," he said, dribbling past, "inadvertent."

That night, Jimmy's taunts made me think of Moby-Dick and his strange name. I got online with my tablet and read that he was based on a notorious sperm whale named Mocha Dick, "white as a sheep," who roamed the Pacific as a menace to whalers for 30 years in the early 1800s. His favorite haunt was near an island called Mocha off the coast of southern Chile, thus the name. As for "Dick," that was just a common name given to him, like Jack or Mike. He could just as well have been Mocha Joe. Or Mocha Jake.

An explorer named Jeremiah Reynolds published an account of him in a magazine called *The Knickerbocker* in 1839, inspiring Melville's novel. Not that he needed prompting: Melville had served as a whaler himself for four or five years.

According to Reynolds, Mocha Dick was a fighter. "Numerous boats are known to have been shattered by his immense flukes, or ground to pieces in the crush of his powerful jaws," he wrote. One time he took on the crews of three English whalers, sending them packing.

He added that Mocha Dick bristled with harpoons, having a "back serried with irons, and from fifty to a hundred yards of line trailing in his wake."

Whalers rounding the Horn of South America were on the lookout for Mocha Dick for decades and eventually he was slaughtered, the oil of his hoary head used, perhaps, to light the lamps of Baltimore or New York.

Mocha Dick's story came on the heels of the wreck of the Essex in 1820, in which a sperm whale rammed the whaling ship, sinking it in minutes. Fearful of cannibals in the islands to the west, the survivors had pushed east against the wind for three months, becoming cannibals themselves.

I thought of men drifting 2,000 miles across the pitiless sea for 95 days in a crowded whaleboat, choking down the salty flesh of five of their fellows who died of exposure and starvation, then drawing lots for two more who received an axe blow to their heads. Only eight survived, their skeletal frames peeled from the bloody ribs of their whaleboat by rescuers off the coast of Chile.

I let Jimmy have his fun with the name thing for a couple of days and then told him to zip it.

"You know, I never would have told you my story if I'd known you were going to go on like this," I said at a lunch stop.

Jimmy looked up in surprise. "What?"

"I mean the names, Ahab, Moby, Ishmael, it's getting old."

"Aw c'mon," he laughed, poking at a pie crust with his fork.

"Listen, everything I told you was a secret with me. I've never told anyone else because I trusted you. But if you go sharing these names around, it makes a joke of what I'm trying to do."

Jimmy grunted, frowned, poked at his pie. "Yeah, I get you."

"So give me a break here, okay?"

"Whatever you say, Moby Jake."

I guess my eyes must have bugged out a bit then because Jimmy looked up and nearly spit out his pie. He started laughing so hard that his eyes watered with the strain of it.

"No, no!" he hiccoughed. "Just messing with you one last time! No more, I swear!"

"Okay then."

"Well, maybe..." he teased.

"Watch it."

He made a sour face and a stink-eye, trying not to grin. "Everything's Jake from now on."

"Let's talk about you for a change," I said.

"Me? What about me?"

"Like what's with the tattoos? The illustrated man thing." I'd never brought up Jimmy's tattoos before, thinking it was too personal. But Jimmy had trampled enough on my space to warrant me trampling on his.

"It's about duality," he said, shrugging, "the duality of the universe."

"Duality."

"Yeah, the yin and yang, light and dark, night and day. I got a thunderbird tattooed on this side of my body and an eagle on the other. Got the devil on one arm and an angel on the other, lion and lamb, sun and moon, everything about me has to be in balance. I don't get a new tattoo unless I've got something else in mind to balance it out.

"I mean," he continued, "have you ever noticed, some dudes have a big-ass tattoo of Popeye or whatever hanging off their right arm and then maybe a skull or their mamma on the other arm? It doesn't fit, it's way off balance."

"Well you've got a point there," I said. "Some of these guys look pretty whacked."

"Right. Like when you see a dude with teardrops coming down off one eye. That's like having a sign on your forehead saying you're messed up. Unbalanced."

"Don't teardrops mean that you've killed someone?"

Jimmy nodded. "That, or you served a long stretch in prison. Unbalanced."

"I don't think that having that teardrops under both eyes would balance things out."

"The idea is not to get there in the first place," Jimmy said. "You might want to remember that."

After a moment, he said, "You got any?"

"What, tattoos?"

"Yeah."

"Sure, a big butterfly tramp-stamp across my ass under my shorts."

"For real?"

"No, I thought about it years ago but could never decide on what to get."

"My advice, get two tattoos that balance each other out."

"Like you."

"Yeah. Shoot the moon. What would you get if you had to? Any combination of tats you can think of."

I thought about it for a bit, considering my cycling gig for starters.

Some weekend athletes tattooed Ironman logos or the number 26.2 on their calves for every race they completed. Maybe I could get some kind of bicycle motif on my arm. But what would I do to balance out the other?

Then it came to me. "I think a heart on one arm and a dagger on the other," I said at last.

Jimmy nodded. "That's sweet. That's you, man."

The next morning we stopped by a tattoo joint in Moab and had it done, a red heart set amid a winding road and distant mountains on my left arm and a dagger within a wheel on my right. Jimmy clucked his approval as the tats glistened wet with blood. "You look like a warrior now," he said. "The real deal."

"Don't get melodramatic," I replied. Still, I was pleased. The new tattoos made me feel powerful, in balance. Maybe Jimmy had something.

We pushed on through the mountains and deserts of Utah in temps over 100. The bloody bandages on my arms slicked off by mid-day from a stream of sweat. At night we took to sleeping under the stars atop our sleeping bags, bathed in sweat and fearful of snakes.

Nonetheless, Utah was a beautiful ride. Far from the strip malls, car lots, fast food restaurants and big box stores that blight America, the country beyond the cities still held its dignity, its mountains rising as blue shadows beyond the umber plain. We stood on a cliff and took it all in as the sun went down with Venus rising over the mountains rimmed by the dying light. And finally, after nearly three years of cycling, I felt that I, too, had become a wild thing of creation. I had become part of the land, as close to its soul as any wolf, elk or eagle.

Jimmy and I hadn't talked about Becker for several days. Whenever I sensed he was angling in that direction, I changed the subject. I didn't really care to talk about it. But considering that Jimmy had seen his share of violence on the streets of Chicago, eventually he couldn't help but ask.

"What are you gonna' do with this guy when you find him? he asked over lunch one afternoon.

"You already asked me that."

"I'm asking again."

"I don't know," I said. "The best case scenario would be killing him with my bare hands."

"You got a lot of experience with that sort of thing?"

"No, I've always been more of a lover than a fighter," I said.

"I thought you said he was a big mother, like maybe a foot taller than you."

"He is."

"That's why people use handguns," Jimmy said. "They just stand back a few feet and blast away. So, do you have a gun?"

"No. Not with me, anyway."

Jimmy sat silent for awhile. Then, "This guy's gonna' kill you if you catch up with him. You know that, right?"

"No, I don't think so."

"You know, the Muslims believe that every man's fate is written in a book by the archangel Gabriel and it doesn't matter what you do with your life; you're still going to kick off when the book says."

"Makes sense to me."

"So, you need to come up with a plan."

"Yeah, sure. I wouldn't be out riding around like this if I didn't have a plan," I said. But that was a lie. I had no plan at all. No knife, no pistol, no hand grenades, no nothing that I might need to bring Becker down. Strangely, I hadn't thought of arming myself.

"I guess I'll turn Becker in to the cops if I find him," I said at last. "And if that doesn't work, then I'll run over him with his own truck, like he killed Jill."

"Revenge can't bring your wife back to life."

"It's not my wife I'm trying to bring back. It's me."

"And you think killing this guy will do it?"

I took a deep breath. "I'm sure of it."

But I wasn't.

"Revenge won't heal you," Jimmy said. "My grandma taught me that peace only comes to those who forgive."

"Did your grandma ever have a loved-one run over by a homicidal maniac?"

"No."

"Well no offense to your grandma, but do you think people ever really forgive?"

"Not really. They just bury it and move on."

"Right. It's not revenge I want, or peace, for that matter," I said. "Revenge isn't a spirit that has much heart as time goes on."

"Hmph... So what do you call what you're doing then?"

"It's retribution, like a price to pay. Becker owes Jill his life and I've been charged with collecting it. I'll never stop until it's paid."

"Retribution."

"Yeah, payment, judgement, whatever you want to call it. I have an obligation to see things through. With retribution you're a force that's got to follow through no matter what to make things right."

Jimmy nodded. "There's no statute of limitation is what you're sayin'."

"Yeah, it's a vow, a duty."

"Duty," Jimmy scoffed. "That's a word used to sucker kids who are young and dumb to go off to war."

"I am at war, Jimmy. A war that can only end up with one of us surviving, him or me."

"I understand, brother, but I wouldn't be getting all sacred about it," Jimmy said. "You'll lose your sense of humor. I'd think of it more as a job, like a bounty hunter."

"Yeah, I like that," I smiled, feeling a crack in the black ice way deep in the back of my head. "A job."

Hit-and-Runs
Chapter 13

Like I said before, there were times during our ride together that I wished that Jimmy would buzz off. I liked him well enough, we had become like brothers, but I was intent on being the Lone Ranger without a Tonto along. Like an old bear, lodged in its winter den, I'd gotten comfortable in my own skin over the past two and a half years of riding mostly solo around the country.

But it was Jimmy who made things rain for me.

"You know, this riding around trying to track this cat without a clue is kind of stupid," he said one day as we rode side-by-side down an empty country road.

"Tell me about it," I said with a grunt.

"You say you've done all this online stuff?"

"Yeah, Facebook, all of the dating sites, RV user sites and online forums. I did that for six months and nothing turned up. The guy's a ghost, online at least."

"Yeah, but have you ever tracked incidents?" Jimmy asked.

"Incidents?"

"Yeah, like hit-and-runs. Bicycle incidents around the country involving RVs. White RVs."

No, it had never occurred to me, and as we skirted Provo, heading north, the possibilities began to spin in my head. Perhaps other cyclists had been among Becker's victims.

"How do you think I'd track down hit-and-runs?" I asked Jimmy later that day.

He gave a laugh. "You ever hear of Google?"

The next day we rolled into Salt Lake City and checked into a hostel downtown.

Hostels have all the online resources you need at $2 per hour on their gummy old PCs. I could use my tablet to search online, but it was easier with the hostel's computer.

Jimmy swanned around town for a bit before deciding that Salt Lake City wasn't a good fit for a heavily-tattoo'ed black man. Not that people there gave him a hard time; he just got bored after a day or two. He joined me in the online search and we sat side-by-side, analyzing bicycle fatalities across the U.S.

Most fatalities were in big cities where cyclists tend to get nailed at intersections. But there were also many cyclists who were killed out on the open road by drunks, distracted drivers and haters who like to buzz cyclists as close as possible.

I read the story of the Kalamazoo Nine, a cycle club in Michigan that did everything right, riding the same route each week, two abreast with fluorescent clothing and flashing tail lights. Yet, on June 7, 2015, Charles Pickett, Jr., 50, smashed into their Chain Gang cycling group with his pickup truck after forcing several vehicles off the road in a drug-addled rampage. Five of the cyclists were killed with four suffering critical injuries.

Reading on, I learned that more than 800 cyclists are killed on the roads each year on the average, with more than 45,000 injured in traffic accidents. Jill had been just another statistic.

Motorists bent on vehicular homicide aren't hard to find online and it turned out there were a lot of hit-and-runs.

But tracking thousands of deaths over the past five years was like chasing mice through a maze, because although it may be true that just about every news item gets uploaded to the Internet these days, not every bit of information is curated to the extent you might imagine. I looked up Jill's death, and although it had been major news in Mississippi at the time, by now almost every mention of it had been washed away in the cyber sea.

Still, we turned things up. A white RV had been involved in a hit-and-run in Michigan's Upper Peninsula, killing a mother of four. They caught the guy, an 84-year-old with bad eyesight driving on a suspended license. Another RV had rammed two cyclists in Texas in a road rage incident; the driver was a Gulf War vet whose defense rested on a case of PTSD.

By week's end Jimmy and I had gone through several dozen reports of bicycle hit-and-runs by every sort of vehicle: RV's, trucks, cars, even motorcycles, but nothing seemed to fit. Except one.

A female cyclist, Jenifer Livingston, 28, had been killed only a week ago while cycling on lonesome Highway 389 between St. George, Utah and the north rim of the Grand Canyon. A triathlete, she made frequent rides of 50-100 miles through the desert. A motorist who arrived soon after the collision told of seeing a white motorhome moving at high speed far off down the highway, disappearing over a low hill about a mile away. Jenifer's killer was still at large.

It was suspected that the motorhome belonged to one of the polygamous Mormon communes that ranged along the highways of southern Utah, outcasts from the Latter Day Saints. Many were hidden away at the end of two-track roadways far out in the desert, making it difficult or impossible for the wives of polygamous renegades to escape, even if they wanted to. More to the point, without any evidence or a search warrant, it wasn't possible for local law enforcement to go snooping around for suspicious RVs.

That in itself wasn't much, but it sharpened our focus. It turned out that there had been a high incidence of hit-and-runs involving cyclists in the desert between Las Vegas, the North Rim, Bryce Canyon and Zion National Park. But, considering the isolation of the area, no suspects had been reported.

The next morning we ate breakfast in the hostel's dining room and I shared my findings with Jimmy.

"It's a long shot, but I'm heading south to look around," I said.

"You know I can't help you with this," he said after a moment, looking a bit sheepish.

"I'm not asking."

"Yeah, look, I been meaning to tell you," he went on. "Coach let me off training this summer to toughen up my legs, but now it's time for me to get home and get with the program. I got my scholarship to think of, you know?"

"Absolutely," I said. "I'm surprised you rode with me this long."

Jimmy gave me a level gaze. "It's been a pleasure."

"Yeah, good times," I nodded.

"But the other thing is, tracking this guy down and killing him all cold, uhn-uhn, I couldn't go along with that," Jimmy went on. "That would be too much like in the movies, where the white guy gets his black buddy to help out and then it's the black guy who gets killed and the white guy rides off with the girl. Or in my case, goes to prison, at least."

Now it was my turn to laugh. "Yeah, you mean like in 'The Shining,' where Scatman Crothers rides to the rescue on a snowcat and gets axed for his trouble."

"That and a dozen other movies," Jimmy said with a shrug.

"Movies made by white men, anyway."

"No good deed goes unpunished."

"That's what they say, but ease your mind. I'm happy to be the lone wolf on this one."

"So, Mr. Wolf, you got no gun, you got no knife, so how you gonna' do him?"

"I don't know, hit him with a pipe or something."

"What if he gets you first?"

"I can't let that happen."

"Your wife will be pissed if he does you too," Jimmy said.

"Believe me, I've given that a lot of thought."

Jimmy snorted. "No you haven't."

"I'll work on it, okay?"

A day later I saw him off on a plane, with his bike boxed up for the trip home to Chicago. He'd been fidgeting for days and now I knew why; he was burning to get home.

"When I get back that way I'll check out a game," I promised. "Northwestern Wildcats, right?"

"That's right, brother," he grinned. "See me on ESPN too if you get a chance."

"I'll make it happen."

"Hey."

"What?"

"I hope you get that whale. Harpoon him, harpoon 'im good," Jimmy said.

"That's the plan, Mr. Queequeg."

"Yeah," he smiled. "Stay cold, Mr. Ishmael."

Then. "Hey man."

"Yeah?"

"I was gonna' build you a coffin, but didn't get around to it."

"Well, I guess I'll have to cut you out of my will then," I said.

We did the three-way handshake and then embraced in a man-hug that I've never felt comfortable with; yet with my thug/college kid friend Jimmy it seemed okay. Then he was off on the plane. I walked out of the airport, got on my bike and rode south.

That night I lay in my tent as a soft rain pattered down from the mountains, a welcome respite from the heat. I thought of all the ways I might kill Becker if it came to that, and of the ways he might kill me.

INCIDENT_____

LIKE MOST HABITUAL CRIMINALS, the man who called himself Peter Becker on his road trips around the country was a risk-taker who knew he could get away with almost anything simply by acting as if he belonged and having a ready excuse if he was caught. Trying doorknobs in quiet neighborhoods while pretending to pass out religious pamphlets, for instance... Strolling into the womens restroom at a department store "by accident".... Sucker-punching a homeless panhandler in the face when no one was looking and then coming back "to help" the dazed man when a crowd gathered... He came across as a hulking, buck-toothed goofball with a Beatle haircut and a harmless, "aw shucks" demeanor, wearing his persona as a disguise like a Texas politician to throw people off. But on the inside, Becker was another person entirely. Inside, he was barely human.

But Becker wasn't stupid. The death of Jenifer Livingston had been a mistake. It turned out she was America's top-ranking woman triathlete, training for the Hawaiian Ironman that fall. There had been speculation on ESPN that she could likely win the race, taking the title back from the Europeans. That, and Livingston was a third-grade teacher whose sobbing students made for riveting clips on the morning news shows. The news coverage had swept Utah and Arizona like a spring blizzard with no sign of easing up. It was a national story, amplified by the fact that there was nothing much going on in the White House that week. All of the big networks were piling on.

Becker read Livingston's story in *The Arizona Republic* with interest at his favorite coffeehouse on the day after the killing. Around him, a dozen college kids sat silently at their tables, headlocked to their laptops. But Becker was old school, preferring the feel of newsprint, which took up most of his table.

A thought crossed his mind that Generation Z made for easy targets with their single-minded focus on their phones and tablets, oblivious to the hazards of the outside world. You could walk right up to any one of them for a bit of naughty fun and the kid plugged into headphones two feet away at the next table wouldn't even know or care. Or, perhaps, they'd pretend not to see. Some people would never learn, he thought, like Jenifer Livingston, cycling all alone on a desert highway.

Becker read that Livingston had dominated her last seven Ironman races in the U.S. and Europe and was poised to win the championship in Kona this October. A college swimmer, she could hold her own on the 2.4-mile ocean swim, but her best event was the 112-mile bike race, finishing under four hours and fifty minutes on the average, with strength enough remaining in her legs to hammer the 26.2-mile marathon.

Becker was pleased to learn that like him, Livingston was a freak of nature, although in a completely different sense. She was able to metabolize oxygen at the rate of an Olympic athlete while having the dual gift of eliminating the build-up of lactic acid in her muscles, which caused incapacitating fatigue in lesser athletes. According to the article in the *Republic*, "She was literally a human machine who could run for hours at high speed without ever getting tired."

The article also noted that the FBI had been called in to assist in the investigation.

Carefully, Becker folded his paper and lowered his coffee cup to the table.

Within an hour he was at the town dump, cleaning out the rat's nest of his RV. He spent the rest of the afternoon scrubbing the interior with a bleach cleanser. By dusk he'd gone over his bull bars with a wire brush and had just finished removing his bumper stickers with the same when the cops showed up that evening.

Becker pulled his nutty professor act with fluttering hands and an

Emmy-worthy expression of concern. Satisfied that he was a harmless kook who'd been working in his shop on the day of the murder, the police left within minutes. There was something about Peter Becker that made people want to get out from under his gaze as fast as possible.

'Have a Great Day'
Chapter 14

It was a little more than 300 miles from Salt Lake City to St. George and as I rode south on Highway 89 the temperature crept over 100 degrees.

For a change, I was riding against the wind. A hot, dry wind blew in my face and combined with the fury of the sun it felt like my skin was being sheared from my skull with a wood rasp. I'd spent the past two-and-a-half years slathered with #50 sunscreen all day and bug spray every evening, but the trek into southern Utah was more than I could bear. Digging in my tool kit, I fished out the oily bandanna I used for cleaning my hands when I changed a tire or slipped a chain and tied it cowboy-style across my face over the bridge of my nose. At last I looked the part of the old cow-punchers who once rode this land, or perhaps like Jesse James.

I rolled south, noting the occasional husk of a dead diamondback imprinted in the road by the crush of a passing vehicle. There were fewer crosses dotting the road than most western states; I guess it was true that the Mormons weren't drinkers, or at least didn't drink and drive.

By now I had a daily ritual of thinking about Jill for an hour each day, willing her back to life by reliving the good times we had shared. Days at the beach, memorable dinners, trips to the relatives, vacations, hot sex, Christmas, the surprise party she'd thrown when I turned 30. I had a catalog of our greatest hits that I played over and over again to keep her alive in my memory.

That included our quiet times too; the many nights we walked down to the ice cream shack for some soft serve under the amber lights beneath the flitting moths; the musing over Merlot or Sauvignon Blanc on

our back porch; splitting sandwiches at Zingerman's Deli in downtown Ann Arbor. I thought of the many nights when she used to lie on the couch with her head in my lap, watching TV with our cat, Mr, Bojangles, nestled on her tummy. I thought of her skill in the kitchen; oven-fried chicken was one of her specialties, with those garlic-crusted potatoes with chives that I liked. I'd never have that again. I'd tried making it from her recipe before selling our home and it wasn't the same.

Mr. Bojangles! I snorted as I pedaled south through a forest of cacti running for miles on either side of the road. He'd gone to live with Jill's best friend Susan when I'd left town, with me promising to come back for him someday. That had been two-and-a-half years ago. I wondered if our old cat was still alive.

That's the thing about biking for weeks turning into months and then years; you start talking to yourself and laughing about some old cat. I'd known for a long time that I'd gone off my rocker and it didn't bother me. What bothered me was when I forgot about Jill and the machine-like quest for justice that I'd set in motion. I'd set myself up as the Terminator and the only time there seemed to be an "off" switch was when I got close to someone like Lynda Martinez, or my good times with Jimmy Christmas. I made a vow to get my head back in gear as I rode south; I wouldn't stop until Becker was dead or behind bars.

I slept under the stars on the way south. Once again the evenings were too warm for a tent and I just flopped down atop my sleeping bag in my running shorts, perspiring through the night. On my second night out of Salt Lake City I woke up about 4 a.m. and the majesty of the Milky Way flowed across the sky in a river of stars, glittering like diamonds in the stream of the night. There were billions of galaxies beyond count up there, each with trillions of stars, planets, perhaps even people looking back at me. I considered that there was a galaxy up there that could be claimed by every single person on earth, all 7.5 billion of us, in fact, a galaxy for every grain of sand on earth, but not for me; I'd wait my turn.

"Starlight, star bright, first star I see tonight, I wish I may, I wish I might, have this wish I wish tonight," I said into the darkness, laughing again to myself, like I had while thinking about Mr. Bojangles. Jesus.

It took me three and a half days to make it to St. George, and that was grinding for 11-12 hours a day against the wind. As usual, I'd kept a lookout for RVs, and Utah had no lack of them, heading for Vegas or the parks at Bryce Canyon, Zion, Red Rocks or the Grand Canyon. I saw scores of them through the day, rolling up behind me in my mirror. Each time, I'd squint, hoping to catch the telltale checker of two bumper stickers, one featuring the symbol of a white star. I always rode with a set of binoculars around my neck, but in the hundreds of times they'd risen to my eyes through the months and years, I'd never marked my prey.

I skirted Bryce Canyon National Park on Highway 89 and then rode Highway 9 west into town, arriving on the outskirts of St. George about 3 o'clock. Kipling said only mad dogs and Englishmen go out in the noonday sun and I was definitely feeling like the former, burned raw, even with my outlaw bandanna covering my face.

I planned to shack up in a cheap motel and rent a car to scope around the region for a few days, expecting to turn up nothing, like usual. But first, I was dying of thirst. I'd ridden south with three water bottles strapped to my bike, but drinking 100-degree H2O is a lot like swallowing hot bath water.

Plus, you lose a lot of electrolytes, sodium and potassium when you sweat for a living and even the salty gas station pizza and fast food burgers that made up my diet couldn't make up the deficit each day. So I tend to guzzle a lot of sports drinks and by that afternoon I was desperate for a couple of cold liters of the stuff.

I rolled up at a gas station convenience store outside of town, feeling as dusty and dry as a salt mine. The front of the store was all glass, so I leaned my bike out of sight around the side of the building.

I pushed through the door and made for the wall of glass at the back of the store where hundreds of soft drinks sparkled like candy behind refrigerator doors. I was pondering whether to go with orange or grape when the white slab of a restroom door opened to the right of me and Peter Becker walked out.

The world seemed to retreat, my vision yo-yoing out and in. Goddamn, it was him; somehow, some way the winds of fate had brought us to this moment, with the monster himself popping out from behind a men's room door like a jack-in-the-box.

We looked right at each other for a fraction of a second, but it was enough. Becker had gone salt-and-pepper above his ears and his hairline had receded, but he still wore the long face of a mournful horse and the same cheap black specs as when we'd sipped lemonade in his rolling dungeon.

But it was clear he didn't recognize me, because I was no longer the same man who'd lingered in that campground in the great state of Mississippi. I'd lost more than 30 pounds since then, and I wasn't heavy to begin with. I was as lean and wiry as a monkey now, a walking twist of beef jerky. Nor had I bothered to get a haircut over the past couple of years. Back then, I had the kind of neatly cropped, shoe-brown haircut favored by car salesmen and fast food restaurant managers, but now my hair was past my shoulders, straggly from lack of brushing and streaked blond by the sun. My tan was so deep I could pass for a Mexican. That, and I had a beard, trimmed close with a pair of scissors once a week, my only concession to vanity.

"S'cuse me, chief," Becker mumbled, brushing past me.

I gazed after him like a hawk. Goddamn, he was a tall motherfucker and he had a sort of herky-jerky, mincing walk that resembled a praying mantis, with his arms held up just so, carrying a bag of chips like some old lady hoisting her purse chest-high with two hands.

Becker was at the counter buying corn chips and a half-pound bag of roll-your-own pipe tobacco when I came up behind him with two bottles of thirst-quencher. Glumly, it settled in on me that this was the time to smash a beer bottle over his head and slice his throat to the bone with the broken glass.

But of course, I couldn't do that, because when push comes to shove, well... Truthfully, I had never expected to actually confront Becker. I thought I'd just ride around the country until hell froze over or I ended up dead in the saddle, but now here he was, standing three feet in front of me and I didn't know what to do.

Becker sensed that I was looking at him. He gazed down at my sweaty legs and dusty shoes.

"Hot day for construction, huh?"

"Yeah, hot day," I said.

He gave me a searching look, but by now I had my shades on and doubt my own mother could have recognized me.

"Well, have a great day," he said awkwardly, pushing for the door.

I nodded, gave a little grunt. It occurred to me that although Becker didn't recognize me, it was still possible that he'd catch something in my voice.

I watched him walk out the door and fold himself into a dusty old pickup truck, which he wheeled carefully out the drive and into traffic. I wrote the license plate on my wrist as Becker headed into town.

"You know that guy?" the store clerk gestured as Becker drove away. He was pale, pink, freckled and short, with a scant trim of reddish hair around his otherwise bald head.

"Not really," I said.

"He's a real fruit loop if you ask me," he went on. "I caught him in here one time stealing a tin of Pringles. Had 'em stuffed down the front of his pants like they was his dick or something. Funny thing is, I think he did it on purpose, like he wanted to get caught."

"So why'd you let him back in the store?"

The clerk looked like he wanted to spit but swallowed instead. "Bidness is bidness," he said.

"You know, now that you mention it, that guy does look kind of familiar," I said. "What is he, a college professor or something?"

He laughed. "Oh, that's a hot one! No man, he repairs air conditioners. Told me he goes all over the country and makes a mint doing it."

"He live around here?"

"Yeah, I guess so. He's in here often enough."

We talked a bit more. The clerk's name was Kevin and he gave me a line on a cheap motel. "There's a big knife and gun show in town this week, so's you better catch a room quick, if you can find one," he said.

There was a run-down motel just a quarter-mile down the highway with only two cars in the lot and the clerk seemed happy enough to see a customer, even if I looked like hell. Suddenly, I was missing Jimmy. Sitting in my motel room off Highway 9 it settled in that I didn't know what to do. I needed someone to talk to. I desperately needed advice, a sounding board. The knife and gun show, was that a sign? A direction?

I tore through the motel phone book. As usual, there were a handful of Beckers in the book: Pat, Susan, Dalton, J.T. It wasn't until I hit the Yellow Pages that it hit me: Becker spelled his name with an "o."

He was right there in the Yellow Pages with a boxed eighth-page ad:

Boecker Industrial Air
Specializing in Multi-Unit Air Handling & Climate Control
No Job Too Big - No Job Too Far
Pieter Boecker, proprietor

Pieter Boecker. No wonder I hadn't found him online. No wonder he'd slipped free of the cops and my P.I. He'd been hidden from us in plain sight the whole time, camouflaged by the letters i and o.

I mused that it would be a cinch to wander over to the gun show and pick up a .12 gauge shotgun, no questions asked thanks to the GOP and the pride of the West, and then blow Boecker's brains out early some morning as I had promised to God Himself something like 10,000 times since Jill died.

But sitting in my motel room staring at Boecker's ad by the thin golden light of a 60-watt bulb, I realized that the heart had gone out of me. I went out for a bad Chinese buffet and snagged a quart of malt liquor on the way back to my room in the hope that it would inspire me to do the right thing. But instead I sat in a fractured chair at the motel, getting stewed while every possible scheme and scenario turned traitor in my brain and fled. I cursed, cried. I felt numb, impotent, powerless to act. I spent the whole night staring at the tube, unable to sleep as a parade of paid programming came and went.

The next morning I gave Smith Freeman a call.

"I found the guy," I said.

"Who?" It had been so long now that even detective Freeman had started to forget.

"Boecker, the guy who killed my wife."

"What! Where?" At the other end of the line I heard Freeman drop his phone. Picking it up, he said, "What the hell. Where are you?"

"Saint George, Utah, about one hundred and fifty miles north of Vegas."

"Utah? Well how about that," Freeman said, his voice so low it was almost a growl. "Never thought to look that far west. Never been there, either. What's it like out there?"

"It's hot, but it's a dry heat," I said. "Boecker's got an air conditioning business here and travels around the country fixing units at hospitals, factories, schools, places like that. He's even in the phone book, but spells his last name B-O-E-C-K-E-R and his first name P-I-E-T-E-R, which is maybe why we couldn't find him in the first place."

"German, I'll bet, or Dutch," Freeman said. "So, have you got a line on where this guy lives?"

"Yeah, I went and checked his place out this morning. He's got this big spread north of town, looks like a ranch, but without any cows."

"What about his RV?"

"It's here. Same old piece of shit parked next to his pole barn."

We talked for more than an hour and I filled Freeman in on my crazy bike ride around the country, following the wind, always searching for the white whale of Boecker's motorhome. I told him about Jimmy Christmas and how he suggested tracking Boecker down by analyzing hit-and-runs among bicyclists.

"It turns out there's been a lot of collisions in the area around St. George," I said.

"Hmm, that could be helpful, but it could also screw your case," Freeman said.

"How's that?"

"If the Utah authorities tie Boecker to any fatalities, they'll be prosecuting him on their home turf. He might be 90 before we can extradite him to Mississippi."

I let that sink in. "What if he doesn't make it to trial?" I asked quietly.

Freeman gave a low laugh over the phone. "Don't be a fool," he said. "Do you think Jill would want to see you go to prison for something this guy should be paying for? I know what you're thinking, Jake, but killing this guy will only hurt you in the end, hurt you bad. Believe me, he'll suffer a lot more in prison than in the grave. It's not pleasant being in prison here in Mississippi. Nobody gets coddled here."

"I'm sure, but..."

"No, don't give me any buts, Jake. Let me make some calls, see what the local sheriff has to say. I want you to just sit tight for a day or two until we can get a plan together."

"You mean an arrest, right?"

"You damn right. An arrest and a trial."

I felt better after we rang off and wandered over to the hall where the gun show was being held that afternoon. I browsed the aisles of engraved knife collections, bayonets and swords; Nazi memorabilia and military gear. There were dozens of booths laden with black powder muzzle-loaders, shotguns and rifles of every description along with hundreds of pistols and revolvers. There were lots of old western Colts and Winchesters proudly displayed as collectors' items and even some Civil War gear. I hefted a Persuader, the home-defense shotgun with the pistol grip that looks like something a bank robber or narco gangbanger would own and considered that it was just such a weapon that I'd vowed to stick up Boecker's ass. But now that Freeman had assured me that the wheels of justice were in motion, buying the gun seemed kind of pointless. Later on, I'd wish I had it.

Things went fast after that. Detective Freeman flew to Vegas and drove up to St. George in a rental car to meet with the local cops. They conferred. Yes, Pieter Boecker was a suspect in the vehicular murder of three cyclists within a 100-mile radius over the past couple of years and there had been other incidents as well, including many near-misses. He'd been named as a person of interest in Arizona's news media, but no one had been able to lay a glove on him.

But now the trap was sprung, and at 8 a.m. on a Monday morning only a week after I hit town, three squad cars pulled up front and back of Boecker's truck as he was heading for work and he was arrested on suspicion of murdering Jill and three other cyclists, including Jenifer Livingston.

Things didn't work out for the prosecutor in St. George. Boecker's RV had a number of deep scratches on his right front fender and a sizable dent in his bumper, but the forensic team failed to find any flecks of paint that might match up to Livingston's bike.

"The guy's a slippery son of a bitch," Freeman said over beers that night. "Slippery as a weasel in tub of vaseline."

"Yeah, but we've got him now, right?"

"Looks like it," he nodded. "I'm heading back to Jackson tomorrow to get Boecker's extradition to Mississippi underway. In case you haven't heard, he's been denied bail."

I nodded. "So what happens now?" Dwight Yoakam was singing "Little Sister" on the jukebox and I had to yell over the din.

"Once he's extradited, we send some federal marshals out this way to escort him back east. Then there's a trial, but I gotta' warn you, this is gonna' take some time. It could be a couple months before we can extradite him, then it'll take some time to put our case together."

"Best guess?"

"I'm hoping we can wrap this up within a year."

"I guess I'll be moving to Jackson, then."

"Might be a good idea," Freeman said, motioning to the waitress for another round. "You want me to look around for a place for you?"

"Thanks, but I've got something else to do in the meantime."

Que Pasa?
Chapter 15

I crossed Death Valley at night, riding under lights beneath an upturned bowl of stars. Even I wasn't crazy enough to cross that expanse of sand and pain in the 120-degree heat, though I had good reason to make the trip.

My "something else to do" had come as a surprise over Facebook while I was idling in the motel that week.

"Hey stranger, que pasa?" It was a friend invite and a message from Lynda Martinez, the lithe Latina cyclist I'd met in Kansas so many months ago.

I wrote back, "How long has it been?"

"A year and a half."

We Skyped. Lynda looked just as I remembered her, better, even, and we still clicked. A lot had happened since we'd met. She'd completed her marketing internship and had accepted an entry-level position ("answering the phone") at a big San Diego boat dealership. Sheer boredom and an undercurrent of sexual harassment from the married boat salesmen had prompted her to ditch the job. Now, she was crewing on a tourist sailboat that made runs back and forth between Catalina Island and the mainland.

"It doesn't pay much, but I get tips," she said to wrap up. "And you?"

"Oh, still just riding around."

"Seriously."

"Yeah, like the Johnny Cash song goes, I've been everywhere, man."

"So, did you ever get your big, dark business done?" she asked.

"It's coming along. Soon," I said.

"Then what?"

"Then I'm going to stuff my bike away somewhere, get my cat back and sink some roots," I said.

"I didn't know you owned a cat," she said, making a little purring sound. A trill ran through me at the sound of it, curling my toes.

"I guess it's out of the bag now. But, yeah, his name is Mr. Bojangles, staying with a friend back in Ann Arbor."

"Are you going home to live in Michigan then?" There was an innocent note in her voice.

That was when my heart skipped a beat, because who asks such a question unless they're hoping the answer is no?

"No," I said cautiously. "I thought I might come and visit you, if you're not doing anything."

Now it was Lynda's turn to pause, and her eyes went wide on the screen of my tablet, because who asks such a question unless they're hoping the answer is yes? In a panic it occurred to me that I'd misread the situation. I was nine years older than her and a homeless person who lived in a tent and traveled around on a bicycle. I looked like a demented hippie. The image reeled in my head as I realized that's exactly what I had become. What could she possibly see in me?

"I.. I... just thought I'd stop by and help you celebrate your birthday," I stumbled on. "You're a Leo, right? You turn 25 this month, if I remember."

"You remembered!" she said, smiling, then, "Yes, I think you could come and see me."

"I'd like that very much."

"Oh, don't look so serious," she teased. "But there is one problem."

Oh-oh.

"Yeah? What's that?"

"My birthday was last month, August."

"Well, we'll have to celebrate twice then to make up for it."

"Only if you promise to take me for a bike ride."

I was thinking more like dinner at the best restaurant on Catalina Island, but I didn't tell Linda that. There was no point in seeming over-eager, though I suppose a 400-mile bike ride through the desert at the tail end of summer just to see her might come across that way.

I was back on the road an hour after we signed off on Skype, pedaling west with the wheels of justice grinding behind me. Late September was still blazing hot and there weren't many other cyclists out riding through Death Valley. Mostly the only people I saw on two wheels were motor-cyclists who gave me a sympathetic thumbs-up as they blew past.

Once again, I found myself riding against the wind, and far from being cool, the breeze in my face was like that of a blast furnace. Around me, a hell in shades of pink and beige stretched to the far horizon with things that could sting, bite or scratch being the only signs of life.

I was riding lean, having sent most of my gear via parcel post to Smith Freeman's place in Jackson, but even so I had to strap on two extra gallons of water along with my three water bottles. It was barely enough and I was choking down hot water by the end of the day.

You get a desperate craving for shade on a ride like that and begin imagining shadows far ahead, hoping for the shelter of a rock-fall or an underpass to catch a respite from the sun. But most of the time those hints of shade were as fleeting as mirages. I'd push for half a mile along a burning stretch of asphalt only to find that what I thought was shade was merely a deeper hue of rock face, hot as a frying pan in the sun.

It was in the depths of Death Valley that I had my last imaginary conversation with Jill. The 120-degree heat had ebbed rapidly as night fell, and I was shivering by the time the moon rose at 1 a.m. I switched off my headlight; there was no need for it with the long ribbon of road glowing silver beneath the moon and stars. Far off, I heard the yip of a coyote and then its mates calling back.

I sensed her spirit moving in the darkness behind my left shoulder. It was as if Jill was riding beside me in the moonlight, silent as a shadow.

"We might as well be riding on the moon," I said. Around me the rock towers and stone piles of the desert were radiant in the moonlight, belted by dark bands of cacti and brush.

"We've been riding on the moon for nearly three years now," Jill replied softly, no hint of sarcasm in her voice.

"Yes we have."

"We must have gone around it a hundred times by now."

"At least." I pedaled on, my legs pumping along the highway like an engine's driving wheel.

"But mostly we've been on the dark side of the moon," she said.

"Yeah, I guess that's true."

"I'm calling it quits, Jake. You've dragged me around long enough."

"I don't have a choice. It's blood for blood," I replied.

"You had a choice," Jill said, "you've always had a choice, but don't you see? It doesn't matter now. I'm gone, we're gone, and we're not coming back."

"There's gonna' be a trial."

"But that won't bring me back. I think you've got me confused with Hamlet's father."

"I see you've still got a sense of humor."

"That's just you talking to yourself Jake. Get over it."

I searched for something to say, but it all seemed so futile. Jill was right: the trial, my plans for retribution and revenge, they were all just for me. What could it matter to her anyway? She was dead. I had placed her memory in a prison and was lodging there myself, having thrown away the key. I had to let her go.

I looked back over my shoulder and for an instant I saw her riding there beside me astride her bike in a flicker of lightning, still in the flower of her womanhood, lithe and strong, her blue eyes flashing. "Goodbye Jake." The words came to me in a whisper.

I pedaled harder after that, trying to outrun the memory. Gradually, thoughts of Lynda crept in and soon I could think of nothing else, and so I rode all night to where she was waiting. It was agony, but it had been so long since I'd known the tenderness of a woman that nothing could stop me from pushing on. I didn't have any great expectations of Lynda; by now I was just a drifter who camped under bushes off the highway, but what man can control his fantasies? Not expecting too much, I hoped that we might at least share some laughs as friends and then I'd get back to my mission, tormented two times over.

We met on the pier where Lynda's boat docked. I'd gone to the laundromat the night before and the barber that morning. I barely recognized myself in the mirror that covered the barbershop wall when he got done shearing me. I'd become a stranger even to myself. What would Lynda think?

So it was all I could do to keep from bursting into tears when she skipped down the dock and threw her arms around me.

"Oh, but what happened to your hair? It was looking so good!" she teased.

"Uh... too many bugs in it, maybe? I can grow it back if you like."

Lynda made a face. "Oh, please, I don't think we're there yet."

"Seriously, your wish is my command."

"Okay," she snapped her fingers. "I give you five minutes to grow it back!"

And so it went. I never did make it out to Catalina with her, but we celebrated her belated birthday at a seafood place at the end of the pier and I could hardly take my eyes off hers. It was as if I could gaze right down deep into them, like they were the pools of her soul, and she looked right back.

I never had told Lynda about what I was really doing and now it spilled out of me. Jill's death, my futile online search for her killer, then the divinely-inspired bike ride, blown by the wind through the Land of Nod. Then, my run-in with Boecker in Utah, his arrest and pending trial. Any other woman might have fled the restaurant screaming, but Lynda sat spellbound, stroking my hand.

"That's amazing," she breathed at last.

"But I've been blabbing on too much about myself," I said at last, my head spinning with wine and the catharsis of sharing. "What about you?"

She laughed. "Oh, nothing so dramatic as you. The high point of my day is spotting dolphins for tourists and encouraging them to drink more."

"Sounds tough, the drinking part I mean."

"Well, they don't need much encouragement."

"Especially from someone as pretty as you, I bet."

"Ooh, creepy," she grimaced. "Some of these guys would keep drinking if the server was a walrus."

"Sorry, I didn't mean to offend. I just couldn't help noticing."

"Really?"

I inched a bit closer. "You know, I read that linda means beautiful in Spanish."

"Is that so? Well my name is spelled with a y," she replied.

"Yes, I know that."

"But?" She cocked an eyebrow.

"But you're still quite beautiful," I said awkwardly.

"Is that true?" She was playing with me now, teasing.

"Yes, muy linda... isn't that how they say it? Very beautiful. And strong. And funny too."

"And smart?"

"Oh yes, very smart."

She purred. "If you think so."

"Do you have someone?"

"What?"

"In your life, a boyfriend."

"I've dated a couple of guys since I saw you, but there was nothing special," she said. "Guys these days text a half dozen girls and whoever hits they take out for a pizza. There's no romance, just guys trying to hook up."

I nodded, wondering what I could do to be more romantic without coming across as silly.

"But you," she cooed, running her hand up my arm, "you're sooo romantic, you're like that knight, Sir Lancelot. And your arm! It's sooo strong."

I'd been called worse things, and though I knew that Lynda was just flirting outrageously, the comparison made me blush. Deeply.

"I think you're just playing with me now," I said with a nervous laugh. Maybe I'd gone too far.

"No," Lynda said, draping her arms around my neck. "I never play when I'm serious."

She looked into my eyes and cocked her head, like, what are you waiting for?

Good question. I pulled her to me there in the restaurant by the rail overlooking the sea and kissed her deeply, tenderly. A torrent of emotion washed through me, driving me under, as if all of the 90,000 miles or so that I'd ridden had led to this moment.

We couldn't get enough of each other in the days that followed. There were more kisses, holding hands, and then things got even better. We hit the clubs and it turned out that Lynda was a good dancer, very good. By the end of the week I was crazy in love with her. Lying naked in her bed I felt like a child who'd been rescued from a terrible ordeal. The analytical part of me said it was just infatuation that could fly away over time but my heart said bring it on. I was ready to feel love again and to give it. Love, lust, whatever Lynda had to offer. But I wondered what I could offer her in return.

Lying in her arms at night I realized that happiness is a momentary thing with a few seconds shared here and there, rather than something that rolls on forever like an eternal summer day. I ached for those moments when we were just nestled in bed, warm and entwined as I listened to her softly breathing beside me.

We stayed together a few weeks doing all the cliche things that lovers do: long walks on the beach, dinners by the bay, art fairs and wine tours. She showed me L.A. and we took that bike ride she wanted down the coastal bike path out of Santa Monica.

She took me swimming in the ocean at her place in Newport Beach. I took a nine-foot wave full force, tumbling ass-over-teakettle like a pair of lace panties in a washing machine, slamming my face against the ocean floor and coming up with a bloody nose.

"Oh Jake! You've got to dive under the wave," Lynda said. "Oh, poor boy, so much you have to learn!"

"We don't have waves like that in Lake Michigan," I said, wiping a long streak of blood across my arm.

"Oh, really?" She laughed. "I can't wait to see you on a surf board."

"Yeah, my nose isn't quite broken, yet."

I knew things had gotten serious when Lynda took me to meet her parents at their place in Riverside. She seemed very nervous on the ride out there in her Honda.

"You know, it's a big deal when a Latina girl takes a boy home to meet her parents," she said as we edged through the freeway traffic.

I laughed. "It's a big deal when a girl takes a guy home anywhere in the whole world."

"Yes, but in Mexico, it's more special," she said somberly, and I could tell she had some doubts about presenting me to her parents so early on.

"Just promise you're not playing me," she said abruptly, looking over with a tight smile. It was only a moment, but I could see she'd been hurt before.

I groaned, laughed. "Oh, you mean like a wolf? No, I think you're stuck with me, more like a stray dog that won't go away."

"Yeah?"

"Yeah. You just whistle and I'll come running."

Lynda's parents were friendly and welcoming, even though they went a bit still when I said I was a U.S. postal worker on an extended leave; in other words, an unemployed bum nearly ten years older than their beloved daughter. Needless to say, I wasn't about to share my cross-country mission with them. There was no point in them thinking I was a certified lunatic in addition to a vagrant. But we got through a dinner of chicken enchiladas washed down with frosty glasses of sangria and her dad, Michel, told me about the time when as a little boy he had accompanied his own father on a fishing trip with Richard Burton. The world's biggest movie star had taken a break from shooting *Night of the Iguana* in Mismaloya and Michel had tagged along to bait the hooks and serve drinks.

"He got very sick on the boat and..." Michel made the universal barf sign, pointing his finger at his open mouth.

We made small talk after that and they asked me my plans. I said I intended to rejoin the post office and perhaps look into starting a business.

To this, Lynda's parents nodded gravely and moved on to dessert.

I felt uncomfortable on the ride home with Lynda, but she seemed happy enough.

"I think they like you," she said.

"Your parents are very nice, considering my status." During the middle of dinner I'd felt suddenly self-conscious and confused. As in, what the hell was I doing with my life? I was still brooding over it on the way back to Lynda's place.

But she didn't pick up on it.

"Your status?"

"Yeah."

She looked at me sideways and shook my leg. "They like you, I like you. That's your status."

"Thanks, but I want you to know that after the trial is over I can do better."

"I know."

We drove on up the coast along the vast Pacific, winding past rocks decked with sea lions and beaches strung with volleyball nets. I could tell that Lynda's thoughts were elsewhere, as buoyant as the waves.

"Maybe you'll come down to Mismaloya sometime with me?" she said.

"Count on it, as long as I don't have to ride a bike there."

"Oh no, you have to ride your bike so I can show you off to my uncle and auntie."

"They'll think you're as crazy as I am if I did that," I said, "but I'd do it for you."

"Just kidding," she said lightly.

I didn't want to tell her, but my other life was ringing a bell. We spent two more days together and then it was time to go. It was all I could do to resist asking her to marry me, but I was still at loose ends, and it didn't feel right. Boecker had been cleared for extradition and there was a trial to prepare for, with Freeman asking me to pull some strings together. I needed to get with the prosecutor back in Jackson so we could build a case. I'd be there for months, maybe even a year before the trial wrapped up.

On our last night together, I gave Lynda a ring and asked her to wait for me. I promised to call her every day and fly out once a month.

"Maybe," she said brightly, but her eyes had retreated as she folded in on herself. "We'll see."

"It won't be long, I'll be back I swear."

"Oh, Jake, you say that, but a year is a long time."

"It might not be a year. It might only be a couple of months."

"A lot can happen in that time."

"Yes, I know."

I had no right to press her further; for all I knew, Lynda had wised up on the advisability of connecting with a guy whose avocation was riding a bicycle. What did I have to offer? I didn't even have a job, and she was young and beautiful and single. Men would be chasing her up one side of the street and down the other as soon as I turned the corner.

But that was the chance I had to take because it was too late to quit now. Linda gave me an ambivalent kiss on a Monday morning and headed off to work. I bought an Amtrak ticket out of Long Beach, rolled my bike onto the train and headed east.

I did a lot of soul-searching on the train, looking out the window as it made the long crawl over the desert, the Rockies and the Great Plains beyond. Despite all of the BS I'd shared with Jimmy about retribution and revenge, I was tired of the chase and the point of it all seemed a distant memory. Tired? I was exhausted.

I tried on different looks for the "new me" in the life I hoped to live with Lynda. I always planned on going to law school, but who knows? Maybe I'd end up teaching history at some junior college. Maybe I'd even teach high school and coach a cycle team. That would be about as normal a life as I could imagine. I'd climb back into the old clothes of my former self and get back to mowing the lawn, watching TV and barbecuing burgers on the weekend. I could be a normal guy again, instead of some ghost out on the highway. Soon, Pieter Boecker would be rotting behind bars and I could forget about him. His memory would drift away until he, too, was a ghost. I'd have my new life with Lynda. I'd go biking on weekends and the past three years would slip away like a dream.

The Trial
Chapter 16

I got an apartment with a month-to-month lease in the gray zone between the black and white halves of Jackson and settled in for the trial. As it turned out, there wasn't that much for me to do and I regretted leaving California. I could have phoned in whatever the prosecutor's office needed.

But I made the best of it. I bought a mountain bike and rode the back roads of Mississippi outside Jackson through the fall and winter. I visited Vicksburg, where General Grant had broken the spine of the Confederacy with a siege that starved the Johnny Rebs of their supplies, starving the town's citizens to boot. I took day trips to Delta Blues country and the haunts of Muddy Waters, Son House and Howlin' Wolf. I made it to the crossroads where Robert Johnson sold his soul to the devil, just shy of being poisoned to death at the age of 27 with stychnine by a jealous husband. It's said he ended up on his hands and knees, barking like a dog as he died.

I rolled through dank, flat fields of cotton which had gone fallow in the winter, bereft of the sharecroppers who once trolled these ruts, dragging nine-foot bags of cotton balls behind them. Like on the Great Plains, the back end of the South was one sprawling rural ghetto that went on for hundreds of miles with no end of tumble-down shacks, abandoned stores and dying towns.

I called Lynda every day, but it was hard maintaining a sense of intimacy over a video link and neither of us were inclined to do the phone-sex thing. She seemed increasingly noncommittal, slipping away, and I couldn't blame her. I flew out to see her at Thanksgiving and we had an awkward three days together with both of us feeling a bit removed. I figured it wasn't going to last; we were like Tristram and Isolde, the medieval lovers torn apart by circumstances, separated by a sea of 21st century insecurity and doubt.

Nonetheless, I told Lynda that I loved her. She took it well, but said she wouldn't be there for me at Christmas. She was headed south to Mismaloya for a family celebration and I wouldn't have stepped into that situation even if she'd asked me, which, significantly, she didn't. She said there was no wi-fi in Mismaloya so she'd get back in touch whenever.

I took a job stocking shelves on the night shift at a grocery store in the poor side of town, which happened to be most of Jackson. I was going nuts just sitting around waiting for the trial and there was no sense plundering my bank account.

The guys at the store called me Shortbread, I never did know why, but they were good-natured about it, so no harm, no foul. Each night I'd wheel out cases of mandarin oranges, string beans, chick peas, frozen pizzas, chicken broth, whatever, and place the items neatly on the shelves, squaring them up in the silence of the store under the buzz of fluorescent lights at 4 a.m. or so. I worked a shift from 10 p.m. to 6 in the morning, which cut into my cycling, but made it possible to show up when I was needed in the court preliminaries and all that came after. I got a gym membership and worked out every day. I had dinner with Freeman's family every Sunday... like with my endless ride around the country, life fell into a routine and the weeks piled into months.

But no matter how much I did to keep busy, I couldn't help growing lonely, far lonelier than I'd ever felt riding around the country for the past three years. Lynda's picture was in a frame next to my bunk and I'd wake up each morning wondering, *when am I going to see you again, girl?* I knew the trial would be a slam-dunk, but there seemed to be endless delays piling up, one after another between the jury selection and rounding up witnesses. Each day was agony as I waited for the trial to begin.

But eventually, the day came around. I didn't look at Lynda's picture on the morning of the trial. Instead I got up, took a shower, got dressed, combed my hair and looked in the mirror. I had sent home to my brother John for my suit, the same one I'd worn to Jill's memorial. I barely recognized the stranger in the mirror, but I could handle it. It was judgement day. I'd been relentless in pursuing justice for Jill; now this day was just for the both of us. It was the day we'd send Boecker to prison for the rest of his life.

The trial was a disaster. Pieter Boecker had plenty of money and he used it to hire a team of the best criminal defense attorneys in Mississippi. He showed up in court in a dust-brown suit, looking like a regular Joe and clutching a copy of the *Book of Mormon*. On the advice of his attorneys, he'd ditched his Prince Valiant haircut, making him seem almost normal. He'd been staged.

"Look at him, trying to make out like he's a preacher or something," I whispered to Smith Freeman, who joined me in court.

"You can put a pig in high-heeled shoes, but it's still a pig," Freeman said. "The jury will see that."

But they didn't.

Boecker had changed since our encounter in Mississippi nearly three years ago. In addition to his graying hair he now sported a glass eye and a raw scar across this forehead, ripping a path through the orb which once nestled there. His attorney said he'd lost his right eye in an accident about a year ago, somewhere out in the desert.

It turned out that Boecker and his parents had emigrated from South Africa when he was 12. His parents had died in a house fire two years later, and though Boecker had been a suspect, the 14-year-old had never been charged. He was an Africaaner, a Dutch-German Boer, and thus the name, Pieter, which had confounded the search engines when I'd been hunting him online. He hadn't gone to Texas A&M as he'd told me so long ago while sitting in his RV, but was, in fact, a graduate of a two-year technical college air conditioning program in Columbus, Ohio, where he'd picked up his Midwestern accent. When I was up on the stand, telling the jury that Boecker had claimed to be an IT trouble-shooter from Plano, Texas, it didn't serve to make him look like a pathological liar; it just made me look dubious and confused.

"I ask you, why would my client make up such a cockamamie story?" his attorney asked the jury during the cross-examination. "The prosecution's witness weaves a wild tale, claiming that my client told him he was Texas, worked as an IT specialist and a dozen other things which are demonstrably false. He even claimed that Mr. Boecker stated he was a bisexual! This, besmirching a man who is a pillar of his church. Are we to believe that my client would make up all of these false assertions off the top of his head to a complete stranger? Ladies and gentlemen of the jury, it beggars the imagination!"

And so it did, but I kept to my story, because despite what Boecker and his attorneys said, it was all true.

Yet, every avenue seemed to lead nowhere.

"The FBI thinks that Boecker was involved in killing the parents of some illegal migrant kids down on the border last year," my attorney told me. "They recovered the bodies in canyon about 40 miles north of the Rio Grande."

"So could that help us?"

"I doubt it would be admissible," he replied. "At any rate, the kids were deported back to their relatives in Guatemala. Their only contacts here were illegals themselves up in Chicago and ICE said no dice to them staying. They've disappeared back home somewhere. The FBI checked around, but nothing turned up. Like they say, it's a jungle down there."

"Poor kids." Circumstantial or not, I didn't need any convincing that Boecker had more blood on his hands.

Boecker's attorneys suppressed any mention of the bicycle murders that had occurred in Utah and the suspicion that he'd been involved. That included the sensational case of Jenifer Livingston. Fair enough, but they also did a good job of character assassination with me. Somehow, they'd learned that I was a homeless loon who'd been riding a bicycle around the country for the past three years. It didn't help with the jury. I came across as unhinged and unreliable, a homeless drifter who worked the night shift, earning minimum wage with black folks at a rundown grocery store in the ghetto, while Boecker was a deacon in his church and a well-respected businessman with nationwide accounts.

Then there was the evidence. There wasn't any, except for my word against his on that terrible night when I saw the backup lights of his RV coming on fast, lighting up the wall of our tent with Jill stirring beside me. Although Freeman had made plaster casts of the tire tracks that rolled over Jill and me, Boecker had long since replaced the tires on his RV, so the tire casts meant zip.

Then there was the matter of the bumper stickers: they had been obliterated and a new one had taken their place: "Dollywood."

Nor could we place him at the scene. The name on the campground slip had been written in a dull pencil and its legibility had gone to mush in the

Mississippi humidity. Boecker had proof that he'd been on a job fixing an air conditioning unit at an auto parts plant in Alabama, some 230 miles away on the weekend that Jill was killed. The prosecutor made the point that Boecker could have driven down to Mississippi prior to the day of Jill's murder, but that of course was inconclusive, "conjecture," as his attorneys pointed out.

My only evidence that could place Boecker at the scene was the cracked kitchen window on his RV, patched with masking tape. The cracks were still there, but Boecker's attorneys produced statistics noting that broken windows were common in RVs.

So it all came down to his word against mine, and that wasn't enough to meet the standard of proving guilt beyond a reasonable doubt. The jury came back deadlocked 10-2, for and against Boecker's guilt and he was acquitted. The gavel cracked a sharp rap from the judge's stand and Boecker was a free man.

I heard his snorting laugh as he threw his hideous horse face back in exultation, exposing his teeth. He towered over his attorneys, slapping their backs and giving high-fives as the glum spectators and press filed out of the courtroom. It had been a sensational case due to the nature of Jill's death, and ten jurors, at least were stricken and even tearful that Boecker was getting off.

"Steady, Jake," Smith Freeman had his hand on my shoulder. It was all I could do not to break into tears. Boecker had never said a word in his defense, never took the stand. He'd let his attorneys do all the talking. He would have denied being in the campground that night anyway, but it would have been something; maybe he would have slipped up. If only the jury could have seen what a psychopathic liar he was, then they would have known what I knew.

"Steady," Freeman repeated. "I'm sorry man, but let it go. There's nothing can be done now."

I was shaking, a little at first, then violently, like I was on the verge of a seizure. Pieter Boecker was getting away with it? I couldn't believe it. It was beyond all reason, beyond justice, beyond the will of God.

"Goddamn it, I swear I'll kill him," I breathed.

"No, no you won't. Come on, out the side door," Freeman said.

He turned to go, but I was still staring at Boecker and the courtroom was almost empty now. He caught my eye and gave me a smile that seemed almost sympathetic.

Then he stuck his tongue in his cheek and cupped his hand to his mouth. Those remaining in the courtroom gasped as he stroked his hand up and down in imitation of a blowjob, pretending to choke on it, giving me a leering wink with his remaining eye.

"I'm going to sue you for everything you've got," he breathed as we drew close, "I'm going to take everything you own, including your piss-ant bicycle. You hear me boy?"

"And I'm going to kill you," I said back to him, as evenly as if I was offering him a dinner mint.

"You hear that, people?" he shouted. "Dick-head here says he's going to kill me!"

But what was left of the crowd in the courtroom seethed behind me, and one querulous voice, that of an old man, rang out, "We hope he kills you too."

That's when I snapped. Pieter Boecker could have ended his days happily fellating his cellmates in the Mississippi State Penitentiary, but now he was a walking dead man. Standing in that courtroom with my world falling apart I once again felt like a creature that was barely human, "old, hoary, monstrous, and swimming alone; who is unspeakably terrible in his wrath." And that monster was rising from the deep.

I made a call to Utah and begged Kevin for a favor. Kevin was the convenience store clerk I'd met when I first rode into St. George. A former sergeant in the U.S. Army, he'd been attached to a reconnaissance unit during Operation Iraqi Freedom and was the ideal candidate for what I had in mind. After Boecker's arrest the story of Jill's death had been all over the newspapers and he'd sent me a way-to-go message and a friend invite on Facebook. We'd been writing back and forth since then.

I wired Kevin $500 via the Western Union outlet at his store and told him to keep the change, along with my undying gratitude.

After that I could take my time. There was no point in sending Boecker to the boneyard immediately after the trial anyway, not unless I wanted to be wearing blaze orange for the rest of my life.

I bought a five-year-old pickup truck from one of the guys I worked with at the grocery store. That's the nice thing about buying a vehicle down south, they're not all pitted and rusted with sodium like up in Michigan, where salt is used to clear the winter roads.

But that's where I was headed. I turned in my notice and had a farewell dinner with Smith Freeman.

"Be good now," he said as we shook hands that evening. "Don't do anything stupid, you hear?"

"Stupid's my middle name," I said.

"Yeah, I think so too," he smiled. "But I'd hate to see you in the papers."

"That's not in my plans. I'm heading home to Michigan, going to see my brother, John."

True enough. The next morning I nosed north and found my way to Highway 61, thinking of that old Dylan song: "Where you want that killin' done? Out on Highway 61."

But of course, that wasn't likely to happen. I rolled into Grand Rapids and spent a couple of days with my brother, catching up on old times. I hadn't seen John in three years and he'd been through a divorce and a custody fight since then. We had a lot to talk about.

But John still had my things boxed up in his basement and I collected what I needed, including the shotgun my dad had given me for Christmas when I turned 12.

As far as weapons go, it wasn't much. Dad had presented me with a breech-loading, single-shot .20 gauge that was more a toy than a killing machine, though I'd been plenty happy to graduate from a BB gun at the time. Over the past 20 years the cheap wood of the front stock had fallen off and I'd reattached it with a spool of electrical tape. It was rickety at best, and when I took it down to the local DNR range to fire off a few shells, some of the other shooters had surveyed my gun with disgust.

But my gun was also untraceable and in my paranoia I imagined that if I went out and purchased a new shotgun it would somehow link me to Boecker's demise, if and when I shot him. There had been witnesses in the courtroom, after all, when I said I'd kill him.

I didn't have the option of buying a gun out of the trunk of a hoodlum's car like you see in the movies and couldn't take a chance buying one legitimately. In Michigan, even the purchase of a shotgun requires filling out a federal Department of Justice form, followed by a phone call to the FBI and NICS, its National Instant Criminal Background Check System. I suppose I could have bought a new weapon from a gun show, but even that would leave some kind of a trail if the authorities suspected me of shooting Boecker.

So my old, taped-together .20 gauge would have to do. I'd never been much of a bird hunter, but back in the day I could knock down 15 out of 20 clay pigeons in a skeet shoot, and I figured that was good enough for a target the size of a moose.

My steel-toe boots were still resting atop the box where I'd placed them three years ago. I looked down at my tattered running shoes and decided it was time for a switch. The boots felt good, well-worn, solid and dependable.

What else? I stopped by an Army-Navy surplus store and bought two outfits, one all black with a balaclava and the other a set of camouflage fatigues. Under glass at the front of the store was a display of combat knives, some of which were a foot long with serrated edges. Throwing knives, throwing stars, throwing axes... switchblades, stilettos, Bowie knives the size of small swords... who buys this junk? I wondered. I opted for a tactical folding knife with a three-and-a-half-inch blade.

I packed the clothes, my gun and the knife in the space behind the bench seat in my truck.

I had a last evening with John at Founders Brewery in downtown Grand Rapids and headed south on 131 the next morning, connecting to I-94 and then west to Interstate 80. It was strange to think that I hadn't ridden this route in the dozen times or more that I'd cycled cross-country. You can ride a bike on the freeway in some states, like Washington, North Dakota and such, but not all the way on I-80, and that was probably the route that Boecker drove the most on his wanderings around America.

But now the rolling hills of Iowa and the endless flats of Nebraska sped by as if a miracle compared to my tortuous, crawling journeys on a bike. Past Denver the Rocky Mountains rose up, a wall reaching to the clouds which had humbled me so often on two wheels. I got a rotisserie chicken at a supermarket in Leadville and ate it in my truck, wondering how anyone could live year-round at 11,000 feet, or work in a molybdenum mine.

Then I was past Gunnison and the Great Divide, rolling down through Durango past Mesa Verde and on through Arizona, past the Grand Canyon and Hoover Dam to Vegas. And then the 300-mile sprint across the desert to L.A. I made it across the country in three days, sleeping a few hours here and there in the back of my truck beside the mountain bike I'd packed along for old times sake.

Humming down the freeways of southern California felt like a home-coming. It was one of those 500-watt days of full sun and an azure sky that seemed bright enough to hurt, or maybe like your heart would burst from the joy of it. I felt a bit dizzy at the wheel, swept away by euphoria; SoCal would be my new home. Maybe I'd take up surfing, that would be a good segue from biking.

At a gas station in Riverside I saw a young guy on a bike laden with panniers and camping gear. He'd stopped for an energy drink and a slice of pizza, the same as me, not so long ago. He had a blue handkerchief wrapped around a thick tussle of curls, doo-rag style, and was wearing bike shorts and a tank top advertising some microbrew from the Pacific Northwest. I noticed that he was riding the same brand of bike that had squired me around the country for three years. He had the aura of a man who's high on life.

"How's the ride?" I called out after filling my tank.

"Free and easy," he replied.

"Where you heading?"

"East," he waved. "All the way to Virginia. It's the trip of a lifetime."

"That right?" I whistled in appreciation. "Damn, I'm gonna have to try that myself sometime."

He should have looked miserable, trying to fight his way clear of L.A,'s urban sprawl, but instead he radiated an inner joy, and for a moment, I envied him. I knew exactly how he felt.

I didn't tell Lynda I was coming; I wanted to surprise her. We hadn't talked much over Skype in the past few weeks and when we did it all seemed kind of disjointed. She seemed distracted, not all that happy to see me. The love-word had fallen out of our vocabulary.

But I still loved her, more than ever. I had walled myself off from the world over the past three years as a nomad who never stuck around anywhere long enough to sink roots or make a true friend. Even the friends I had made, Jimmy Christmas, Smith Freeman and the guys I'd met at the grocery store were situational, belonging to a time and place that was now buried in the past. Really, there was no one, only Lynda and my promise to a dead woman who was once my wife.

I picked up some flowers at the market in Newport Beach, carnations, daisies, a sweetheart rose and a sprig of fern, the kind they sell everywhere for $2.40. That and a bottle of Lynda's favorite wine, a Sauvignon Blanc. Her place was only two blocks away.

My powers of observation had been sharpened by the past few years of hunting Pieter Boecker, but now they deserted me. Almost anyway. I drove around the block, trembling with the anticipation of seeing Lynda again, and, hopefully, repairing the divide between us. I didn't notice the two of them walking as I eased into a parking spot across from her apartment. And then she was passing by my window, holding a bag of groceries to her chest with a big, handsome guy in a tight red t-shirt trailing alongside, laughing about something in the morning sun. She glanced my way and froze.

"Jake!"

"Lynda."

"What are you doing here?"

"I... I came to see you." Obviously.

There was an awkward silence and a puzzled look settled over her companion's face. He was on the verge of putting things together, and I already had.

"Jake, this is Dave," Lynda said at last. "Dave, this is Jake."

'I'm Not a Killer'
Chapter 17

"What did you expect?"

It was the next day and Lynda wore a pinched, pale face as we sat in the local coffeehouse.

"You've been gone for eight months," she went on. "No, nine! Do you know how many times I've been asked out since then? Do you know how many offers I've turned down? I had a submarine commander ask me out, for Christ's sake, and an airline pilot!"

"Jesus."

She waved it aside with a grimace. "They were both too old, but still."

"I'm sorry, Lynda, I'm really sorry!" I said, and meant it. "It's just that the trial took so much time and I had to see it through. There was nothing else I could do, but I thought about you the whole time and I thought about us being together again."

"Yes, but it's not through is it?" She gave me an accusing look, revealing a side I'd never seen before; the bright Latina lioness was angry now, baring her teeth. Mexican hellcat, that's what crossed my mind, but she looked good when she was angry and I felt myself stirring.

"It will never be through for you, Jake."

"Yes, yes it will! It's almost over and then..."

"And then? And then? Then you will be a murderer yourself! Do you think I want to know such a thing? Do you think I want to be with such a man? A murderer? Oh, Jake!" she stroked my hand, "That would haunt you the rest of your life!"

I waved her words aside. "Oh, murderer, come on! You know that's not me. I'm not a killer, I could never do that."

"No, Jake, I don't know," she jabbed her finger into my chest. "I only know you're crazy enough to chase this guy around the country for three years and leave me hanging right when we get together. Do you think I liked that? Huh?"

"What about Dave? I asked wearily. "Is he my replacement?"

"Your replacement!" Lynda jumped to her feet and for a moment I thought she was going to throw her coffee in my face.

"Lynda, please!" I threw up my hands. "I'm begging you, please sit down and talk to me. I don't know what he means to you. I only know that I drove across most of the country thinking of you every minute of the way and it crushed my heart down to a grain of sand to see you with someone else. That's all. That's all I ask. I just want to know if you still care or if there's someone new."

Lynda shook her head, her eyes moist in exasperation.

"We've been on one date, riding bikes, and there was a hug, but no kiss," she said at last. "He's still married anyway, separated from his wife."

Relief trickled through me. I still had a chance. "Thank you."

But Lynda wasn't finished.

"You know, Jake, you can't expect too much from me," she said. "Between our time biking out west and your visit last year we've only been together for about a month if you add up the days. Maybe I've dated around a bit more than you have, but I've found that couples don't really reveal themselves to each other until they've been together at least three months. That's when you drop whatever mask you're wearing and start acting like your real self."

"But I've never been fake with you," I protested. "What you see is what you get with me. I mean, it's not like I'm some kind of player."

"Yes, but you have secrets, Jake, you have the sin of omission, and that's what's fake about you. There's a part of you that I can't reach and I know you'll never let me. I don't know about you, Jake, I just don't know."

She wouldn't meet my eyes, glaring straight ahead. What could I say? I was a fake, there were things I could never tell her.

"All I can tell you is that I love you," I said miserably. "There's no one else but you."

Slowly, she turned my way. "Stop that!" she snapped.

"What?"

"The puppy eyes. Stop looking so sad."

I forced a crooked grimace, trying to smile.

"Oh, Jake..."

We sat and looked at each other, not saying a word for five minutes or so. I reached out and locked her pinky finger in mine.

"I've missed you."

"I've missed you too," she said in a small voice.

"So, what do we do now?"

"I don't know," she said, shrugging. "It's up to you, Jake. You're still married to another woman; a woman who's been dead for three years now and I can't compete. Can't you give her up? She's gone, Jake, and I'm here. Why do you hang on to her?"

"Jill's gone, there's only you, but..."

"But?"

"I made a promise."

"But Jake," she gripped my hands hard. "You have to give this up! The only way you'll ever get beyond this is to forgive and move on. If you want us to be together, you have to decide, right here, right now if it's going to be Jill or me. Do you understand? I can't be with a man who's chasing a ghost."

Lynda was giving me everything she had with her eyes, imploring me to be human again, offering the chance to heal with her love. It was a make-it-or-break-it moment and I wanted more than anything to say, yes, Lynda, yes, I'm yours forever and in my heart there will be only you, forever and ever.

But forgive? A blanket of gloom settled over me like the morning fog over the town pier. I had never told Lynda the whole story. I had never her about the baby.

There were two lives to pay for, Jill and our unborn child.

Three years ago, lying in the hospital in Mississippi, a woman doctor had entered the room and sat on the edge of my bed. I don't remember her name, can't even recall her face, but she said she was an OB/GYN. She told me that Jill had been six weeks pregnant when she died.

If it had been only Jill I still would have vowed to track Boecker down, but the incidental murder of our unborn child sealed his tomb. Our baby would never beam with happiness in Jill's arms in the morning, never experience the first day of kindergarten, never learn the ABCs, go to the prom, drive a car, fall in love. Never get married, have children, then grandchildren, see us pass away, retire and visit Europe, Hawaii, and then die of old age with a life that had been sweet and fulfilled. All that and so much more were things that I had thought about on all of those mornings when I woke up at 4:30 a.m., staring at the wall of my tent. On that score, my heart was cold as a toad's.

All that ran through my thoughts while Lynda waited for an answer and I knew there were only seconds before she saw into the heart of me, slapped my face and walked out of my life forever.

I had to choose and there was no other possible choice, so I did what any man would do in that situation. I lied.

"For you Lynda, only for you I will forget," I said glumly.

"But can you forgive, Jake?"

I threw my head back, closed my eyes and groaned. "I don't know, Lynda, but I can try. For you, I can try."

"And you'll give up chasing this psycho around? You will do that for me?"

I sighed. "Yes. Yes, I will. He's gone anyway. He sold his home in Utah and hit the road. I'd never be able to find him again if I had three lifetimes. It's time to move on."

I knew she wanted to ask me if I could forget Jill too, but that would be too much. She had moved the goal posts in her direction and that was good enough for now.

"So what should we do?" The tenderness had crept back into her voice.

"Look," I said. "I want you to know that this is real between us, too. I want you more than anything, but I want you to be sure about me. I'm going back to Michigan to collect my things and then I'm moving out here for good. I'll be back in two weeks and that will give you time to think things over."

"But what if we don't work out? You say your search is over, but what if you can't give it up?"

"Hey, whatever happens between you and me, I'm still not going back to live in Michigan," I said. "I like California, and if anyplace can help me get past my demons, it's out here with you in Newport Beach. If things don't work out for us we can still be friends, can't we?"

"Yes, I think so," Lynda said hopefully.

We spent the night together and then another and it was like old times, waking in the morning in each other's arms with the sun pouring gold through the window. Lynda said that I was the one she wanted to share her life with, and I believed her. "You're a traveler," she said. "I like that, I need that in a man."

No problem there.

The next day I got online and applied for a job with the U.S. Postal Service anywhere within a 20-mile radius of Newport Beach. I tracked down a couple of distribution centers and called their managers. Yes, they'd take a look at my qualifications; there had been some turnover lately and they might be able to fit me in.

That afternoon we took a walk on the beach and sat for awhile on a bench by the sea. I shared my job search with Lynda along with my hope of getting back on with the USPS within a month, and then, hopefully, law school.

"So I'm going to marry a postman?" she said when I told her the news.

She'd never mentioned anything about marriage before.

"Well, until I get my law degree," I said slowly. "Wait, was that a proposal?"

"Oh Jake, you silly man. Latina girls don't make proposals. They get them."

"And you would marry a poor postal worker?"

She shrugged. "I think so. I think that yes, I would. I think you have potential, how do they say? I think you are a diamond in the rough. Besides, I've heard that the postman always rings twice."

"Lynda, will you please marry me?"

She put a finger to her lips, as if thinking it over. "I might. But only if you ask me from down on your knees."

I did. I got down on my knees with the joggers and cyclists passing by on the bike path and asked again.

Lynda looked into my eyes and smiled. "Yes Jake. Yes."

We hugged, kissed, and sat for awhile holding hands, each of us lost in our dreams. Far out on the Pacific, I watched a line of brilliant clouds sculpted in fantastic shapes - animals, houses, cars, trees and more - creeping in a stately procession along the horizon. I imagined my life with Lynda moving forward like that line of clouds into a future of peace and happiness.

"You know Lynda, you don't have to be poor," I said after a bit.

"No? I don't mind so much. Poor is the natural condition of the human race. When you're from Mexico you get used to being poor."

"Let me show you." I pulled out my phone and logged into my stock market app. Up came my S&P-indexed fund with the earnings made over the past three years while I'd been riding around, living on nickels and dimes.

A line of figures crawled across the screen of my phone and then a number in neon green letters: **$1,203,941.07...**

Lynda's eyes went as wide as I'd ever seen them.

"This is yours?" she said in disbelief. "Jake, that's more than a million dollars!"

"Yeah, quite a bit more," I nodded. "The stock market doubled or tripled in value while I was out riding. I just sort of forgot about it until a week ago."

"But Jake!"

I shrugged. "It was a pleasant surprise. It's not much in terms of the real estate market around here, but maybe enough for us to buy a small place off the beach. That, and get me started in law school."

Lynda gaped at me and punched my arm in play. "Well you are just full of surprises!"

"I try."

"But you're kidding yourself if you think you could ever be a lawyer."

"Why not?"

"Sitting in a chair for sixty or a hundred hours a week? Please, you're way too antsy. You need to do something physical; I hate to say it, but something like being a mail carrier."

"Or a cowboy. A garbage man, maybe."

"Yes, something like that," she nodded, a bit more vigorously than I would have liked.

"But what would you do?"

Lynda paused and smoothed her hand across my cheek. "Let's make a deal," she murmured. "We'll reinvent ourselves, and promise that we'll love whatever we do."

"That will take a lot of reinventing. Most people don't figure out what they want to do until they're in their 30s and then they just fall into something. They settle."

"Yes," she nodded somberly.

But a moment later her face brightened as she thought of something. "You know, maybe we don't need to buy a house."

"What?"

"Or get jobs. Or go back to school."

I waited.

"There's another way for us to live with the kind of money you have." she smiled. "Do you know how to sail a boat?"

We shared a few more nights together and dinner at "our" restaurant on the beach. We were going to be married! We talked about it. Lynda wanted a year's engagement so we could truly get to know each other. That was fine by me because I wanted to get back on my feet in the "real" world before saying "I do."

We went shopping for boats. Lynda had this idea that we'd start a charter service, ferrying couples back and forth to Catalina Island, serving wine and shrimp hors d'oeurves and scouting out whales. I didn't know crap about sailing, but I could learn, and Lynda already knew the ropes of playing hostess. We could live on the boat and who knows? Maybe take off for Bora Bora, the Bahamas or the Mediterranean when we felt like it. I was pretty sure there would be a devil or two in the details, but had to admit, it sounded better than my plan to go to law school or become a history teacher. That stuff could be my fall-back if the boat thing didn't work out. But for now, we were building our castle in the sky and it filled me with bliss to see her so happy.

Even so, I felt like a rat for lying to Lynda about what I planned to do before I got back in town. But not too much, because as the saying goes, what you don't know can't hurt you.

That, and my love for her was true. True to the bone.

"I can't wait to see Mr. Bojangles!" she said as we kissed goodbye through the window of my truck the next morning.

"Who?"

"Your cat!"

"Oh, right, duh!" I slapped my head. "He's a pretty one. You're going to like him."

"I'm sure. I love cats."

"Well, you are Leo the lioness, after all," I teased.

"See you in two weeks, hombre."

"Hasta la vista, sweets."

Then I was on my way, with Lynda, the renewed love of my life waving goodbye in the rear view mirror. And somewhere along the way I took a left turn and headed due north instead of northeast toward Michigan. As I headed up Interstate 15 I wondered what I'd do about Mr. Bojangles, since kitty had died of feline diabetes only two months before. I'd have to find a replacement.

The Highway of Death
Chapter 18

"...to the last I grapple with thee; from hell's heart I stab at thee; for hate's sake I spit my last breath at thee."

- Herman Melville, *Moby-Dick or, The Whale*

My dad had been a political junkie and took pride in being an un-wavering independent long before that came into vogue. Sometimes he voted Republican and sometimes Democrat, even, on occasion, Libertarian. He had voted for Obama in 2008, but for George Bush, Sr., in 1992.

He had a collection of video clips of famous moments in politics: John F. Kennedy's "Ask not what your country can do for you" speech, along with his vow to take America to the moon and save the world through the efforts of the Peace Corps. Lyndon Johnson's 1968 message to the American people that he wouldn't run for a second term. Richard Nixon's "I am not a crook" speech and his farewell wave from the helicopter after Watergate in 1972. Ronald Reagan's "Mr. Gorbachev, tear down that wall" demand in the late '80s. We used to sit and watch some of those great moments in politics while Dad was dying of cancer back in 2009. They made me proud to be an American.

I remember one time we watched a clip from a famous debate in the 1988 campaign between the first George Bush and Michael Dukakis, the Democratic governor of Massachusetts. Dukakis opposed capital punishment and the GOP was trying to paint him as being soft on crime, since his state had freed a black felon, Willie Horton, who had raped and murdered a woman upon his early release from prison.

Dukakis stepped on a land mine during the debate when the moderator asked him what he'd do if someone raped and murdered his wife, Kitty. Dukakis gave a namby-pamby answer to the effect that he'd feel bad about it, but would let the authorities handle it. His mild answer shocked the nation to its core.

"That's where he blew the election right there," Dad said as we watched the clip. "He should have said he'd kill the guy with his bare hands. He should have said he'd tear the guy's head off and to hell with the consequences. If a man rapes your wife, you have to kill him right?"

"I guess so," I said.

"With your bare hands if you can."

I nodded.

"And if a man kills your wife, you're honor-bound to kill him. Am I right?"

"You're right Dad," I said, pulling the tab on a second can of beer. "You're always right. You and John Wayne."

"No, I'm serious," he leaned in, gazing at me under his heavy, gray brows with a look that reminded me of an eagle. "You'd have to kill the son of a bitch. A man's got to do what a man's got to do. Do you believe that?"

"I guess so."

"Well good."

"I'd do it with an arrow through his window at night, a broad-tip," I said, humoring him. "Razor sharp."

Dad snorted. "I know you would, son," he patted my knee, "though an arrow would be a foolish way to go about it."

Talk about honor and revenge was easy for Dad to say; he was a killer. He'd been in Vietnam and unlike a lot of old soldiers, he didn't mind talking about it. I knew he wasn't just bullshitting me about sticking it to those who deserved it.

But I was something less, with a lot of ground to make up if I hoped to have him smiling in his grave.

I thought about that clip and Dad's words as I rolled through Vegas and north to Utah. I had wondered back then if I had some of the killer gene, like Dad, and I guess I was still wondering. It was true, there were some things that a man had to do if he really was a man, and for starters that meant killing whoever harmed your wife.

I felt bad about lying to Lynda, but the secret of what I planned to do was safe with me. I'd never breathe a word of it for the rest of my life, even on my death bed. She'd never know. Men keep secrets from women and women do the same, no harm, no foul.

Then there was the matter of my immortal soul and the killing at hand. I had long since sealed that ugly truth into a box buried within my mind and removed it from introspection, yet somehow "murder" always managed to creep out, rising again and again in my thoughts. I pushed it away, straining to believe I was just an executioner, the sword of justice. I had long since compartmentalized the task at hand. Does a hunter feel bad when he kills a deer? Maybe a little bit, but he gets over it. I knew Boecker was guilty and deserved to die by lethal injection under the auspices of the great state of Mississippi. There had been a miscarriage of justice; nonetheless, I would save the state millions in Death Row expenses, years of appeals and what it took to finally send Boecker down the karmic chute to hell.

It's said that at any one time there are an estimated 70,000 Americans on the loose who have killed another human being, be it in warfare or on the city streets, or, in Boecker's case, for the sheer thrill of it. I didn't mind being in that club if it would bring Boecker the justice he deserved.

As for my eternal soul and the blight that a killing might bring, I'd never been all that religious. That, and I still had the mentality of a U.S. postal worker where everything had to be done exactly right, every mistake corrected, every package inspected and stamped. I had a duty to correct the mistake known as Pieter Boecker.

I caught up with Boecker on MT-200, a lonely ribbon of road that winds through low-lying mountains and forests from Sand Point, Idaho to Missoula, Montana and beyond. I'd ridden highway 200 once before on my way through Dixon. It's as narrow as a country lane and there's no shoulder to speak of; if you're crowded off the highway on a bike you can mostly expect a plummet down a steep embankment on either side. Dozens of tiny crosses dot the highway along its length as it passes through lands once and still owned by various tribes: the Blackfeet, Salish, Kootenai and Flathead Indians. Two years before, I'd named this scenic route the Highway of Death, owing to those crosses and its speed limit of 70 mph. It was a nightmare to ride on a bike.

I'd camped in the foothills north of here back then, creeping into the woods with a storm coming on. The forest had been dry as a dynamite depot in the desert beneath a canopy of cedars that towered out of sight overhead. Beneath their boughs lay a carpet of pine needles six inches long and six inches deep, so thick and spongy that they made walking difficult. In the afternoon heat the trees had seemed as brittle as breadsticks, literally carbon bombs that were ready to explode at the slightest spark. I had nestled beneath them on the cushion of needles, nervous about prowling grizzly bears. Back then, I had mused on the rampage of western forest fires and the thought that no cyclist could outrun their maelstrom of fire.

But I was in a pickup truck now and according to the information on my phone, Boecker's RV was only a couple of miles up ahead, parked alongside the Clark Fork River at a fishing access site. This I knew because my pal, Kevin, had attached two GPS trackers under the front and rear bumpers of Boecker's motorhome before he got back from the trial in Jackson.

I'd been following his meanderings all over the country ever since, watching the green icons of the trackers flashing on a laptop as Boecker's RV made its way around Montana. Closer and closer I came, and then in the late afternoon I spotted him pulling out of a gas station on Highway 93 south of the National Buffalo Range. A mixed thrill of dread and anticipation ran through me, knowing that I had reached the brink of all my travels.

I followed him at a distance of two miles back in my truck, passing by when he pulled in next to the river. It was the perfect spot for an ambush. The fishing site was on the downslope of the Bitterroot Range, miles from the nearest house, let alone any town. No one would hear gunfire out here or think anything of it if they did. An hour later I changed into my all black outfit and doubled back, taking my foot off the gas as I reached the public access to quiet my engine. I cut my lights and rolled into the far entrance. I could see Boecker's RV glowing in the moonlight at the far end of the drive, a ghostly white whale in the moonshade of the pines.

This would be the tough part, because it's one thing to say you're going to shoot a man through the window of his home as he puttered around in his robe or sat watching TV, and quite another to go ahead and do it. But I'd rehearsed this many times in my mind and had even practiced breathing exercises to help me keep steady when the time came. I had also performed visualization exercises, like what boxers and professional athletes do to transform themselves into winners.

I told myself that I was a warrior. I had the tattoos on my arms and a black ninja suit to prove it. I was the dead man who got up and walked... I was the Crow. I had a gun, a knife, and the element of surprise. I had Dad's words of vengeance still lingering in my thoughts. I had prepared for this for three long years and more than 90,000 miles on the road. I was psyched up to kill, to do it for Jill and the baby we never had. I was locked in and loaded.

Still, I felt shaky. Shaky as the last leaf on an oak tree with the first big winter storm coming on. How's that for a metaphor? But that's how I felt. A lonely dry husk, rattling in the wind.

Far away, I heard a whistle blow as a train crept up the spine of the mountains, across the river from M-200. You see trains almost every day out West, steel anacondas dragging hundreds of boxcars filled with coal or colossal steel tubes of toxic chemicals or deadly industrial gases. On many nights, lying alone in my tent, I had thought of abducting Boecker at gunpoint and tying him to the tracks so that he could see the lights of a train coming on, just as I had seen the lights of his RV. But that would take too much work and entail too much risk. That, and I'd have to be even more demented than Boecker himself.

By now it was full dark. I switched off the dome light in my truck and edged the door open. With my hands shaking almost out of control I folded the seat down and pulled out my shotgun and my knife. I broke the breech and loaded a shell, filling my pockets with five more from the glove compartment. A .20 gauge shotgun shell doesn't look like much, it's about the size of a beefy tube of lipstick, but if I managed to pump three or four of them into Boecker it would get the job done. With luck, just one would do it.

I crept down the drive along the river in the dark with my gun held up before me like I was holding a flag. The RV loomed closer, the staccato glow of a television flickering in its windows. My chest was booming so hard it felt like I was having a heart attack; me, the guy who'd cycled more than three times the circumference of the earth over the past few years. It was unnerving, and for the 10,000th time I repeated my mantra, *a man's got to do what a man's got to do. A man's got to...*

I smelled the odor of frying fish. The RV was only a few feet away now and Boecker would be there by the cracked kitchen window, working on his dinner or watching TV. *A man's got to do what a man's...*

BANG! There was a flash of light and the sense that I'd been kicked ten feet by a mule. I was on the ground, my body convulsing, writhing; I couldn't control my limbs, I was shaking in a violent seizure.

Then there was Boecker leaning over me, shining what had to be a military grade flashlight in my eyes. I couldn't see him through the glare, but I could hear him well enough.

"Well, if it isn't my old friend the bicycle boy," he said, chuckling. "You're just two sticks of dynamite in an orange juice can, aren't ya? Well, I've been waiting for you, chief. Waiting all this time for just this moment."

He hit me hard on the side of the head with the light, but he didn't need to. I couldn't move from the effects of the taser. Boecker had been hiding around the side of the RV when I'd come peeking in his kitchen window and had hit me with 50,000 volts. At least, that's what a standard taser packs, but by the time it hits you, it delivers receive a mere 1,200 volts. It was enough.

"Wait here."

I heard the screen door of his RV open and then slam. Then he was back again, rolling me over, binding my hands and feet. I still couldn't move, it was as if a lethargy as thick as tar had settled over my joints and my brain had assumed mindset of a turtle. Even so, I knew I was fucked.

"Ho-ho! You're mine now, buddy, all mine," Boecker gloated as he finished his work. He'd zip-tied me behind my back and had my legs bound together at the ankles.

I suppose an Olympic weight-lifter could bust out of a set of simple plastic zip-ties measuring no more than 3/16ths of an inch across, but he'd have to cut his wrists to the bone to do it. That's why cops, gangsters and foreign torture squads use zip-ties instead of handcuffs these days, some of them, anyway.

Boecker grabbed me by the arms and dragged me across the rocky ground and up the steel mesh of the RV's stairs. Then down the hall toward what I knew was his bedroom. I started to scream and he slammed me to the floor.

"Shut the fuck up or you'll be wearing a smile twice as wide the next time you open your mouth," he said, his face looming close to mine. "You get me mister?"

I nodded and he shoved me through a doorway to the right. It was the bathroom.

"Here's your new home, laddie," Boecker said, breathing close in my face again, his breath reeking of fried fish. "Til I decide what to do with you, that is."

My eyes began to clear enough to see the outlines of his face. Boecker was wearing lipstick and had darkened his eyebrows with what looked like a felt marker. He'd drawn lightning zig-zags on his cheeks. It gave him the look of a malevolent clown.

"Warpaint my friend," he said, as if guessing my thoughts. "Welcome to the fun house."

I tried to speak but my mouth still wasn't working right.

"I heard you lost your spleen," he went on. "We'll have to check out that scar in a bit. You and I got a lot to talk about. It's lonely in here and I like company."

I managed something like a growl.

He gave me a look of mock chagrin.

"Don't be mad. I had quite a laugh when I heard about your bike ride around the country. After I took care of your missus, I headed south of the border for a few months until things cooled down. I was down in Baja the whole time, camping on the beach with all the other RV monkeys, drinking beer and grilling fish. Had a whole lot of fun down there."

He paused, looking up and around toward the ceiling as if following the flight of a fly or trying to remember something just as fleeting. Slowly, sensation was returning to my limbs and my thoughts grew clearer. Whether Boecker sensed I was coming around or not, I don't know, but he started hammering my head against the bathroom floor. The wood beneath the linoleum had long since rotted to a spongy mush, otherwise I might have blacked out again.

I was completely at his mercy as he loomed over me, filling my vision. The toilet was six inches from my head, the sink located the same distance to my left. My universe had dwindled to this tiny space as I lay helpless with no chance of escape. As for Boecker, he had no more sense of mercy than a pterodactyl, and I knew it.

"Do you like eating out of a toilet?" he huffed, slamming the back of my skull against the floor. "Drinking out of a toilet? Because that's where all your meals will be served over the next few weeks, and you'll get thirsty soon enough."

Boecker's bathroom was a horror on par with the rest of his place. My nostrils filled with the stench of cidered urine and I could see that his toilet was crusted with tendrils of vomit. A matrix of flies buzzed over a wastebasket overflowing with tissue covered with blood. I retched, grateful that he hadn't duct-taped my mouth; I would have suffocated on my vomit.

Boecker gave my head another slam, a cat now, playing with a mouse, but it was useless against the spongy floor. I was coming to fast, half hog-tied in a room barely big enough for the two of us.

I turned to look at him and he was holding my knife, inches from my face.

"Sharp little thing," he mused. "Could come in handy. Have you ever thought of being a candidate for a penis transplant? This could be the way forward."

At last I was able to speak. "I... I been looking for you."

"That so?"

I nodded.

He looked down at me. "You know, I've been thinking about you, too. I even went looking for you, but you had disappeared without a forwarding address. How was I to know you were looking for me?" he chuckled.

"Too bad we didn't exchange emails," I said.

"Yeah, too bad," he said, his face a yellow blur in the dim light of the bathroom. "Like I told you long ago, I create scenarios, little games that play out over time, but you were hidden from me. Perhaps we passed each other in the night on some country road."

"Your scenarios are going to get you killed." I had to keep him talking, recalling that Boecker couldn't seem to shut up when we'd met at the campsite in Mississippi, chit-chatting about Paris, tropical fish and smooth jazz.

Boecker chuckled again. "So says the fly to the spider."

"You're a spider alright. You ever stop to consider that?"

"Yesss... Maybe so. But you fell right into my web, didn't you? Did you think I wouldn't check for your trackers? I found one of them on my first day on the road and the second one a week later. I lured you here, my friend, to this lonesome place."

"So what's the point of your scenarios?"

"You'll see soon enough," he chuckled again. "They amuse me, especially when they play out as planned. We're going to have a holiday, you and I. We're going to get to know each other real good over the next few weeks out here in God's country, but I'm afraid you're not going to like it unless you give in."

"Give in?"

"Yeah, like they used to advise young ladies getting raped years back in the good old days. Lean back and try to enjoy it."

By now I was coming wide awake fast, my mind speeding up from its earthworm crawl.

"Cut the shit. You don't think I showed up here on my own do you?"

Boecker gave me a whimsical look.

"Yes, I do," he said. "You're the same as me, a lone wolf. You had to do alone or it wouldn't count."

"Yeah, but I'm not stupid. I've got friends in Missoula waiting for me to check in."

"Oh really? Tough guys like you, I suppose."

"They're not so tough, but they know how to use a phone. I told them to call the sheriff if I didn't check in. They'll be calling by now."

It was bullshit, but the only thing I could think of with my face pressed to the bathroom floor.

Boecker called my bluff.

"Let's give these buddies a call then."

He had me there.

"My phone's in my truck," I said, "and it's got a passcode."

"Yeah? What county are we in then? What sheriff's department did you tell them to call?"

'They're locals. Biking friends from Montana. They'll know who to call."

"And suppose they did call the police and they showed up. What would you tell them? That you tried to kill a harmless RV'er and I got the drop on you?"

"At least I'd stay alive." To try killing you again.

Boecker smiled. I could tell he didn't believe me. He knew as well as me that it was just we two, way out in a remote Montana forest, literally up a river. Still, some part of him hesitated. I'd planted a seed and he couldn't ignore it.

"Well you'd better hope it works when I fetch it," he said at last. "Because after dinner I'm going to take a stroll down to your truck and then we'll call these friends of yours. God help you if you're lying." He raised the knife and gave me a sharp jab under the chin, drawing blood.

"Chin up."

For once I had nothing to say; no smart-ass remark, no message of defiance. This wasn't the time to play out the shower scene in *Scarface* with Al Pacino spitting "fuck you" in the face of the Colombians wielding a chain saw. Somberly, it settled upon me that I wasn't going to see Lynda again, and that all of our dreams were going to wash down some drain, most likely with what was left of me. If my body turned up, Lynda would know that I had lied to her and had broken my promise. That stabbed at my heart, worse than the pain in my chin. Maybe they'd never find a trace and she'd spend the rest of her life wondering. I'd let her down. I'd let Jill down. All I could do now was wait.

But then I remembered something. That, and I could still smell the fish frying on his stove.

"So what's for dinner?" I said it deadpan.

Boecker's long face spread in a slow grin.

"Dinner? Well, yesss, dinner. I've been a bad host, haven't I?" he beamed in the half light of the bathroom. "I've got my own dinner to tend to and then we'll have yours in your special place. I'd like that. We'll try a little spoon-feeding."

I pushed a little more.

"You going to serve lemonade too, you piece of shit?" It was a B'rer Rabbit and the briar patch gambit to buy time. "Isn't this part of your goddamned scenario?"

Boecker's eyes narrowed, wondering what I was trying to pull, and for a moment I figured I'd gone too far. But I was bound up tight with cable ties and his excitement over the coming coprophagiac feast got the best of him.

"Lemonade? Ah-ha, you mean from the time we bonded..." he said, as if remembering a family get-together. "Lemonade, yes, I think we could have some lemonade, if you don't mind me making it from a powder."

I nodded. It was no surprise to me that the monster who planned to have me eating fish and drinking lemonade from his toilet would be contrite about serving a powdered mix.

"Now you just make yourself at home and momma will be back soon with dinner," Boecker said, patting my cheek.

He rumbled down the fiberboard hall, humming a tune to the kitchen, maybe 12 feet away. There was, as the saying goes, no time to waste.

I'd learned a lot in all of those years of browsing the Internet searching for Pieter Boecker, including plenty of paramilitary moves and survival techniques when I got bored of sifting data. One of them was how to escape when your hands are bound behind your back with zip-ties.

I wriggled up against the wall and pushed myself up, sitting on the edge of the toilet with my arms looped behind my legs. It was easy to untie the laces of my left boot and unstring about 14 inches of its braided cord. The tricky part was threading it through the zip-tie fastening my wrists, but I had plenty of motivation. I got the boot lace through the loop and wedged the tip of it under the heel of my other boot. Now I had a saw.

My steel-toe boots had been sitting atop a box in my brother's basement for three years and I'd owned them for maybe five years before that. The laces were a tough, industrial-grade stretch of braided cord, but things wear out over time from simple lack of use: humidity, dust mites, atomic disintegration, who knows? I hadn't sawed for more than ten seconds when the boot lace broke. Just a few feet away around the corner I could hear Boecker hogging down the rest of his dinner. He was a fast eater.

Desperately, I began unstringing the other lace, wrenching my hands in the effort until my wrists bled. I secured another length of boot lace, threaded it through the zip-tie again, anchored it under my boot and began sawing back and forth, easier this time, just enough to keep the pressure on.

I had no idea if it would work. I'd learned the technique from a YouTube video, but for all I knew it was with a far thinner zip-tie or a stronger boot lace, or just simply bullshit. I kept sawing, gentle enough to keep from breaking the lace, but keeping the pressure on. But I couldn't tell if the cord was gnawing into the plastic tie. My heart was hammering, I was pouring with sweat. I could feel my only chance slipping away in seconds.

Then, the zip-tie snapped and my hands were free. In another 30 seconds my legs were free too. I glanced around the bathroom for some kind of weapon. There was nothing but a plastic disposable razor on the sink and a rusted can of deodorant with so much grime around its rim that it didn't look like it had been used in years.

But I still had something.

I heard the clatter of dishes down the hall, then water running and the tinkle of a spoon. Then the slosh of liquid in a glass. Then, there was Boecker, standing in the narrow bathroom doorway with a frying pan of sunfish in one hand and a glass of lemonade in the other, with me sitting up on the toilet with my hands behind my back, like they were still bound.

He looked down on me and smiled. "So, making ourselves comfortable, are we?"

I didn't answer. Instead, I kicked for the goal posts with my steel-toe boot, right where I figured Boecker's left kneecap would be waiting for the blow. Sitting on the toilet, I had an angle that gave my kick a machine-like precision. I couldn't miss.

He gave a high-pitched scream as his knee cap flew at least two inches off the joint with a sickening pop. That's when I kicked him with my other boot, scoring hard on his right shin.

Boecker didn't feel the pain in his shin immediately. He was too busy screaming over his damaged kneecap. But then the damage to his right leg hit him like a speeding train and he cut off in mid-scream and scrambled down the hall, hopping on one leg.

I wobbled up, my head still woozy from the taser, my body feeling like a gumby. But I stumbled down the narrow hallway, banging right and left against its walls until I was on him. I smashed into his back with everything I had. He fell forward, banging his head on a kitchen counter, collapsing in a corner of the kitchen next to the door. If it fazed him, he didn't show it. He hooked his hands on the sink and scuttled up like a crab, bracing himself on the counter with his elbows. He was breathing heavy, his chin running wet with saliva.

That's when I ran out of options. Like I said way back, I haven't been in a fight since I was 16 and Boecker stood more than a foot taller than me. Busted knee or not, a panic seized me that Boecker was going to win this one. We were only six feet apart, close enough to grapple, but though I'd gone wiry with muscle over the past couple of years, Boecker easily had more than a hundred pounds on me and longer arms. My shotgun was beside him, propped up by the doorway in easy reach. All he had to do was grab the gun and blow my guts out.

But for me there was nothing in reach but Boecker's cheap aluminum frying pan, lying on the floor, greasy with the remains of fried fish. I grabbed it and hit him hard on the side of the face, knocking his head sideways. He laughed, brushing it off like he'd been slapped by a little girl. The pan flew off the handle, bouncing against the kitchen wall.

Boecker was sprawled in the doorway, holding my shotgun like a walking stick to brace himself up. I got ready for an all-or-nothing rush, but it seemed hopeless. His bulk filled the doorway in a wall of flesh and he had my loaded gun.

"You ain't gonna' make it to dinner now, chief," he said, panting, with tears of pain streaming down his face. "About thirty seconds from now you're going to be biking with Jesus."

Who knows? Maybe Boecker had said the magic word, but I've been saying my prayers ever since. He leaned down to push himself up with my shotgun, using it as a crutch, and the frayed electric tape gave out on the wooden stock that I'd patched up something like 15 years ago. It gave way and Boecker slipped, catching himself by coming down hard on his left leg and the screaming pain of his wrecked knee. He screamed again, an octave higher than the last time, as high as the whistle scream of a diva. He flayed his arms, trying to catch his balance. He caught the door frame with the tips of his fingers as it slammed open behind him.

He was tottering there in the doorway with only an instant to spare before he regained his balance. I rushed him, slamming into his chest with both hands as he crashed backward through the flimsy screen door into the darkness.

It was at least an eight-foot drop in the arc from where Boecker's head left the threshold of the doorway to when it hit the rocky ground of western Montana. I heard a soft *ponk* and then nothing more.

I gazed from the door. Boecker was lying on the ground, a shadow in the darkness, moaning. My wrecked shotgun was lying on the floor, still serviceable enough to shoot him, but I held off. He didn't look like he was going anywhere.

I switched on the outside light, probably a stupid thing to do if anyone came driving down M-200 and decided to investigate, but vehicles had been almost nonexistent after darkness fell and I doubted that Montana's state police made it out this far. It was just me and Boecker and another far-off train coming up the valley.

Boecker kept moaning and I watched as his head began to swell. It started expanding, growing bigger and bigger until it looked like an oblong pumpkin. He'd cracked his skull and his badly-concussed brain was swelling, pushing the fractured bone beyond its limits.

I suppose I could have tried an emergency trepanation. The ancient Aztecs knew how to pull it off. Simply drill a hole in the skull with a shard of obsidian or one of Boecker's kitchen knives to relieve the pressure. Or, I could have piled Boecker into the back of my pickup truck and driven 100 miles or so to a trauma center in Missoula. I did neither.

Instead, I noticed that there was a basketball game on Boecker's TV. It had been playing all this time while we'd been fighting to the death. And, what the hell, it was Northwestern University playing South Carolina. What a coincidence. I settled into one of Boecker's stinking captain chairs and watched the game for a bit, unable to concentrate. I glimpsed Jimmy Christmas sitting on the bench, but he never got on the court. What were the chances?

Outside, Boecker lay dying. A more vengeful man might have gone out and pissed on him, but I was done. A better man might have tried to comfort him in his final minutes, but that wasn't going to happen either. It was enough for me just to sit there and breathe.

A half hour later — it seemed like night crawling toward eternity -- I went out to check on him. He looked like the Elephant Man with his head ballooned up and his eyes bugging into the darkness. I didn't need to check his pulse like in the movies. I knew that Pieter Boecker was dead.

I crept back into the RV and collected the zip-tie shreds, the broken gun and my shoe lace from the bathroom floor. But otherwise, I didn't try to cover anything up. The broken pan and the dishes scattered across the floor fit right in with the general disarray of Boecker's RV. Nor was there any sense trying to bury Boecker in that stony ground. Some fisherman or highway patrolman would find him at sunup and figure he'd fallen down the steps in a drunken stupor. Happens all the time. Maybe Smith Freeman would hear of Boecker's death back east and figure it was me that did him in, but he'd be cool with it.

I switched out the lights and sat on the porch in the darkness, thinking things over. It occurred to me that life is a series of coincidences that line up to mark your destiny for good luck or bad. If I hadn't seen that Jesus bumper sticker in Ann Arbor I wouldn't have gone biking around the country. If I hadn't gone biking, I wouldn't have met Lynda. If my running shoes were still good, I wouldn't have been wearing my steel-toe boots when I needed them most. If I had a better shotgun than a piece of junk that fell apart in a critical moment, then I'd be dead right now. The check marks and more had lined up like a row of cherries in a slot machine. But to take it back a few steps, they hadn't lined up for Jill. For better or worse, that's life.

I walked the hundred yards to where my truck sat waiting in the darkness with the keys still in the ignition. A hush had settled over the valley, but I could hear the river flowing gently along just down the hill. What now? A wind was rising from a cleft in the mountains. I wondered which way it was blowing.

The End

About the author

Robert Downes has cycle-toured across most of Europe, the British Isles and the United States. He has also bicycled throughout Asia, Australia, Latin America, Canada, and along many of the U.S. routes mentioned in *Bicycle Hobo*.

He is the author of several adventure-travel books and the prizewinning historical novel, *Windigo Moon - A Novel of Native America*. He and his wife, Jeannette, live in Traverse City, Michigan.